Financial Models Using Simulation and Optimization II

Investment Valuation, Options Pricing, Real Options & Product Pricing Models

Wayne L. Winston
Kelley School of Business
Indiana University

Published by:

Palisade Corporation
31 Decker Road
Newfield, NY USA 14867

(607) 277-8000
(607) 277-8001 (fax)
http://www.palisade.com (website)
sales@palisade.com (e-mail)

Preface

I have been thrilled by the positive reception received by my book *Financial Models Using Simulation and Optimization*. In the last few years I have developed many more financial models that are included in the present volume. Many of these models have been used successfully in classes at companies such as GM, Microsoft, Intel, Cisco, and Canyon Partners (a Beverly Hills based hedge fund). The book is broken into sections, which I have tried to make as self-contained as possible.

Section I (Chapters 1-18) deals with modeling future stock prices and hedging the risk associated with changes in stock prices and exchange rates. Much of this material was used in a class at Canyon Partners, and I am indebted to Mitch Julis and Mike Kao of Canyon Partners for stimulating my interest in these areas.

Section II (Chapters 18-27) deals with the problem of valuing a firm or a stock price. My major contribution is adding uncertainty to some basic deterministic valuation models. I am indebted to Professor Sreenie Kamma of the Kelley School for suggesting some of the applications in these sections.

Section III (Chapters 28-51) contains a self-contained introduction to the important field of real options. After reading this section the reader should be able to apply the important tool of real options in their corporation. Most of Section III has been used successfully as a text at Indiana University and University of Texas (Austin).

Section IV (Chapters 52-62) contains a variety of marketing oriented models including several examples of nonlinear pricing and an introduction to conjoint analysis.

Section V (Chapters 63-68) contains some cool miscellaneous material including important Excel tips on the XNPV and text functions.

My thanks go out to the wonderful people at Palisade Corporation. Their great software makes books like this possible. In particular, I want to thank Sam McLafferty for his unwavering support of my publishing efforts. Crystal Winters did an outstanding job preparing the manuscript for publication. I also want to thank Jennifer Skoog, Norm Tonina, and Nancy Sartor for supporting my efforts at Microsoft Finance. Final thanks go to my wonderful wife Vivian and my children, Gregory and Jennifer, for their patience and encouragement.

As usual, I have tried as much as possible to write the book in a modular fashion. The chapters of each of Sections I-III should be read in order but the chapters in Sections IV and V may be read in any order.

Let me know what you think. My e-mail is <u>Winston@Indiana.edu</u> and my phone number is 812-855-3495.

Table of Contents

Chapter 1: The Discrete Random Variable

Suppose Microsoft stock is selling on July 29, 2000 for $80. How might we model its stock price in six months? Clearly Microsoft's stock price on January 29, 2001 is an unknown **random variable**. Let's suppose that in six months we believe that Microsoft will sell for $60, $70, $80, $90, $100, or $110. Clearly this is unrealistic because other prices are possible, but it is a start. In this case we are modeling MSFT's future stock price as a **discrete** random variable. A discrete random variable takes on a finite number of possible values. Let's suppose we have subjectively estimated the probabilities of these stock prices as follows:

Price	Probability
$60	.1
$70	.15
$80	.25
$90	.30
$100	.10
$110	.10

The mass function for this random variable looks as follows.

 Figure 1.1

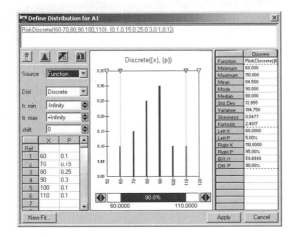

How can we have @RISK "play out" the MSFT stock price hundreds or thousands of times? See file **Discrete.xls** and Figure 1.2.

Figure 1.2

	A	B	C	D	E	F	G
1	Discrete						
2	Random						
3	Variable						
4				Price			
5				80	Value	Prob	
6					$ 60.00	0.1	
7					$ 70.00	0.15	
8					$ 80.00	0.25	
9					$ 90.00	0.3	
10					$ 100.00	0.1	
11					$ 110.00	0.1	
12							
13							

Step by Step

Step 1: We enter the possible values of the random variable in E6:E11 and the corresponding probabilities in F6:F11.

Step 2: Enter in cell D5 the formula

  =RiskDiscrete(E6:E11,F6:F11).

10% of the time this formula will enter a $60 in D5, 15% of the time a $70, etc.

Step 3: To ensure that hitting F9 will "recalculate" the random variable select the @ RISK simulation settings icon

and then choose Sampling Tab and select Standard Recalc and change it to Monte Carlo. Now hitting F9 will change value in D5 in accordance with probabilities you have entered.

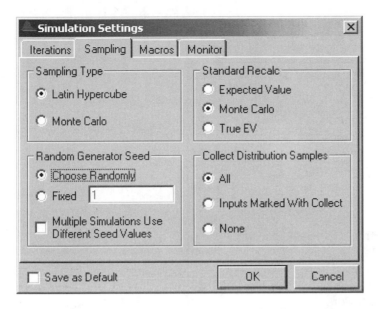

Note if Standard Recalc is set to TRUE EV you obtain the mean of the random variable ($84.50).

Step 4: To run, say 1000 MSFT prices you select cell D5 as an output cell with the Select Output Icon

Then select Simulation Settings Icon and Iterations and change number of iterations to 1000.

Step 5: To run the simulation simply select the Run Simulation Icon.

Step 6: You will obtain statistical output that looks as follows:

Figure 1.3

	D	E
16	Name	Price
17	Description	Output
18	Cell	D5
19	Minimum =	60
20	Maximum =	110
21	Mean =	84.5
22	Std Deviation =	13.96227
23	Variance =	194.9449
24	Skewness =	4.77E-02
25	Kurtosis =	2.396943
26	Errors Calculated =	0
27	Mode =	90
28	5% Perc =	60
29	10% Perc =	60
30	15% Perc =	70
31	20% Perc =	70
32	25% Perc =	70
33	30% Perc =	80
34	35% Perc =	80
35	40% Perc =	80
36	45% Perc =	80
37	50% Perc =	80
38	55% Perc =	90
39	60% Perc =	90
40	65% Perc =	90
41	70% Perc =	90
42	75% Perc =	90
43	80% Perc =	90
44	85% Perc =	100
45	90% Perc =	100
46	95% Perc =	110

Note average price is $84.50 and standard deviation is $13.96. This distribution exhibits little Skewness. We simply copied and pasted this output in the spreadsheet with the Windows Clipboard.

To obtain a graph simply put the cursor on the output cell in the "Explorer" list on the left side of the @RISK-Results window, right-click, and select Graph Histogram.

Figure 1.4

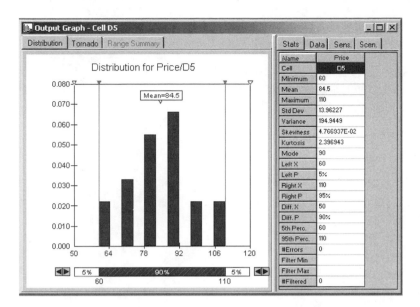

Note that the histogram from output is a virtual exact match for our inputted values and probabilities. Again we used the Windows clipboard to copy and paste our graph into the spreadsheet.

Chapter 2: The Triangular Random Variable

Clearly the future stock price of MSFT is a **continuous random** variable. That is, any price for some range of values (say $50 to $120) is possible. Probably the most commonly used continuous random variable in Monte Carlo simulation is the **triangular random variable.** This is because unlike the normal random variable, the triangular random variable does not require an assumption of symmetry. At GM, Lilly, Intel, Pfizer, and many other companies the triangular random variable is often used to model market share for a new product. To specify a triangular random variable all you do is specify the worst case, most likely, and best case for the random variable. For example, if you believe that the worst-case scenario for MSFT price on January 29, 2001 is $50, most likely case is $85, and best case is $105 you would enter the formula

=*RiskTriang(50, 85, 105).*

Upon doing that we obtain the following statistical output: See Figure 2.1 and file **Triang.xls**.

Figure 2.1

	C	D	E
9	Name	Price	Price
10	Description	Output	Triang(D5,E5,F5)
11	Cell	C5	C5
12	Minimum =	50.99054	50.99054
13	Maximum =	104.1766	104.1766
14	Mean =	80.00036	80.00036
15	Std Deviation =	11.37078	11.37078
16	Variance =	129.2946	129.2946
17	Skewness =	-0.254405	-0.2544051
18	Kurtosis =	2.394822	2.394822
19	Errors Calculated =	0	0
20	Mode =	85.80085	85.80085
21	5% Perc =	59.77173	59.77173
22	10% Perc =	63.83656	63.83656
23	15% Perc =	66.94127	66.94127
24	20% Perc =	69.60744	69.60744
25	25% Perc =	71.93345	71.93345
26	30% Perc =	74.01499	74.01499
27	35% Perc =	75.94006	75.94006
28	40% Perc =	77.71969	77.71969
29	45% Perc =	79.42284	79.42284
30	50% Perc =	80.99464	80.99464
31	55% Perc =	82.50976	82.50976
32	60% Perc =	83.96925	83.96925
33	65% Perc =	85.35621	85.35621
34	70% Perc =	86.81703	86.81703
35	75% Perc =	88.41389	88.41389
36	80% Perc =	90.14555	90.14555
37	85% Perc =	92.14463	92.14463
38	90% Perc =	94.49156	94.49156
39	95% Perc =	97.53962	97.53962
40	Target #1 (Value)=	90	
41	Target #1 (Perc%)=	79.60%	
42	Target #2 (Value)=	65	
43	Target #2 (Perc%)=	11.75%	

Our specification of the triangular random variable implies a mean price of $80 and a standard deviation of $11.37. Note that the median (or 50% percentile which is $80.99) does not equal the mean because our specification of the triangular random variable was not symmetric.

Suppose we wanted to know the probability that the stock price would be less than or equal to $90 or $65. In the @RISK-Results window, simply display the Detailed Statistics window, go down to Targets and enter in the values $90 and $65. We find that there is a 79.6% chance of a $90 or smaller price and a 11.75% chance of a $65 or lower price.

The density function implied by our triangular random variable is as follows:

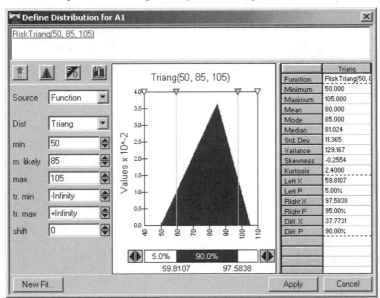

Total area under density equals 1. Note that area under a density represents probability. Thus area to left of $65 is around .12. The relative likelihood of a stock price is proportional to the height of the density. Thus a stock price of $95 is half as likely as a stock price of $85.

Chapter 3: The Normal Random Variable

If you believe a continuous random variable is symmetric, then you can model the random variable with the normal random variable. Recall that the normal random variable is specified by a mean and standard deviation. Here are two important properties of the normal random variable

- The normal random variable is symmetric about its mean. For example, IQs (which have mean = 100 and sigma, or standard deviation, = 15) are as likely to be around 80 as 120, etc.

- 68% of the time a normal random variable is within one standard deviation of its mean, 95% of the time a normal random variable is within two standard deviations of its mean, and 99.7% of the time a normal random variable is within 3 standard deviations of its mean. For example, 95% of people have IQs between 70 and 130.

Let's use the normal random variable to model the price of MSFT on January 29, 2001. Let's suppose you believe the most likely price is $85 and you believe that symmetry is a reasonable assumption. To estimate the standard deviation for the 01-29-01 MSFT price simply answer the following question. You are 95% sure that the MSFT price on 01-29-01 will be between ___ and ___. Suppose you are 95% sure that MSFT price on 01-29-01 will be between $50 and $120. Then we are estimating 2*sigma = 85 – 50 = 120 –85 = $35 or sigma = $17.50. Then we can model the price of MSFT on 01-29-01 with the formula

=*RiskNormal (85,17.5).*

Our output and histogram look as follows. See file **Normal.xls** and Figures 3.1-3.2.

Figure 3.1

	G	H
8	Name	Price
9	Description	RiskNormal(C4,D4)
10	Cell	E4
11	Minimum	29.65406
12	Maximum	141.5562
13	Mean	85.00065
14	Std Deviation	17.49442
15	Variance	3.06E+02
16	Skewness	4.77E-04
17	Kurtosis	2.955692
18	Errors Calculated	0
19	Mode	86.98035
20	5% Perc	56.17757
21	10% Perc	62.54925
22	15% Perc	66.83866
23	20% Perc	70.21091
24	25% Perc	73.15628
25	30% Perc	75.80623
26	35% Perc	78.2411
27	40% Perc	80.52512
28	45% Perc	82.79804
29	50% Perc	84.99211
30	55% Perc	87.15738
31	60% Perc	89.39811
32	65% Perc	91.72847
33	70% Perc	94.13226
34	75% Perc	96.773
35	80% Perc	99.72083
36	85% Perc	103.0768
37	90% Perc	107.3299
38	95% Perc	113.6571

Figure 3.2

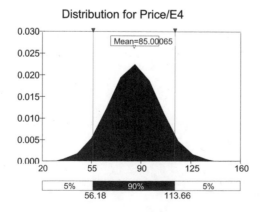

Distribution for Price/E4

Chapter 4: The Lognormal Random Variable and VAR

The lognormal model for asset value (or stock price) assumes that in a small time Δt the stock price changes by an amount that is normally distributed with

$Standard\ Deviation = \sigma S \sqrt{\Delta t}$

$Mean = \mu S \Delta t$

Here S = current stock price.

μ may be thought of as the instantaneous rate of return on the stock. By the way, this model leads to really "jumpy" changes in stock prices (like real life). This is because during a small period of time the standard deviation of the stock's movement will greatly exceed the mean of a stock's movement. This follows because for small Δt, $\sqrt{\Delta t}$ will be much larger than Δt.

In a small time Δt, the natural logarithm (Ln (S)) of the current stock price will change (by Ito's Lemma) by an amount that is normally distributed with

$Mean = (\mu - .5\sigma^2)\Delta t$

Let S_t = stock price at time t . It can be shown that at time t Ln S_t is normally distributed with

$Mean = Ln\ S_0 + (\mu - .5\sigma^2)\ t\ and$

$Standard\ Deviation = \sigma \sqrt{t}$

We refer to $(\mu - .5\sigma^2)$ as the **continuously compounded rate of return** on the stock. Note the continuously compounded rate of return on S is less than instantaneous return. Since Ln S_t follows a normal random variable we say that S_t is a **lognormal random variable.**

To simulate S_t we get Ln (S_t) by entering in @RISK the formula

$= LN(S_0) + (\mu - .5\sigma^2)t + \sigma\sqrt{t}RISKNORMAL\,(0,1)$

Therefore to get S_t we must take the antilog of this equation and get

$$S_t = S_0 e^{(\mu - .5\sigma^2)t + \sigma\sqrt{t}RISKNORMAL\,(0,1)}$$

Estimation of μ and σ

Estimation of μ is very difficult. This is because knowledge of μ is equivalent to knowledge of the stock's future mean return. Probably the best we can do is hypothesize some equally likely values for μ. We can do much better in estimating σ. We simply find the value of σ that makes the Black-Scholes price match the trade price for an option on the underlying stock. This is called the **implied volatility** of a stock. Here is an example.

Implied Volatility Example

On June 30, 1998 Dell Computer sold for $94. A European put with an exercise price of $80 expiring on November 22, 1998 was selling for $5.25. The current 90 day T-Bill rate is 5.5%. What is the implied volatility of Dell computer?

Solution   Our work is in the file **Varduniform.xls**, sheet **imp vol**. See Figure 4.1. This file contains a "Black-Scholes template" which computes the price of a European put or call given the current stock price, option duration in years, option exercise price, risk-free rate (should be a compounded rate), and value of σ (called the annual volatility) of the stock.

Figure 4.1

	A	B	C	D	E	F
1	**Black-Schole's Option Pricing Problem**					
2	**Using the Option Price to Find the Implied Volatility**					
3						
4	Input data					
5	Stock price	$94			today	6/30/98
6	Exercise price	$80			expire	11/22/98
7	Duration	0.39726				
8	Interest rate	5.35%				
9						
10	Implied volatility (stdev)	53.27%				
11						
12	Call price	Actual		Predicted		
13			=	$21.06		
14	Put price	$5.25		$5.25		
15						
16						
17	Other quantities for option price					
18	d1	0.715534		N(d1)	0.76286	
19	d2	0.37981		N(d2)	0.647957	

Step by Step

Step 1: Enter the duration of the option (145/365) years in B7, the current Stock and exercise prices in B5 and B6, and in B8 the risk free rate Ln(1+.055).

Step 2: Now use Goal Seek (see below) to change the volatility until the predicted BS price for a put matches *actual* price.

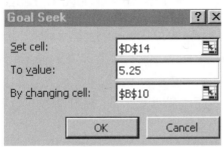

We change volatility (B10) until predicted put price (D14) equals $5.25 (actual put price). From Figure 4.1 we obtain a 53.27% annual volatility.

Value At Risk (VAR)

Recently the concept of **value at risk (VAR)** has been used to help describe a portfolio's uncertainty. Simply stated, **value at risk** of a portfolio at a future point in time is the loss implied by the fifth percentile of the portfolio's value at that point in time. In short, there is only one chance in 20 that the portfolio's loss will exceed the VAR. To illustrate the idea suppose a portfolio today is worth $100. We simulate the portfolio's value one year from now and find there is a 5% chance that the portfolio's value will be $80 or less. Then the portfolio's VAR is $20 or 20%. The following example shows how @RISK can be used to measure VAR. The example also demonstrates how buying puts can greatly reduce the risk, or **hedge**, a long position in a stock.

Modeling Stock Prices

Let's suppose we own one share of Dell computer on June 30, 1998. The current price is $94. Let's assume the mean annual return on Dell during the next four months is equally likely to be 0%, 10%, 20% or 30%. To hedge the risk involved in owning Dell we are considering buying (for $5.25) a European put on Dell with exercise price $80 and expiration date November 22, 1998.

    a. Compute the VAR on November 22, 1998 if we own Dell computer and do not buy a put.

    b. Compute the VAR on November 22, 1998 if we own Dell computer and buy the put.

Our work is in file **Varduniform.xls** in the sheet **model.** See Figure 4.2.

Figure 4.2

	A	B	C
1			
2	**Stress Testing Dell**	Range Name	
3	Current price	S	$ 94.00
4	Put exercise price	x	$ 80.00
5	put duration	d	0.39726
6	risk free rate	r_	0.053541
7	actual growth rate	g	0.2
8	volatility	v	0.5327
9	put price	p	$ 5.25
10			
11	Dell price at expiration	96.19541584	
12	put value at expiration	0	
13			
14	% age Gain without put	2.3%	
15	%age Gain with put	-3.1%	
16			

We have created range names as indicated in Figure 4.2.

Step by Step

Step 1: In cell C7 we create the (random) mean growth rate (value of μ) for the next four months with the formula

    $= RiskDuniform(\{0,0.1,0.2,0.3\}).$

Step 2: In cell B11 we generate Dell's price on November 22, 1998 with the formula

    $=S*EXP((g-0.5*v^2)*d+RiskNormal(0,1)*v*SQRT(d)).$

Step 3: In cell B12 we compute the payments from the put at expiration with the formula

    $=IF(B11>x,0,x-B11).$

Computing Percentage Return

Step 4: If we just own Dell the percentage gain on our portfolio is given by

$$\frac{Ending\ Dell\ Price - Beginning\ Dell\ Price}{Beginning\ Dell\ Price}.$$

In B14 we compute the percentage gain on our portfolio if we do not buy a put with the formula

=(B11-S)/S.

Step 5: The percentage gain on our portfolio if we own Dell and a put is

$$\frac{Ending\ Dell\ Price + Cash\ Flows\ from\ Put - Beginning\ Dell\ Price - Put\ Price}{Beginning\ Dell\ Price + Put\ Price}$$

In cell B15 we compute the percentage gain on our portfolio if we buy the put with the formula

=((B12+B11)-(S+p))/(S+p).

Running and Interpreting the Simulation Output

Step 6: After selecting B14 and B15 as output cells and running 1600 iterations we obtained the @RISK output in Figure 4.3.

Figure 4.3

	D	E	F
19	Name	% age Gain without put / p	%age Gain with put / p
20	Description	Output	Output
21	Cell	B14	B15
22	Minimum =	-0.6768757	-0.1939547
23	Maximum =	2.284537	2.110795
24	Mean =	6.20E-02	5.28E-02
25	Std Deviation =	0.3682485	0.3003744
26	Variance =	1.36E-01	9.02E-02
27	Skewness =	1.050841	1.716306
28	Kurtosis =	4.961527	6.92E+00
29	Errors Calculated =	0.00E+00	0
30	Mode =	-1.60E-02	-1.94E-01
31	5% Perc =	-4.25E-01	-1.94E-01
32	10% Perc =	-0.3450871	-1.94E-01
33	15% Perc =	-0.2940845	-1.94E-01
34	20% Perc =	-0.2484266	-0.1939547
35	25% Perc =	-0.2057383	-0.1939547
36	30% Perc =	-0.1627831	-0.1939547
37	35% Perc =	-0.1170508	-0.1637559
38	40% Perc =	-7.99E-02	-0.1285334
39	45% Perc =	-3.39E-02	-8.50E-02
40	50% Perc =	6.97E-03	-4.63E-02
41	55% Perc =	5.19E-02	-3.76E-03
42	60% Perc =	9.57E-02	3.77E-02
43	65% Perc =	1.46E-01	8.52E-02
44	70% Perc =	2.01E-01	1.37E-01
45	75% Perc =	0.2563464	1.90E-01
46	80% Perc =	0.3314393	0.2610105
47	85% Perc =	0.4285794	0.3530122
48	90% Perc =	0.5389413	0.4575363
49	95% Perc =	0.7528516	0.6601315

The simulation output provides three ways to show how the purchase of a put has hedged our risk.

- We find our VAR by looking at the 5th percentile of the @RISK output. If we do not buy the put, we find this to be 43% of our invested cash while if we buy the put our VAR drops to 19% of the invested cash. The reason for this is, of course, that if Dell stock drops below $80, every one-dollar decrease in the value of Dell is countered by a one-dollar increase in the value of the put.

- Also note that if we do not buy the put, Dell (despite its high growth rate) might lose up to 69% of its value. If we buy the put the worst we can do is lose 19%.

- We also find that the standard deviation of our percentage return with the put is 30% while without the put the standard deviation is 37%.

Note, however, when we buy the put the mean return on our portfolio is reduced from 6.2% to 5.3%. This leads people to refer to the cost of the put as **portfolio insurance.**

The following histograms give the distribution of the percentage gain on our portfolio with and without the put.

Figure 4.4 –
Percentage
Return With
Put

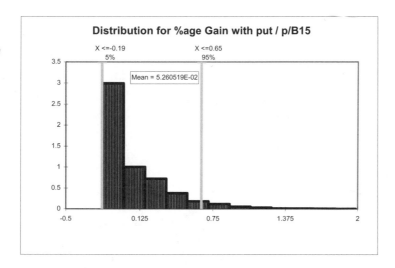

Figure 4.5 –
Percentage
Return
Without Put

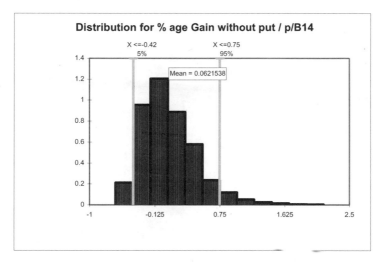

The huge spike in Figure 4.4 corresponds to our minimum loss when hedged of 19%. Note that without the put we can easily go below a 50% loss!

Overlaying Graphs

We can easily report the histograms for our return with and without the put on the same graph. Simply right click on a histogram for either output cell. Select Graph Format, choose Variables to Graph and select the variables you want to graph (return with put and without put). You will obtain the following result.

Figure 4.6 – Overlaying Return with Put and Without Put

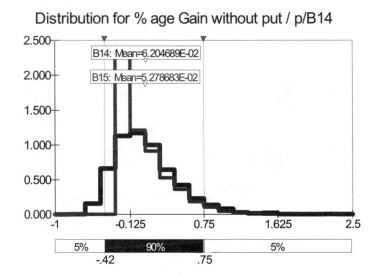

Distribution for % age Gain without put / p/B14

Chapter 5: The RiskGeneral Random Variable

Perhaps the normal or triangular random variable does not incorporate your view of MSFT future prices. Do not despair. You can specify **any** density function with the RiskGeneral random variable. All you do is specify the minimum value for the random variable, the maximum value for the random variable, some intermediate values for the random variable and their relative likelihoods.

For example, we may specify the following information for the 01-29-01 MSFT stock.

Price	Likelihood
$55	Min
$130	Max
$70	1
$80	5
$100	6
$110	2
$120	.5

Thus we believe MSFT price will be between $55 and $130. $80 is five times as likely as $70, etc.

In the file **GeneralMSFT.xls** we have generated stock prices with the following formula. See Figure 5.1.

=RiskGeneral(C4,C5,B8:B12,C8:C12).

Figure 5.1

	A	B	C	D	E
1	**General**				
2	**Random**				
3	**Variable**				
4		Min	$ 55.00		
5		Max	$ 130.00		Price
6					91.87243
7		Price	Likelihood		
8		$ 70.00	1		
9		$ 80.00	5		
10		$ 100.00	6		
11		$ 110.00	2		
12		$ 120.00	0.5		
13					

This formula generates a graph that looks as follows:

Figure 5.2

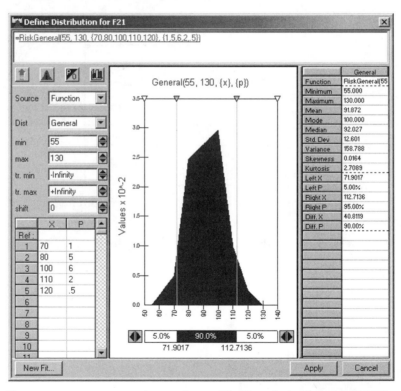

Between any two points whose likelihood is input, @RISK assumes that the likelihood changes in a linear fashion. For example, $75 would have a likelihood of 3.

Running the stock price through 1000 times yields the following output:

Figure 5.3

	B	C
16	Name	Price
17	Description	Output
18	Cell	[generalmsft.xls]$
19	Minimum =	57.37582
20	Maximum =	128.9175
21	Mean =	91.87708
22	Std Deviation =	12.6072
23	Variance =	158.9415
24	Skewness =	2.20E-02
25	Kurtosis =	2.70509
26	Errors Calculated =	0
27	Mode =	99.88175
28	5% Perc =	71.85423
29	10% Perc =	75.85638
30	15% Perc =	78.46812
31	20% Perc =	80.57681
32	25% Perc =	82.55334
33	30% Perc =	84.52263
34	35% Perc =	86.44759
35	40% Perc =	88.34077
36	45% Perc =	90.20241
37	50% Perc =	92.01555
38	55% Perc =	93.78883
39	60% Perc =	95.58018
40	65% Perc =	97.30399
41	70% Perc =	99.03092
42	75% Perc =	100.74
43	80% Perc =	102.6297
44	85% Perc =	104.8981
45	90% Perc =	107.7945
46	95% Perc =	112.691

For instance, our model implies that MSFT has a 5% chance of selling for $71.85 or less and a 5% chance of selling for $112.69 or more.

Chapter 6: The RiskCumulative Random Variable

Instead of estimating relative likelihoods of various stock prices we may estimate fractiles or percentiles of MSFT prices. For example we may estimate the following:

- Worst case price is $55.

- Best case is $130.

- 25% chance price will be $65 or less.

- 50% chance price will be $90 or less.

- 75% chance price will be $120 or less.

The RiskCumulative random variable (see file **cumulativemsft.xls**) lets us model a random variable based on its fractiles, minimum, and maximum values. See Figure 6.1.

Figure 6.1

	A	B	C	D
1	Cumulative Random			
2	Variable			
3				
4		Min	$ 55.00	
5		Max	$ 130.00	
6				
7		Fractile	%age	
8		$ 65.00	0.25	
9		$ 90.00	0.5	
10		$ 120.00	0.75	
11				
12			Price	
13			$ 91.88	

The formula

$$=RiskCumul(C4,C5,B8.B10,C8:C10)$$

generates a random variable with the given fractiles, minimum and maximum values. Between any two given fractiles, @RISK assumes the cumulative probability increases linearly. For example, $77.50 would have a cumulative probability of .375.

Running 1000 iterations of this random variable yields the following output.

Figure 6.2

	D	E
16	Name	Price
17	Description	Output
18	Cell	C13
19	Minimum =	55.00946
20	Maximum =	129.9878
21	Mean =	91.87442
22	Std Deviation =	25.67815
23	Variance =	6.59E+02
24	Skewness =	5.90E-02
25	Kurtosis =	1.478685
26	Errors Calculated =	0
27	Mode =	61.59955
28	5% Perc =	56.98421
29	10% Perc =	58.98927
30	15% Perc =	60.99473
31	20% Perc =	62.98562
32	25% Perc =	64.97955
33	30% Perc =	69.93971
34	35% Perc =	74.9854
35	40% Perc =	79.96487
36	45% Perc =	84.9803
37	50% Perc =	89.98432
38	55% Perc =	95.9315
39	60% Perc =	101.9491
40	65% Perc =	107.9413
41	70% Perc =	113.9312
42	75% Perc =	119.9933
43	80% Perc =	121.9976
44	85% Perc =	123.9779
45	90% Perc =	125.9867
46	95% Perc =	127.9823

Mean price is $91.87 and 25 percentile, 50 percentile and 75 percentile match up with what we put in.

A histogram and cumulative graph for the stock price follow:

Figure 6.3

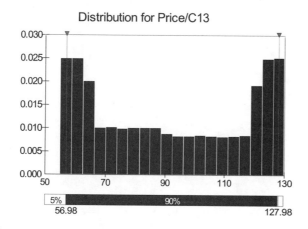

Distribution for Price/C13

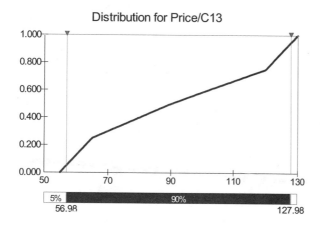

Distribution for Price/C13

Note the bimodal nature of our histogram.

Chapter 7: Incorporating Analyst Forecasts

Bulldogresearch.com gives a consensus 12-month view on all stocks. For example, the consensus view (on June 29, 2000) is that MSFT in 12 months will be selling for $112.27. Today's price (June 29, 2000) is $79.44. We can use this information to back out a Lognormal random variable model for MSFT price. We need to estimate mu (mean) and sigma (standard deviation) for MSFT. We simply use implied volatility to estimate sigma. From CNBC.com we find that an $80 put on MSFT expiring on January 20, 2001 (in 205/365 = .56 years) sells for $7.94. Using Goal Seek (see file **impliedvolmsft.xls**) and Figure 7.1 we obtain an annual volatility of 37.3%

Figure 7.1

	A	B	C	D	E	F
1	**Black-Schole's Option Pricing Problem**					
2	**Using the Option Price to Find the Implied Volatility**					
3						
4	Input data					
5	Stock price	$79				
6	Exercise price	$80				
7	Duration	0.561644				
8	Interest rate	5.0000%				
9						
10	Implied volatility (stdev)	37.32%				
11						
12	Call price	Actual		Predicted		
13			=	$9.60		
14	Put price	$7.94		$7.94		
15						
16						
17	Other quantities for option price					
18	d1	0.215134		N(d1)	0.585169	
19	d2	-0.064556		N(d2)	0.474264	

File **Lognormal.xls** lets us compute the mean and standard deviation for a stock price on any future date. Since we know sigma, we may use Goal Seek to back out a mu that implies an average price in one year of $112.27. See file Lognormal.xls and Figure 7.2.

Figure 7.2

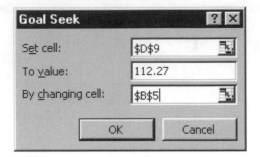

	A	B	C	D
1	Confidence interval for stock price			
2				
3	S=current price	79.44		
4	t=time	1		
5	mu	0.345905		
6	sigma	0.373		
7	alpha	0.95		
8				
9	Mean for ln S(T)	4.651342	Mean S(T)	112.27
10	Sigma for ln S(T)	0.373	var S(T)	1881.511
11				
12	CI			
13	Lower(for ln S(T))	3.920277		
14	Upper (for ln S(T))	5.382408		
15	Lower for S(T)	50.41439		
16	Upper for S(T)	217.5454		

We find that the analyst consensus implies a mu = 34.6%. We can now simulate MSFT's price in six months in sheet **MSFTanalyst.xls** by entering (see Figure 7.3) in cell B9 the formula

$$=B9*EXP((B6-0.5*C6\char`\^2)*0.5+SQRT(0.5)*C6*RiskNormal(0,1)).$$

Figure 7.3

	A	B	C	D
1				
2		**Bulldog**		
3		**Simulation**		
4				
5		Mean	Sigma	
6		0.346	0.373	
7				
8		Today Price		
9		79.44		
10		Six month price		
11		91.21503763		
12				

We obtain the following statistical output.

	D	E
13	Name	Six month
14	Description	Output
15	Cell	B11
16	Minimum =	41.65692
17	Maximum =	216.4833
18	Mean =	94.4696
19	Std Deviation =	25.45064
20	Variance =	647.7349
21	Skewness =	0.847738
22	Kurtosis =	4.292611
23	Errors Calculated =	0
24	Mode =	83.8613
25	5% Perc =	59.01973
26	10% Perc =	64.95518
27	15% Perc =	69.37183
28	20% Perc =	72.96737
29	25% Perc =	76.32859
30	30% Perc =	79.33075
31	35% Perc =	82.28365
32	40% Perc =	85.22157
33	45% Perc =	88.20525
34	50% Perc =	91.17208
35	55% Perc =	94.23479
36	60% Perc =	97.46803
37	65% Perc =	100.8726
38	70% Perc =	104.5947
39	75% Perc =	108.9527
40	80% Perc =	113.6911
41	85% Perc =	119.858
42	90% Perc =	127.5178
43	95% Perc =	140.4433

We find an average price in six months of $94.46. There is a 5% chance price will go as low as $59.01 or as high as $140.44.

Incorporating Analysts' Biases

It is well known that analysts' forecasts are biased upward. Suppose we know the extent of this bias (say 5%). Then we just knock down the consensus forecast by 5% and re-estimate mu. See Figure 7.4.

Figure 7.4

	A	B	C	D
1	Confidence interval for stock price			
2				
3	S=current price	79.44		
4	t=time	1		
5	mu	0.294646		
6	sigma	0.373		
7	alpha	0.95		
8				
9	Mean for ln S(T)	4.600084	Mean S(T)	106.6602
10	Sigma for ln S(T)	0.373	var S(T)	1698.182
11				
12	**CI**			
13	Lower(for ln S(T))	3.869018		
14	Upper (for ln S(T))	5.331149		
15	Lower for S(T)	47.89534		
16	Upper for S(T)	206.6754		

Then we would use mu = 29.5%.

Incorporating the Strong Buy/Strong Sell Consensus

The July 10, 2000 *Business Week* reported the results of a study that estimated how well analysts' consensus of Strong Buy (a 1) to Strong Sell (a 5) forecast annual returns on a stock. They found the following predictions for annual returns (relative to the market)

Rating	Average Excess Return (over Market)
Strong Buy = 1	+4.5%
Buy = 2	+3.5%
Hold = 3	+0.5%
Sell = 4	-1.0%
Strong Sell = 5	-8.5%

We can use this approach to model a future stock price as follows:

- First subjectively estimate the broad market return.

- Find from Yahoo! the consensus view on the stock. (Ford was a 1.74)

We can now generate the mean return on the stock.

Combine this mean return with an implied volatility estimate (Ford is 31.8%) to use a lognormal random variable to generate future prices.

Let's suppose we want to use this approach to model Ford's stock price in three months (current price is $43.38). Ford's consensus rating of 1.74 implies that Ford should beat the market by .74*3.5 + .26*4.5 = 3.75%. Let's suppose for next three months the market is equally likely to have an annual return of -10%, 0%, 5%, 10% or 15%. We can now generate Ford's price in three months as follows (see file **Fordan.xls**).

Step by Step

Step 1: In cell D35 generate annual market return for the next three months with the formula

> =RiskDuniform(A39:A43).

Step 2: In cell E35 add 3.75% to market return to generate Ford's mean return.

> =D35+.0375.

Step 3: In cell F35 generate Ford's price in three months with the lognormal random variable

$$=B35*EXP((E35-0.5*C35\^2)*0.25+SQRT(0.25)*C35*RiskNormal(0,1)).$$

Step 4: After making F35 an output cell we obtain the histogram in Figure 7.6.

Figure 7.5

	A	B	C	D	E	F
30						
31	Ford Price					
32	in 3					
33	Months					3 months
34		Price now	Vol	Market Return	Ford Mean	Actual Ford Price
35		43.38	0.318	0.05	0.0875	43.78244795
36						
37						
38	Market Return					
39	-0.1					
40	0					
41	0.05					
42	0.1					
43	0.15					
44						
45						
46						
47						

Figure 7.6

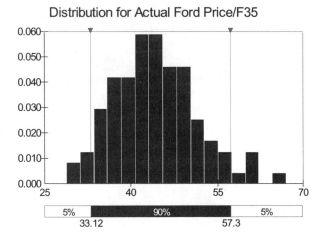

Distribution for Actual Ford Price/F35

Incorporating the Strong Buy/Strong Sell Consensus

Chapter 8: Generating Correlated Stock Forecasts

We all know that stock prices are correlated. If we own Ford, Microsoft and Pfizer, we know that if Pfizer goes up this increases the chance that Ford and Microsoft will also go up. How can we incorporate this correlation? We begin by estimating the correlations between the returns on our stocks. Then we use the method of Chapter 7 to generate a lognormal random variable for each stock. @RISK makes it a snap to generate correlated stock price paths. After analyzing Ford, Pfizer and Microsoft we obtained the following parameters.

Stock	Today's Price	Mu	Sigma
MSFT	$79.44	34.6%	37.3%
Ford	$43.38	47.3%	31.8%
Pfizer	$50.56	6.6%	35%

In file **correlation.xls** we are given last six months of daily returns on the three stocks. We can use these returns to estimate the correlations between the stocks.

Figure 8.1

	A	B	C	D	E	F	G
1	Date	MSFT	Ford	Pfizer	MSFT R	Ford R	Pfizer R
2	29-Apr-00	90.875	44.7287	37.9259	MSFT R	Ford R	Pfizer R
3	30-Apr-00	88.5625	46.6916	39.6724	-0.025447	0.043885	0.04605
4	1-May-00	86.375	46.9295	38.5496	-0.0247	0.005095	-0.028302
5	2-May-00	86	47.5243	38.3001	-0.004342	0.012674	-0.006472
6	3-May-00	89.0625	45.7994	38.7368	0.03561	-0.036295	0.011402
7	4-May-00	86.0625	48.5949	39.7348	-0.033684	0.061038	0.025764
8	5-May-00	83.875	49.4276	39.7348	-0.025418	0.017136	0
9	6-May-00	79.375	51.0336	40.2962	-0.053651	0.032492	0.014129
10	7-May-00	79.25	51.8068	39.5477	-0.001575	0.015151	-0.018575
11	8-May-00	74.125	49.725	37.8635	-0.064669	-0.040184	-0.042587
12	9-May-00	75.875	54.305	37.9259	0.023609	0.092107	0.001648
13	10-May-00	80.5625	52.699	39.4853	0.061779	-0.029574	0.041117

Step 1: Go to Tools>DataAnalysis>Correlations.

Step 2: Select the range E2:G64 and check the labels box. You will find the following information.

	J	K	L	M	N
5					
6					
7					
8		**MSFT R**	**Ford R**	**Pfizer R**	
9	**MSFT R**	**1**			
10	**Ford R**	**-0.075423**	**1**		
11	**Pfizer R**	**-0.084439**	**0.052139**	**1**	

Note these stocks are virtually uncorrelated. We could ignore the correlations, but we will incorporate them into our analysis.

Let's suppose 50% of our money is in MSFT and 25% each in Pfizer and Ford. Let's compute an average return and VAR on our portfolio over a six-month period.

To model the returns of these stocks over the next six months look at file **Corrvar.xls**.

Figure 8.2

	B	C	D	E	F	G	H	I	J	K
1		Modeling								
2		Correlated stocks								
3										
4										
5	Correlations									
6		MSFT R	Ford R	Pfizer R						
7	MSFT R	1	-0.075423	-0.084439						
8	Ford R	-0.075423	1	0.052139		Weights	0.5	0.25	0.25	
9	Pfizer R	-0.084439	0.052139	1			MSFT	Ford	5	
10						Mu	0.346	0.473	0.066	
11						sigma	0.373	0.318	0.35	
12						price	79.44	43.38	50.56	
13							1	2	3	
14						Time	MSFT pr	Ford Pr	Prizer Pr	
15						0	79.44	43.38	50.56	
16						1	72.91699	43.93892	57.6522	
17						2	78.41884	44.82833	46.17412	
18						3	87.39169	48.79079	48.148	
19						4	84.55157	56.98359	58.76752	
20						5	87.61849	62.03682	51.46882	
21						6	95.28541	73.28624	41.21995	
22						Return	0.217307	0.680632	-0.162007	
23										
24						Portfolio return	0.23831			
25										

Step 1: To generate the monthly stock prices for MSFT, Ford and Pfizer over the next six months simply copy from H16 to H16:J21 the formula

$=H15*EXP((H\$10-0.5*H\$11\^2)*(1/12)+H\$11*SQRT(1/12)*RiskNormal(0,1,RiskCorrmat(\$C\$7:\$E\$9,H\$13,\$G16)))$.

Without the RiskCorrmat portion of the formula, this would generate stock prices that vary according to independent lognormal random variables with the estimated means and volatilities. The returns on the three stocks during each month (**and different months**) would be independent random variables. The RiskCorrmat portion of the formula has three parts:

- (\$C\$7:\$E\$9) is the matrix where the correlations between the monthly returns on MSFT, F, and PR are entered.

- H\$13 gives the column of the correlation matrix that applies to the given random variable.

- \$G16 makes copies of the correlation matrix so that returns **within** each year on different stocks are correlated but returns **between** years are independent.

Step 2: In cells H22:J22 we compute the return on each stock for the six-month period by copying from H22 to H22:J22 the formula

$=(H21-H15)/H15$.

Step 3: In cell H24 we compute the six-month return on our portfolio with the formula

$=RiskOutput() + SUMPRODUCT(H8:J8,H22:J22)$.

Step 4: After making H24 an output cell we obtain the following output.

	E	F
26	Name	Portfolio return / MSFT pr
27	Description	Output
28	Cell	H24
29	Minimum	-0.3228264
30	Maximum	0.9004612
31	Mean	0.1534894
32	Std Deviation	1.75E-01
33	Variance	0.0306924
34	Skewness	3.94E-01
35	Kurtosis	3.246321
36	Errors Calculated	0
37	Mode	9.67E-02
38	5% Perc	-0.1122939
39	10% Perc	-6.02E-02

Mean portfolio return is 15.3% and VAR is 11.2% of the portfolio.

	E	F
28	Name	Portfolio return / MSFT pr
29	Description	Output
30	Cell	H24
31	Minimum	-0.5481239
32	Maximum	1.61E+00
33	Mean	0.1550649
34	Std Deviation	2.70E-01
35	Variance	7.28E-02
36	Skewness	0.5800508
37	Kurtosis	3.781696
38	Errors Calculated	0
39	Mode	0.128358
40	5% Perc	-2.49E-01

If we made all stocks have a .8 correlation we find the following output (see file **corrvar.8.xls**)

Mean return is 15.5% and VAR is now 24.9% of invested portfolio! The higher VAR is due to the fact that the high correlation between the stocks reduces the diversification benefits from owning three stocks.

Chapter 9: Generating Stock Returns by Bootstrapping

As an alternative approach, we can use bootstrapping to model future stock prices. We simply take a recent sample of returns on the three stocks and assume that **for any future day, the day's return is equally likely to equal one of the days from our sample.** See file **Bootstrap.xls**. We will simulate six months of stock prices for Microsoft, Ford and Pfizer.

Figure 9.1

	A	B	C	D	E	F	G	H
1		Date	MSFT	Ford	Pfizer	MSFT R	Ford R	Pfizer R
2		29-Apr-00	90.875	44.7287	37.9259	MSFT R	Ford R	Pfizer R
3	1	30-Apr-00	88.5625	46.6916	39.6724	-0.025447	0.043885	0.04605
4	2	1-May-00	86.375	46.9295	38.5496	-0.0247	0.005095	-0.028302
5	3	2-May-00	86	47.5243	38.3001	-0.004342	0.012674	-0.006472
6	4	3-May-00	89.0625	45.7994	38.7368	0.03561	-0.036295	0.011402
7	5	4-May-00	86.0625	48.5949	39.7348	-0.033684	0.061038	0.025764
8	6	5-May-00	83.875	49.4276	39.7348	-0.025418	0.017136	0
9	7	6-May-00	79.375	51.0336	40.2962	-0.053651	0.032492	0.014129
10	8	7-May-00	79.25	51.8068	39.5477	-0.001575	0.015151	-0.018575
11	9	8-May-00	74.125	49.725	37.8635	-0.064669	-0.040184	-0.042587
33	31	30-May-00	67.6875	50.3002	45	-0.026079	-0.015276	0.011236
34	32	31-May-00	66.1875	51.5007	45.1875	-0.022161	0.023867	0.004167
35	33	1-Jun-00	65.0625	51.3206	44.1875	-0.016997	-0.003497	-0.02213
36	34	2-Jun-00	64.1875	49.2198	43.9375	-0.013449	-0.040935	-0.005658
37	35	3-Jun-00	63.1875	49.3398	44.1875	-0.015579	0.002438	0.00569
38	36	4-Jun-00	65.5625	49.8801	44.25	0.037587	0.010951	0.001414
39	37	5-Jun-00	61.5	48.6796	45.6562	-0.061964	-0.024068	0.031779
40	38	6-Jun-00	61.4375	46.2786	45.125	-0.001016	-0.049323	-0.011635
41	39	7-Jun-00	63.375	47.119	44.1875	0.031536	0.01816	-0.020776
42	40	8-Jun-00	62.5625	46.6388	44.5	-0.012821	-0.010191	0.007072
43	41	9-Jun-00	64.5625	47.5391	45	0.031968	0.019304	0.011236
44	42	10-Jun-00	66.3125	48.0193	43.5625	0.027106	0.010101	-0.031944
45	43	11-Jun-00	66.875	48.6196	42.75	0.008483	0.012501	-0.018651
46	44	12-Jun-00	69.625	48.0193	43.4375	0.041121	-0.012347	0.016082
47	45	13-Jun-00	70.5	47.4791	43.5	0.012567	-0.01125	0.001439
48	46	14-Jun-00	68.8125	47.0589	44.25	-0.023936	-0.00885	0.017241
49	47	15-Jun-00	68.8125	47.8993	46	0	0.017858	0.039548
50	48	16-Jun-00	66.875	48.1394	44.375	-0.028156	0.005013	-0.035326
51	49	17-Jun-00	67.875	47.9593	45.8438	0.014953	-0.003741	0.0331
52	50	18-Jun-00	70.5	46.3386	46.5938	0.038674	-0.033793	0.01636
53	51	19-Jun-00	72.375	44.1778	47	0.026596	-0.046631	0.008718
54	52	20-Jun-00	72.5625	43.2174	47.9375	0.002591	-0.021739	0.019947
55	53	21-Jun-00	73.6875	42.8572	46.75	0.015504	-0.008335	-0.024772
56	54	22-Jun-00	74.9375	41.2966	46.25	0.016964	-0.036414	-0.010695
57	55	23-Jun-00	80.6875	41.9569	46.875	0.076731	0.015989	0.013514
58	56	24-Jun-00	79.875	42.6171	45.75	-0.01007	0.015735	-0.024
59	57	25-Jun-00	77.6875	42.6772	45.875	-0.027387	0.00141	0.002732
60	58	26-Jun-00	79.5	41.1766	46.25	0.023331	-0.035162	0.008174
61	59	27-Jun-00	78.8125	41.1766	47	-0.008648	0	0.016216
62	60	28-Jun-00	78.9375	42.257	46.4844	0.001586	0.026238	-0.01097
63	61	29-Jun-00	77.1875	43.25	46.2344	-0.022169	0.023499	-0.005378
64	62	30-Jun-00	80	43	48	0.036437	-0.00578	0.038188

	I	J	K	L	M	N	O
1	**Bootstrapping**						
2							
3							
4							
5					6	7	8
6				Scenarios'	MSFT	Ford	Pfizer
7					$ 79.44	$ 43.38	$ 50.56
8			1	50	82.51227	43.12925	49.61699
9			2	43	83.21218	42.87995	48.032
10			3	6	81.09713	42.63209	46.49764
11			4	21	81.89504	42.38566	45.0123
33			26	19	94.41586	37.31045	45.63633
34			27	22	94.2486	37.09478	47.08658
35			28	30	94.41842	36.88036	47.15318
36			29	61	92.32522	36.66718	47.21988
37			30	50	95.89581	36.45523	47.28667
38			31	36	99.5002	36.24451	47.35355
39			32	23	100.4714	36.035	47.42053
40			33	34	99.12016	35.82671	47.69035
41			34	24	97.29106	35.61962	47.9617
42			35	18	97.20396	35.41372	48.2346
43			36	16	95.27739	35.20902	48.50905
44			37	20	90.65542	35.0055	48.78506
45			38	49	92.01102	34.80315	48.50905
46			39	22	91.84802	34.60198	48.2346
47			40	21	92.75172	34.40197	47.9617
48			41	34	91.50434	34.20311	47.69035
49			42	35	90.07876	34.00541	47.42053
50			43	36	93.46451	33.80884	46.37111
51			44	48	90.8329	33.61342	45.34492
52			45	23	91.71947	33.41912	44.34143
53			46	14	77.41326	33.22595	43.36016
54			47	4	80.16999	33.03389	42.4006
55			48	58	82.0404	32.84294	42.57727
56			49	59	81.33093	32.6531	42.75467
57			50	34	80.23715	32.46435	42.93282
58			51	17	82.37582	32.2767	43.1117
59			52	39	84.97363	32.09013	43.29134
60			53	8	84.83982	31.90463	43.77775
61			54	30	84.99268	31.72021	44.26964
62			55	4	88.01931	31.53686	44.76705
63			56	27	90.26343	31.35457	45.27005
64			57	9	84.4262	31.17333	45.7787
65			58	44	87.89794	30.99313	46.29892
133			126	32	106.4871	20.89608	59.76727
134	Total return			Return	0.290561	-0.515501	0.204573
135	0.067548			Weights	0.5	0.25	0.25

40

Step 1: We have named the range A1:H64 as Lookup. In cells L8:L135 we generate 126 scenarios (half a year) of daily returns by copying from L8 to L9:L135 the formula

$=RiskDuniform(\$A\$3:\$A\$64).$

This formula is equally likely to choose a 1, 2, …, 62.

Step 2: Copying from M8:O133 the formula

$=M7*(1+VLOOKUP(L8,Lookup,M\$5))$

generates stock prices for the next 126 days. Note that we have "implied correlations" because we choose an entire row of returns as the returns on the three stocks. Thus if MSFT and Ford tend to go up and down together bootstrapping will catch it.

Step 3: Copying from M134 to M134:O134 the formula

$=(M133-M8)/M8$

generates the six-month return on each stock.

Step 4: Cell I135 (our output cell) generates the return on our portfolio with the formula

$=SUMPRODUCT(M134:O134,M135:O135).$

Step 5: Our @RISK output yields the following.

	F	G
138	Name	Total return
139	Description	Output
140	Cell	I135
141	Minimum =	-0.5820336
142	Maximum =	0.9726494
143	Mean =	-0.1439344
144	Std Deviation =	0.2001531
145	Variance =	4.01E-02
146	Skewness =	0.8652029
147	Kurtosis =	5.722406
148	Errors Calculated =	0
149	Mode =	-0.111545
150	5% Perc =	-0.4424216
151	10% Perc =	-0.3938472
152	15% Perc =	-0.3513991
153	20% Perc =	-0.3115693
154	25% Perc =	-0.2790683
155	30% Perc =	-0.2434133
156	35% Perc =	-0.2161472
157	40% Perc =	-0.1927143
158	45% Perc =	-0.1672658
159	50% Perc =	-0.1446542
160	55% Perc =	-0.1248541
161	60% Perc =	-0.1073746
162	65% Perc =	-8.92E-02
163	70% Perc =	-6.51E-02
164	75% Perc =	-4.11E-02
165	80% Perc =	-6.80E-03
166	85% Perc =	3.47E-02
167	90% Perc =	9.35E-02
168	95% Perc =	0.1826005

Note the mean return is –14% and VAR is –44%. This is because these stocks did poorly during the last three months. Bootstrapping has the advantage that it "creates" the actual shape of the stock's return distribution and is not confined to a lognormal assumption. If we bootstrap off a bull market that suddenly turns into a bear, however, we will be in trouble.

Combining Bootstrapping With Analyst Forecasts

Suppose we bootstrap MSFT ahead six months. We get a mean price of $66.19. Say that analyst consensus is $90. How could we adjust the bootstrapping to incorporate the analyst consensus? Simply add a constant r to each daily return where

$$(1+r)^{126}\,66.19 = 90 \ \ or\, r = \left(\frac{90}{66.19}\right)^{1/126} - 1 = .00242.$$

This preserves the shape of the stock return distribution (so it can be non lognormal) but makes the stock land on average at the analyst consensus.

Chapter 10: Portfolio Optimization

In this chapter we will show how to find desirable portfolios when several investments are available. We will assume that the distribution of future returns will be similar to past returns. For our example (see file **Hitechport.xls, data** tab) let's suppose we are given monthly returns on Microsoft, Intel, and GE for the years 1993-1997.

*onthly
*eturns From
itechport.xls

	A	B	C	D	E
3	Code		MSFT	INTC	GE
4	1	1/29/93	0.013177	0.228161	0.00731
5	2	2/26/93	-0.03613	0.091335	-0.02322
6	3	3/31/93	0.109445	-0.01288	0.066924
7	4	4/30/93	-0.07568	-0.17196	0.01683
8	5	5/28/93	0.083333	0.165572	0.023448
9	6	6/30/93	-0.04993	-0.00789	0.039137
10	7	7/30/93	-0.15909	-0.04909	0.028721
11	8	8/31/93	0.015203	0.229665	-0.00254
12	9	9/30/93	0.09817	0.101167	-0.01776
13	10	10/29/93	-0.02879	-0.1053	0.011734
14	11	11/30/93	-0.00156	-0.02767	0.014175
15	12	12/31/93	0.007813	0.00813	0.073393
16	13	1/31/94	0.055814	0.053226	0.027414
17	14	2/28/94	-0.03084	0.05364	-0.02204
18	15	3/31/94	0.027273	-0.01818	-0.04418
19	16	4/29/94	0.091445	-0.09556	-0.0475
20	17	5/31/94	0.162162	0.02459	0.044619
21	18	6/30/94	-0.03953	-0.064	-0.05558
22	19	7/29/94	-0.00242	0.013932	0.080429
23	20	8/31/94	0.128641	0.109705	-0.01241
24	21	9/30/94	-0.03441	-0.06464	-0.02543
25	22	10/31/94	0.122494	0.011138	0.015584
26	23	11/30/94	-0.00198	0.016097	-0.05882
27	24	12/30/94	-0.02783	0.011881	0.117609
28	25	1/31/95	-0.02863	0.087045	0.009804
29	26	2/28/95	0.061053	0.149549	0.063107
30	27	3/31/95	0.128968	0.064263	-0.00621
31	28	4/28/95	0.149385	0.206893	0.037037
32	29	5/31/95	0.035933	0.096459	0.035714
33	30	6/30/95	0.067159	0.128062	-0.02095
34	31	7/31/95	0.001383	0.027285	0.046563
35	32	8/31/95	0.022099	-0.05577	-0.00212
36	33	9/29/95	-0.02162	-0.01833	0.089766
37	34	10/31/95	0.104972	0.160415	-0.00784
38	35	11/30/95	-0.12875	-0.1288	0.061265
39	36	12/29/95	0.007174	-0.06776	0.079479
40	37	1/31/96	0.054131	-0.026	0.065972
41	38	2/29/96	0.066892	0.064781	-0.01629
42	39	3/29/96	0.044965	-0.03294	0.03755
43	40	4/30/96	0.098182	0.191912	-0.00803
44	41	5/31/96	0.048565	0.114391	0.071197
45	42	6/28/96	0.011579	-0.02732	0.048338
46	43	7/31/96	-0.01873	0.02366	-0.04657
47	44	8/30/96	0.039236	0.062396	0.010638
40	45	9/30/96	0.076531	0.195771	0.100271
49	46	10/31/96	0.040758	0.151801	0.063187
50	47	11/29/96	0.142987	0.154721	0.074935
51	48	12/31/96	0.053386	0.03202	-0.04428
52	49	1/31/97	0.234493	0.239523	0.046776
53	50	2/28/97	-0.04412	-0.12558	-0.00604
54	51	3/31/97	-0.05962	-0.01938	-0.03018
55	52	4/30/97	0.325153	0.100988	0.118388
56	53	5/30/97	0.020576	-0.01061	0.087838
57	54	6/30/97	0.019153	-0.06394	0.076605
58	55	7/31/97	0.119683	0.295267	0.082846
59	56	8/29/97	-0.06581	0.003404	-0.10784
60	57	9/30/97	0.000946	0.002035	0.092068
61	58	10/31/97	-0.01748	-0.16555	-0.0505
62	59	11/28/97	0.088461	0.008117	0.143134
63	60	12/31/97	-0.08657	-0.09501	-0.00271

How could we determine what fraction of our assets we should allocate to each investment during the next year? We begin by bootstrapping off our 1993-1997 returns to generate many (say 1000) possible distributions of returns for these three stocks. Then we will use Solver or Evolver to solve for an optimal asset allocation for the following criteria:

- Minimize risk of the portfolio (standard deviation) subject to a desired mean return of at least 35%.

- Minimize probability of a loss subject to a desired mean return of at least 35%.

- Maximize the portfolio's Sharpe Ratio. The Sharpe Ratio of a portfolio equals $\dfrac{\mu - r}{\sigma}$.

- Minimize the portfolio's "downside risk" subject to a constraint on desired mean return.

Here μ = mean return on the portfolio, r = risk-free rate and σ = portfolio standard deviation. It turns out that whatever your risk-return preference, you should invest your money in the risky portfolio that maximizes the Sharpe Ratio.

Bootstrapping to Future Annual Returns

To generate, say, 1000 samples of annual returns for the next year we simply generate 12 months of MSFT, INT and GE returns **assuming that each of these 12 months is equally likely to be one of the last 60 months.** We proceed as follows:

Step by Step

Step 1: Name range A4:E63 (where returns lie) "Lookup".

Step 2: Assume current price of each stock is $1.

Step 3: In cells H5:H16 generate the "scenario" or month of 1993-1997 that is chosen to generate each month's returns for the next year by copying from H5 to H6:H16 the formula

   =RiskDuniform($A$4:$A$63).

The RiskDuniform function makes it equally likely that any of the numbers 1, 2, ..., 59, 60 are chosen.

Step 4: Copying from I5 to I5:K16 the formula

$$=I4*(1+VLOOKUP(\$H5,Lookup,I\$2))$$

generates 12 months of MSFT, INT and GE returns. For each month the new price equals the old price times the return on the stock generated by the Column H scenario for that month. For example, in Month 1 we chose Scenario 30, so returns for the stocks come from Row 33. Note that this approach implicitly models the correlations between the returns on the assets.

Figure 10.1

	G	H	I	J	K
2			3	4	5
3	Month	Scenario	MSFT	INTC	GE
4	0		1	1	1
5	1	30	1.067159	1.128062	0.979052
6	2	30	1.138828	1.272524	0.958542
7	3	30	1.21531	1.435486	0.938462
8	4	30	1.296929	1.619317	0.918803
9	5	30	1.384029	1.82669	0.899556
10	6	30	1.476978	2.06062	0.880712
11	7	30	1.57617	2.324507	0.862262
12	8	30	1.682024	2.622188	0.844199
13	9	30	1.794986	2.95799	0.826515
14	10	30	1.915535	3.336796	0.809201
15	11	30	2.04418	3.764113	0.792249
16	12	30	2.181464	4.246153	0.775653

Step 5: We now select cells I16:K16 as output cells and run 1000 iterations. Clicking on the Data window icon extracts the results of each iteration, which we then paste to a spreadsheet. We are now ready to solve each of our portfolio problems.

Minimize Risk of Portfolio (Standard Deviation)

We now show how to minimize the portfolio's standard deviation while ensuring that we have an expected return of at least 35%. See sheet Scen(min stdev).

Figure 10.2

	B	C	D	E	F	G	H	I	J	K
1	Mean	1.495564	1.558791	1.333413						
2					Sum					
3	Weights	0.111726	0.029346	0.858928	1					
4	Name	MSFT	INTC	GE						
5	Description	Output	Output	Output						
6	Iteration#	I16	J16	K16	Port Return					Required
7	1	1.15606	1.423145	1.258973	0.252293		Mean	0.358143	>=	0.35
8	2	1.844068	2.361518	1.376689	0.457808					
9	3	1.513937	1.748734	1.156956	0.214206		stdev	0.218459		
10	4	1.757936	1.186947	1.047859	0.131275					
11	5	0.947717	1.929377	1.640597	0.571659		Min St dev			
12	6	1.05338	1.461804	1.646367	0.574699		with 35% return			

Step 1: In cells C3:E3 we enter trial fractions for the percentage of our money invested in each stock.

Step 2: In F7:F1006 we compute the actual return on our portfolio for each scenario by copying from F7 to F8:F1006 the formula

   $=SUMPRODUCT(\$C\$3:\$E\$3,C7:E7)-1.$

Step 3: In I7 we compute the mean return on our portfolio by just averaging the portfolio return for each scenario with the formula

   $=AVERAGE(Scenarios).$

Note: The range Scenarios refers to F7:F1006.

Step 4: In cell I9 we compute the portfolio's standard deviation under the assumption that each scenario occurs with probability 1/1000.

   $=STDEVP(Scenarios).$

$$\sum_{all\ scenarios} \frac{1}{999}(Scenario\ Return - Mean)^2$$

Note: If we used =STDEV formula we would have obtained

when we actually want to divide by 1000 (not 999!).

Step 5: In cell F3 we compute total fraction invested with the formula

   $=SUM(C3:E3).$

Step 6: We now are ready to use Solver. Even though the problem of minimizing standard deviation is nonlinear, Solver is guaranteed to solve it correctly. This is because the objective function is a convex function and our constraints are linear functions. Our Solver Window follows:

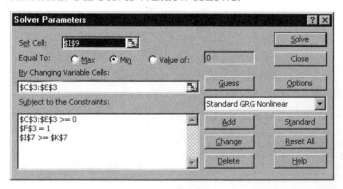

We minimize portfolio standard deviation (I9) by changing the fraction invested in each stock (C3:E3). We ensure that each fraction is non-negative (this rules out short-sales) and the total fraction invested equals 1 (F3 =1). To ensure at least a 35% mean return we add constraint I7>=K7. After selecting Solve we find that (see Figure 10.3) we should use the following investment strategy

Figure 10.3

	B	C	D	E
3	Weights	0.111726	0.029346	0.858928
4	Name	MSFT	INTC	GE

A mean return of 36.8% and standard deviation of 21.8% is obtained.

Finding the Efficient Frontier

By varying the required mean return and minimizing the portfolio standard deviation, we can obtain the efficient frontier. This is easily done with Add-in. We note from cells B1:E1 that mean return on portfolio will be between 33% and 54%. Here is how we use SolverTable.

Step by Step

Step 1: Under Tools>Add-Ins>Browse, find SolverTable and click OK to install it.

Step 2: We will change only one parameter (required mean return) so choose one-way SolverTable and fill in the dialog box as follows:

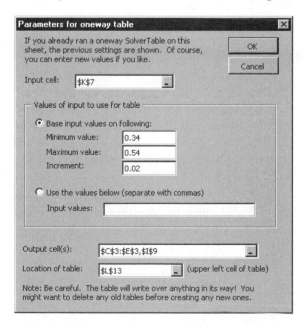

We change required mean return (K7) between .34 and .54 in increments of .02. For each value of mean return SolverTable will find the problem's optimal solution and then keep track of the fraction placed in each stock (C3:E3) and portfolio standard deviation (I9). The results follow:

Figure 10.4

	L	M	N	O	P
13		$C$3	$D$3	$E$3	$I$9
14	0.34	0.111726	0.029346	0.858928	0.218459
15	0.36	0.116666	0.03403	0.849304	0.218505
16	0.38	0.169728	0.084593	0.745679	0.224703
17	0.4	0.22279	0.135157	0.642053	0.240565
18	0.42	0.275852	0.185721	0.538428	0.264358
19	0.44	0.328913	0.236284	0.434802	0.294163
20	0.46	0.381975	0.286848	0.331177	0.328348
21	0.48	0.435037	0.337412	0.227551	0.365686
22	0.5	0.488099	0.387976	0.123926	0.405306
23	0.52	0.54116	0.438539	0.020301	0.446602
24	0.54	0.297204	0.702796	0	0.503044

For example, with a 40% required return, we place 22% in MSFT, 14% in Intel, and 64% in GE and obtain a portfolio sigma of 24%.

To graph the efficient frontier, we recopy the portfolio standard deviations to K14:K24

Figure 10.5

	K	L
13	Sigma	Mean
14	0.218459	0.34
15	0.218505	0.36
16	0.224703	0.38
17	0.240565	0.4
18	0.264358	0.42
19	0.294163	0.44
20	0.328348	0.46
21	0.365686	0.48
22	0.405306	0.5
23	0.446602	0.52
24	0.503044	0.54

and use the Chart Wizard's X-Y Option to graph the efficient frontier.

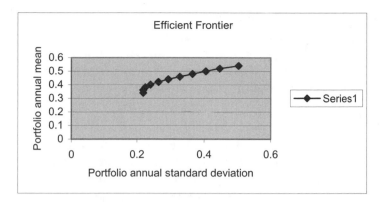

Note the efficient frontier, as expected, gets flatter. This tells us that each additional unit of sigma allowed increases our mean return by less and less!

Minimizing the Probability of a Loss

Suppose we still want to have an expected annual return of at least 35%, but our goal is to minimize the probability of losing money. In cell I8 of sheet Scen (Min Prob Loss) we compute the (See Figure 10.7) probability of a loss with the formula

$= PERCENTRANK(Scenarios,0).$

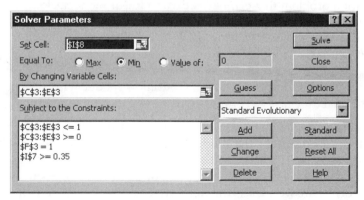

This formula gives fraction of iterations that yield a non-positive annual return.

Our Solver window simply minimizes the probability of a loss (cell I8). We have all the previous constraints and we have added the constraint that each fraction invested is <=1. We will soon see why this constraint was added. If we choose a starting solution which puts 50% of our money in Intel and Microsoft and none in GE the Solver tells us this is the optimal solution. Thus with this starting solution Solver tells us that the minimum chance of a loss is 8.7%. We will soon see that this is an incorrect answer to the problem.

Evolver and Genetic Algorithms

The Target cell of minimizing probability of loss is, unlike portfolio standard deviation, **not a convex function of our changing cells. Unfortunately, the ordinary Solver often finds incorrect answers when a problem requires minimizing a non-convex function.** Fortunately, we have Evolver, which handles this type of problem well. To use Evolver, we need to put a lower and upper bound on each changing cell. This is why we added constraints that C3:E3<=1.

In previous chapters we used the Excel Solver to solve many interesting and important problems. Unfortunately, there are many interesting and important optimization problems for which the Solver is ill-suited to find optimal solutions. Fortunately, however, **genetic algorithms** often perform well on optimization problems for which the Excel Solver performs poorly. The Excel add-in Evolver has a user interface similar to the Excel Solver and can easily be used to solve many optimization problems that cannot be solved with the Excel Solver. Before discussing genetic algorithms and Evolver let's look at the strengths and weaknesses of the Excel Solver.

Consider an optimization problem in which the target cell is a linear function of the changing cells, the left-hand and right-hand sides of each constraint are linear functions of the changing cells, and all changing cells may assume fractional values (e.g. changing cells are not required to be integers). For such problems (called **linear models)**, the Excel Solver is guaranteed to find (if one exists) an optimal solution. The Excel Solver is an excellent tool to use for modeling solutions for any optimization problem that can be set up as a linear model as long as the model does not exceed the size constraints (up to 200 changing cells and 200 constraints) of the Excel Solver[1]. Most larger linear models are difficult to handle in a spreadsheet format. Such larger models are often solved using a **modeling language** such as LINGO, GAMS or AMPLE. With a modeling language a user can generate, say 10,000 supply constraints for a transportation model with one line of computer code. This makes it easy to compactly represent and solve a large model.

It is important to note that if a spreadsheet uses =IF, =ABS, =MAX, =MIN functions which depend on any of the model's changing cells, then the model is nonlinear and Solver may have great difficulty finding an optimal solution. If Solver starts with an initial solution near the problem's optimal solution, then Solver will usually find the correct answer. Unfortunately, we have no way of knowing whether or not or initial solution is near the problems optimal solution.

---

[1] Solvers that handle problems involving thousands of changing cells may be purchased from Frontline Systems (web address www.frontsys.com).

An Introduction to Genetic Algorithms

In the early 1970s John Holland of the University of Michigan realized that many features of natural evolution (such as survival of the fittest and mutation) could be used to help solve difficult optimization problems. Goldberg (1989), Davis (1991) and Holland (1975) are good references on genetic algorithms. Since his methods were based on behavior observed in nature, Holland coined the name **genetic algorithms** to describe his methods. Simply stated, genetic algorithms provide a method of intelligently searching an optimization problem's feasible region for an optimal solution. Biological terminology is used to describe the algorithm. For example, the target cell is called a **fitness function**. A specification of values for all changing cells is called a **chromosome.** For most problems, a genetic algorithm codes changing cells in binary notation. For example, 1001 represents $1(2^3) + 0(2^2) + 0(2^1) + 1(2^0) = 8 + 1 = 9$.

Here is a rough outline of how a GA (genetic algorithm) might work. To illustrate, suppose we are trying to solve the following optimization problem:

Maximize $x^2 + y^2 - 3xy - 6x^2y$

Subject to $0 \le x \le 10$ and $0 \le y \le 10$.

In our discussion we assume our problem has no constraints except for lower and upper bounds on each changing cell; later we discuss how GAs handle constraints.

Step by Step

Step 1: Randomly sample values of the changing cells between the lower and upper bounds to generate a set of (usually at least 50) chromosomes. The initial set of chromosomes is called the population. For example, two members of the population might be

Chromosome 1: $x = 1001$ and $y = 0000$ (or $x = 9$ and $y = 0$)

Chromosome 2: $x = 0100$ and $y = 0010$ (or $x = 4$ and $y = 2$)

The initial population is constructed by randomly choosing points from throughout the problem's feasible region.

Step 2: Generate a new generation of (hopefully improved chromosomes). In the new generation chromosomes with a larger fitness function (in a max problem) have a greater chance of surviving to the next generation. In our example Chromosome 1 has a fitness value of 81 and Chromosome 2 has a fitness value of -196. Clearly, Chromosome 1 should have a larger chance of surviving to the next generation. The ideas of **crossover** and mutation are also used to generate chromosomes for the next generation.

Crossover (fairly common) "splices" together two chromosomes at a pre-specified point. For example, if the Chromosomes 1 and 2 were combined by crossover and the crossover point is between the 2nd and 3rd digit the resulting chromosomes would be

Chromosome 1': x = 1000 y = 0010

Chromosome 2': x = 0101 y = 0000

Mutation (very rare) randomly selects a digit and changes it (from 0 to 1 or 1 to 0). For example, if we chose to mutate the first digit of x in Chromosome 1, then Chromosome 1 would become x = 0001 y = 0000.

Step 3: At each generation the maximum fitness in the generation is recorded. If after many consecutive generations no improvement in the maximum fitness is observed, then the GA terminates.

How would a GA handle a constraint such as x + y≤50? Simply subtract (in a maximization problem), say 100*(x + y -50) from the fitness function. Now any chromosome violating the constraint will have a low value of the fitness function (because -100(x + y - 50) will greatly reduce the value of the new fitness function). This causes the GA to stay away from chromosomes that violate the constraint.

Strengths and Weaknesses of GAs

If you let a GA run long enough it is guaranteed to find the solution to any optimization problem. The problem is that the sun may supernova before the GA finds the optimal solution! In general, we never know how long we should run a GA. For the problems discussed in this chapter, an optimal solution was always found within 120 minutes. Therefore, we will usually tell Evolver to run for 120 minutes and report the best solution found. Again, we will not know if the best solution we have found is optimal, but it is usually a good solution in the sense that the best value of the fitness function we have obtained is close to the actual optimal value of the fitness function.

As a rule, GAs do very well in problems with few constraints (excluding bounds on changing cells, which are required by Evolver). **The complexity of the target cell does not bother a GA.** For example, GAs thrive on =MIN, =MAX =IF, =ABS functions in spreadsheets. This is the key advantage of GAs. Evolver usually does not perform as well, however, on problems having many constraints. Now it's time to see what Evolver can do!

We are now ready to use Evolver! The Evolver toolbar looks as follows:

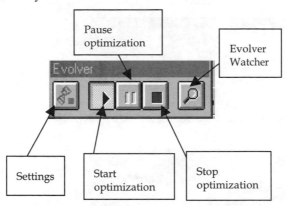

We will not use the Evolver Watcher icon (Evolver Watcher allows you to view Evolver's progress as it solves your problem). The functions of the other icons will be described as we proceed with our example.

Step by Step

Step 1: Click on the Settings icon. This allows you to set the cell you are optimizing, the adjustable cells (analogous to Solver changing cells), and constraints. You will see the following dialog box:

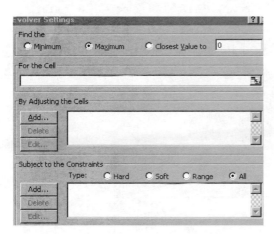

Step 2: Select cell I8 (Probability of loss) to minimize.

Step 3: Select Add under Adjust the Cells, and fill in dialog box as follows:

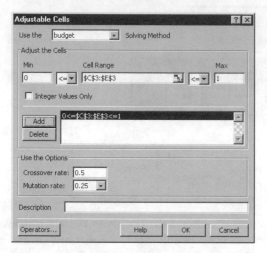

We use the Budget solving method to ensure that fractions invested add to 1 (this requires your starting values of changing cells add to 1!). We recommend a mutation rate of .25 (if you have Industrial or Professional version set mutation on AUTO). Also we recommend (if you have the Industrial or Professional version) choosing Operators and selecting ALL. Now select OK to return to Evolver Settings dialog box.

Step 4: Now select Add Constraint and fill it in as follows:

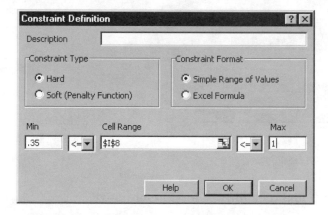

This ensures a mean gain of at least 35%.

Step 5: Our Evolver Settings dialog box now looks as follows:

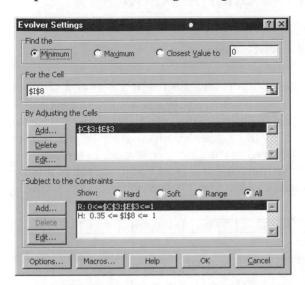

After selecting the Start button we find the optimal solution given in Figure 10.7.

Figure 10.7

	B	C	D	E	F	G	H	I
1								
2					Sum			
3	Weights	0.290231	0.116649	0.593121	1			
4	Name	MSFT	INTC	GE				
5	Description	Output	Output	Output				
6	Iteration#	I16	J16	K16	Port Return			
7	1	1.15606	1.423145	1.258973	0.248255		Mean	0.406764
8	2	1.844068	2.361518	1.376689	0.627216		Prob Loss	0.013
9	3	1.513937	1.748734	1.156956	0.329593			
10	4	1.757936	1.186947	1.047859	0.270169			
11	5	0.947717	1.929377	1.640597	0.473188		Min probability of a los	
12	6	1.05338	1.461804	1.646367	0.452735		with >=35% return	

Thus we can hold probability of a loss to 1.3% and still obtain a mean return of at least 35%. We invest 29% of our money in MSFT, 11% in Intel, and 59% in GE.

Maximizing the Sharpe Ratio

The Sharpe Ratio of a portfolio equals $\dfrac{\mu - r}{\sigma}$.

Here μ = mean return on portfolio, r = risk-free rate and σ = portfolio standard deviation. It turns out that whatever your risk-return preference, you should invest your money in the risky portfolio that maximizes the Sharpe Ratio. Many Wall Street firms evaluate their traders based on their Sharpe Ratios. This requires traders who choose risky trading strategies to attain expected returns commensurate with the high risk they have taken. We can easily use Evolver to find the portfolio that maximizes the Sharpe Ratio. We assume a risk-free rate of 5%.

Figure 10.8

	B	C	D	E	F	G	H	I
1								
2					Sum			
3	Weights	0.182682	0.096921	0.720397	1			
4	Name	MSFT	INTC	GE				
5	Description	Output	Output	Output				
6	Iteration#	I16	J16	K16	Port Return			
7	1	1.15606	1.423145	1.258973	0.256084		Mean	0.384879
8	2	1.844068	2.361518	1.376689	0.557522		Sigma	0.227737
9	3	1.513937	1.748734	1.156956	0.279526		risk free	0.05
10	4	1.757936	1.186947	1.047859	0.191058		Sharpe Ratio	1.470461
11	5	0.947717	1.929377	1.640597	0.542009			

Step by Step

Step 1: In cell I10 compute the Sharpe Ratio with the formula

$=(I7-I9)/I8$.

Step 2: Our Evolver Settings Window is as follows:

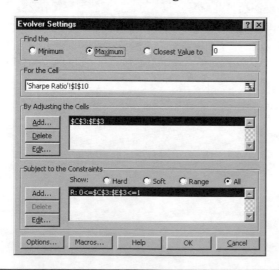

We maximize (cell I10) the Sharpe ratio by changing fraction invested in each stock (cells C3:E3). We ensure that the fraction invested in each stock is between 0 and 1. Finally to ensure a total (cell F3) of 100% of our money is invested we selected the Budget solving method when choosing our Adjusting Cells. We find that 18% in MSFT, 10% in Intel, and 72% in GE will yield the highest Sharpe Ratio (1.47).

Minimizing Downside Risk

Although most finance professionals measure the riskiness of a portfolio by its variance or standard deviation, this is a flawed approach to measuring risk. For example, a portfolio with a .5 chance at yielding a 100% return and a .5 chance at yielding a 20% return has a standard deviation of 40% while a portfolio which has a .5 chance at losing 40% and a .5 chance of breaking even has a 20% standard deviation. Clearly, the second portfolio is more risky **even though it has a lower standard deviation**. The problem is the risk we really care about is the chance of failing to meet a goal. The downside risk approach attempts to minimize the average amount by which we fail to meet a target. For example, we might set a target of 10% on our investment. A reasonable approach to portfolio selection is to set a desired expected return (say 30%) and then choose a target (say 10%) and minimize the average amount by which target is not met (this is the **downside risk**) subject to meeting the constraint on desired expected return. We implement this approach in the sheet Downside Risk. By copying from G7 to G8:G1006 the formula

=IF(F7<$I$8,$I$8-F7,0)

we determine the downside risk for each scenario. Then in cell I9 we compute the average downside risk with the formula

=AVERAGE(G7:G1006).

Our Evolver Settings Window is set as follows (again we use the Budget solving method).

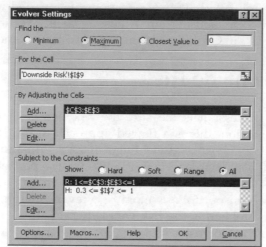

We find the optimal solution in Figure 10.9.

Figure 10.9

	B	C	D	E	F	G	H	I
1								
2					Sum			
3	Weights	0.31818	0.065166	0.618626	1.001972558			
4	Name	MSFT	INTC	GE				
5	Description	Output	Output	Output				
6	Iteration#	I16	J16	K16	Port Return	Shortfall		
7	1	1.15606	1.423145	1.258973	0.23941001	0	Mean	0.402323
8	2	1.844068	2.361518	1.376689	0.592293048	0	Target	0.1
9	3	1.513937	1.748734	1.156956	0.311386456	0	Downside risk	0.005008

Thus we can achieve a downside risk of .5% by putting 32% in MSFT, 7% in Intel, and 62% in GE.

Chapter 11: Long a Stock; Short Some Puts?: The Nortel Trade

On January 4, 2000 Nortel was selling for $93.72. Let's suppose we buy 10,000 shares of Nortel. Perhaps we may want to trade in some 3 month $75, $80, and $85 puts to hedge our risk.

The historical volatility of Nortel was 48%. Plugging into Black-Scholes we find the following prices for these puts.

Put exercise Price	3 Month Put Price
$75	$1.43
$80	$2.50
$85	$4.02

We will evaluate our trades on NPV. **When investment strategies involve shorting investments** this makes more sense than evaluating trades based on return. We will assume the investment firm desires an expected return of 20%, so a hurdle rate of 20% will be used. We will solve for an optimal investment strategy using the following criteria:

- Minimize variance subject to a mean NPV that is non-negative.

- Maximize our VAR (the 5th percentile of our NPV).

- Maximize our absolute worst-case scenario.

To begin (see file **Nortel.xls**) we generate 400 "scenarios" for Nortel's price in 3 months. Let's suppose we expect 20% annual growth for Nortel. If we combine this with the volatility of 48% we may model Nortel's stock price on the date the options expire by entering the formula

$=I8*EXP((0.2-0.5*0.48\^2)*(55/252)+SQRT(55/252)*0.48*RiskNormal(0,1))$

into cell I10. See Figure 11.1.

Then we run 400 iterations and click on the Show Data Window icon to extract the data.

Figure 11.1

	C	D	E	F	G	H	I	J	K		L
2	Close	Return	Ln(1+Ret)				Buy 10000 shares				
3	24.8988					Today 01/04/2000		75 put price	$	1.43	
4	25.3967	0.019997	0.0198			3 month hedge		80 put price	$	2.50	
5	28.3223	0.115196	0.10903			expires 03/24/00		85 put price		4.02	
6	28.9759	0.023077	0.022815			55 trade days					
7	27.8866	-0.037593	-0.038318				Price	Scenario	Min		55
8	27.7621	-0.004465	-0.004475			Today	93.72		Max		130
9	27.1708	-0.021299	-0.021529			Price March 24	53.61978		60		1
10	26.3927	-0.028637	-0.029055						70		2
11	26.3927	0	0						80		6
12	26.3304	-0.002361	-0.002363						90		12
13	28.0422	0.065012	0.062986						100		24
14	27.5754	-0.016646	-0.016786						110		12
15	27.1397	-0.0158	-0.015926						120		10
16	26.8907	-0.009175	-0.009217						Mean $99.87from riskgene		

We now compute the NPV of our trades for each scenario. See Figure 11.2.

Figure 11.2

	I	J	K	L	M	N
1						
2	Buy 10000 shares					
3	0	75 put price	$ 1.43		-9551.512023	
4		80 put price	$ 2.50		6283.977604	
5		85 put price	4.02		-223.5293632	
6						
7	Price	Scenario	Min	55		
8	93.72		Max	130		
9	53.61978		60	1		
10			70	2		
11			80	6		
12			90	12		
13			100	24		
14			110	12		
15			120	10		
16			Mean $99.87from riskgeneral!			
17						
18					VAR	-309245.8
19	Name				mean	-5011
20	Description				stdev	211010.4
21	Iteration#	Price	Cost of Stock	Put costs	Put payoff	NPV
22	1	94.54641	937200	1152.694	0	-37910.69
23	2	131.7515	937200	1152.694	0	316423.5
24	3	117.7525	937200	1152.694	0	183099.7
25	4	96.36205	937200	1152.694	0	-20618.88
26	5	93.10383	937200	1152.694	0	-51649.55
27	6	79.71183	937200	1152.694	628.7925538	-178593.6
28	7	89.46455	937200	1152.694	0	-86309.36
29	8	96.73312	937200	1152.694	0	-17084.88
30	9	116.2253	937200	1152.694	0	168554.9
31	10	118.2846	937200	1152.694	0	188167.3
32	11	67.05098	937200	1152.694	1434.058565	-298406.2

Step by
Step

Step 1: In cell K22 we compute the cost of purchasing our 10,000 shares of Nortel with the formula

> *=10000*$I$8.*

Step 2: In cell L22 we compute the cost of buying the puts with the formula

> *=SUMPRODUCT($M$3:$M$5,$K$3:$K$5).*

Step 3: In cell M22 we compute the cash received from the puts in three months with the formula

> *=IF(J22<75,75-J22,0)*$M$3+$M$4*IF(J22<80,80-J22,0)+IF(J22<85,85-J22,0)*$M$5.*

Step 4: In cell N22 we compute the total NPV of our transactions with the formula

> *=10000*J22/1.05-K22-L22+M22/1.05.*

Step 5: In cells N17-N19 we compute the VAR, mean, and standard deviation of our NPV with the formulas

> *= PERCENTILE(N22:N421,0.05) (VAR)*

> *= AVERAGE(N22:N421) (Mean)*

> *= STDEVP(N22:N421) (Standard Deviation).*

Step 6: We now use Solver to find the minimum variance portfolio having a mean NPV of at least -$5011 (this is mean of NPV if we just own stock).

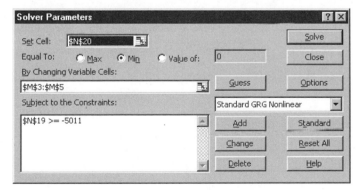

We find that we should short 9552 $75 puts, long 6284 $80 puts and short 224 $85 puts.

Step 7: We copy all our work to a new worksheet and now maximize VAR. This requires we use Evolver, so we bound number of puts of each type bought or sold by 100,000. Our Evolver Window follows:

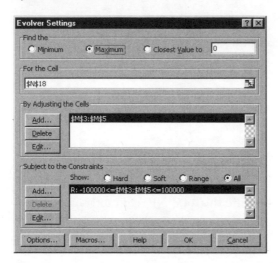

Note we use the Recipe solving method when selecting Adjusting Cells, because there is no need for the Adjusting Cells to add to any particular number. The Recipe method essentially makes Evolver act like the ordinary Solver when conducting an optimization.

Figure 11.3 gives the VAR maximizing trades.

Figure 11.3

	H	I	J	K	L	M	N
1	0.482718773						
2		Buy 10000 shares					
3	Today 01/04/2000		75 put price	$ 1.43		3047.760859	
4	3 month hedge		80 put price	$ 2.50		-7859.830611	
5	expires 03/24/00		85 put price	4.02		14807.26093	
6	55 trade days						
7		Price	Scenario				
8	Today	93.72					
9	Price March 24	85.84671					
10							
11							
12							
13							
14							
15							
16							0.634
17							
18						VAR	-163705.2
19		Name				mean	-14700.09
20		Description				stdev	173284.5
21		Iteration#	Price	Cost of Stock	Put costs	Disc Put payoff	NPV
22		1	94.54641	937200	44233.91	0	-80991.91
23		2	131.7515	937200	44233.91	0	273342.3
24		3	117.7525	937200	44233.91	0	140018.5
25		4	96.36205	937200	44233.91	0	-63700.1
26		5	93.10383	937200	44233.91	0	-94730.77
27		6	79.71183	937200	44233.91	76038.34565	-149856.2
28		7	89.46455	937200	44233.91	0	-129390.6
29		8	96.73312	937200	44233.91	0	-60166.1
30		9	116.2253	937200	44233.91	0	125473.7
31		10	118.2846	937200	44233.91	0	145086.1
32		11	67.05098	937200	44233.91	188225.4308	-163590.8

We go long 3048 $75 puts, go short 7860 $80 puts and go long 14,808 $85 puts. Our VAR has increased from losing $309,000 to losing $164,000. Of course, our mean NPV has decreased but so has our standard deviation.

Stress Testing

An extremely conservative approach to risk management is to look at the absolute worst case (minimum profit). In Figure 11.4 we computed minimum NPV in cell N17 we computed the minimum NPV obtained with the formula

=MIN(N22:N421).

Then we used Evolver to determine the "best" worst case with the following Evolver window.

Figure 11.4

	H	I	J	K	L	M	N
1	0.482718773						
2		Buy 10000 shares					
3	Today 01/04/2000		75 put price	$ 1.43		-1329.789976	
4	3 month hedge		80 put price	$ 2.50		1138.48142	
5	expires 03/24/00		85 put price	4.02		10000.0053	
6	55 trade days						
7		Price	Scenario	Min	55		
8	Today	93.72		Max	130		
9	Price March 24	95.47071		60	1		
10				70	2		
11				80	6		
12				90	12		
13				100	24		
14				110	12		
15				120	10		
16				Mean $99.87from riskgeneral!			0.628
17						MIN	-168820.8
18						VAR	-168820.8
19		Name				mean	-14179.43
20		Description				stdev	175468.3
21		Iteration#	Price	Cost of Stock	Put costs	Disc Put payoff	NPV
22		1	94.54641	937200	41144.63	0	-77902.63
23		2	131.7515	937200	41144.63	0	276431.6
24		3	117.7525	937200	41144.63	0	143107.8

From Figure 11.4 we find that we can improve the worst case to a loss of $168,821.

Chapter 12: Evaluating Trading Rules: The Moving Average

A common trading rule is the following: Buy the stock if the price is higher than the K day moving average and sell the stock if the price is below the M day moving average. We can use Evolver to find the optimal trading rule of this form. In file **Ibmma.xls** we have 2 years of daily IBM prices. We will seek the optimal moving average trading rule where K and M can be at most 30.

Step by Step

Step 1: We begin 30 days into our data (March 19, 1998) and compute the 1, 2, …30 day moving averages of prices by copying from I37 to I37:AL571 the formula

    =AVERAGE(OFFSET($B37,-I$35,0,I$35,1)).

This formula begins with the current price (in cell B37) and creates a range that begins I35 cells above cell B37. The range consists of I35 rows and 1 column. This range is then averaged. Copying this formula computes 2 day moving averages in column J, etc.

Step 2: In D32 and E32 we enter trial values for K and M.

Step 3: In G37 we compute the cutoff for buying with the formula

    =OFFSET($I37,0,$D$31-1,1,1).

This formula goes K –1 columns to the right of the one day moving average. This yields the K day moving average.

In H37 we compute the cutoff for selling with the formula

    =OFFSET($I37,0,$E$31-1,1,1).

This formula goes M-1 columns to the right of the one day moving average to yield the M day moving average.

Step 4: In C37 we enter No to indicate we do not own the stock. In D37 we determine if we buy the stock today with the following formula

    =IF(AND(C37="No",B37>=G37),"Yes","No").

We buy the stock if and only if we do not own it and price exceeds buy cutoff.

Step 5: In cell E37 we determine if we sell the stock with the formula

=IF(AND(C37="Yes",B37<H37),"Yes","No").

We sell the stock if and only if we owned it and price is below cutoff point for sale.

Step 6: In cell F37 we determine today's cash flows with the formula

=IF(D37="Yes",-B37,IF(E37="Yes",B37,0)).

This ensures that we pay for the stock if we buy it and receive price of stock if we sell it.

Step 7: In cell C38 we determine if we own stock at beginning of 2nd day of trading with the formula

=IF(D37="Yes","Yes",IF(E37="Yes","No",C37)).

If we bought the stock yesterday we own it. If we sold it yesterday we do not own it. Otherwise our status is whatever it was yesterday.

Step 8: We now copy the formula in columns C:F down to the bottom of the spreadsheet.

Step 9: In cell F35 we compute our total profit from trading

=SUM(F37:F573)+IF(C573="Yes",B573,0).

Note if we own the stock at end of period we "cash it in" for the last day's price.

Step 10: We now use Evolver to determine the profit maximizing values of K and M. Our Evolver Window follows. Again we use the Recipe method. We find that we should buy when price exceeds the 2-day moving average and sell when price is lower than the 27 day moving average. Total profit is $75.93. Note buy and hold beats our strategy (buy and hold makes $84.00) but in a bear market our strategy might help a lot! We maximize profit (F35) by changing K and M to be an integer between 1 and 30. Again we choose the Recipe method.

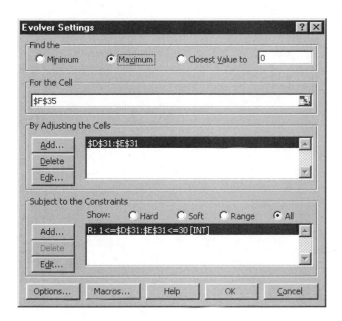

Figure 12.1

	C	D	E	F	G	H	I	J	K	L	M	N
29												
30		MA Buy	MA Sell									
31		2	27									
32												
33												
34				Total								
35				75.9343			1	2	3	4	5	6
36	Own	Buy?	Sell?	Cash Flow	Buy Cut	Sell Cut	MA 1	MA 2	MA 3	MA 4	MA 5	MA 6
37	No	Yes	No	-31.2095	30.58965	26.02699	30.8686	30.58965	30.3727	29.8923	29.75904	29.49973
38	Yes	No	No	0	31.03905	26.33008	31.2095	31.03905	30.79627	30.5819	30.15574	30.00078
39	Yes	No	No	0	31.1165	26.62056	31.0235	31.1165	31.03387	30.85308	30.67022	30.30037
40	Yes	No	No	0	30.7291	26.88694	30.4347	30.7291	30.88923	30.88408	30.7694	30.63097
41	Yes	No	No	0	31.08555	27.18662	31.7364	31.08555	31.06487	31.10103	31.05454	30.93057
42	Yes	No	No	0	31.7209	27.49662	31.7054	31.7209	31.29217	31.225	31.2219	31.16302
43	Yes	No	No	0	31.45745	27.78253	31.2095	31.45745	31.55043	31.2715	31.2219	31.21983
44	Yes	No	No	0	31.44195	28.05929	31.6744	31.44195	31.52977	31.58143	31.35208	31.29732
45	Yes	No	No	0	31.6744	28.32573	31.6744	31.6744	31.51943	31.56593	31.60002	31.4058

Remark

Katz and McCormick (2000) give a discussion of many different trading strategies. Evolver is well-suited to optimize virtually any mechanical trading system.

Reference

Katz, J, and McCormick, D., *The Encyclopedia of Trading Strategies*, McGraw Hill, 2000

Chapter 13: Evaluating Stop Loss Trades

Many traders advocate selling a stock if your loss exceeds, say 5%. The idea is you will truncate your downside risk. Of course, you may also lose some winners. Let's use the following example to explore stop loss trading.

Example 13.1

Junkco is currently selling for $100 and has a 50% volatility. We do not know the mean return on Junkco, but we believe it is equally likely to be –10%, 0%, 5%, 10%, 15% or 20%. Compare and contrast the merits of a Buy and Hold and stop loss strategies. Consider 5%, 4%, 3%, 2%, and 1% stop loss strategies.

Solution

Our work is in file **Stoploss.xls**. See Figure 13.1.

Figure 13.1

	A	B	C	D	E	F	G	H	I
1									
2	Stop Loss Trading				Stop Loss	0.05			
3					Mu	0		Total Stop	Hold
4					sigma	0.5		-6.653308	-0.364983
5				Day	Price	Sell?	Sold Already?	Profit	
6				0	100	no	no		
7				1	101.7897	no	no	0	
8				2	105.8422	no	no	0	
9				3	106.6385	no	no	0	
10				4	107.1105	no	no	0	
11				5	106.9566	no	no	0	
12				6	108.4836	no	no	0	
13				7	106.9538	no	no	0	
14				8	112.6868	no	no	0	
15				9	110.3391	no	no	0	

Step by Step

Step 1: In F3 we generate the mean return on the stock (unknown to us) with the formula

$$=RiskDuniform(\{-0.1,0,0.05,0.1,0.15,0.2\}) .$$

Step 2: We use the RiskSimtable function to generate different stop loss parameters by entering in cell F2 the formula

$$=RiskSimtable(\{0.05,0.04,0.03,0.02,0.01\}).$$

On our first simulation this will put .05 in the cell. Then in the second simulation .04 will be entered in the cell, etc.

Step 3: By copying from E7 to E8:E132 the formula

$$=E6*EXP(($F$3-0.5*$F$4\wedge2)*(1/252)+SQRT(1/252)*$F$4*RiskNormal(0,1))$$

we generate daily stock prices for the next six months.

Step 4: Since stock will not be sold on day 0 we enter no in F6 and G6.

Step 5: By copying from F7 to F8:F131 the formula

$$=IF(AND(G6="no",E7<$E$6*(1-$F$2)),"yes","no")$$

we determine (if the stock was sold before the last day) the day the stock was sold. If the stock was not sold so far and the price drops below the stop loss cut, we sell; otherwise we hold the stock. In cell F132 we ensure that if the stock has not been already sold it will be sold with the formula

$$=IF(G131="no","yes","no").$$

Step 6: By copying from G7 to G8:G132 the formula

$$=IF(OR(G6="yes",F7="yes"),"yes","no")$$

we determine if the stock has already been sold. This formula returns a yes if and only if the stock has been already sold or is sold today.

Step 7: In cells H7:H132 we determine the profit for selling the stock by copying from H7 to H8:H132 the formula

$$=IF(F7="yes",E7-$E$6,0).$$

Step 8: We compute our total profit from the stop loss strategy in cell H4 with the formula

$$=SUM(H7:H132).$$

Step 9: We compute our Buy and Hold profit in cell I4 with the formula

$$=E132-100.$$

Step 10: We now select H4 and I4 as Output cells and change simulations to 5. This is one simulation for each stop loss parameter in the RiskSimtable function. The first simulation puts in 5% for the stop loss parameter, the second simulation puts in 4%, etc.

The statistical results follow:

	J	K	L	M	N	O	P
11		5%	4%	3%	2%	1%	No stop
12	Minimum =	-13.75023	-12.06004	-11.60002	-10.6096	-9.484633	-65.92669
13	Maximum =	219.4751	219.4751	219.4751	219.4751	219.4751	213.1479
14	Mean =	1.991801	1.790236	1.299773	0.946293	1.28616	3.538156
15	Std Deviation =	26.22898	24.98213	22.18828	20.34021	19.46234	38.52449
16	Variance =	687.9594	624.1069	492.3198	413.7243	378.7827	1484.136
17	Skewness =	4.080042	4.505787	4.812166	5.614514	6.08673	1.243218
18	Kurtosis =	23.47426	27.81749	31.50931	41.58032	47.99221	5.757193
19	Errors Calculated =	0	0	0	0	0	0
20	Mode =	-5.538232	-4.414807	-3.520229	-2.010273	-2.542478	-11.23865
21	5% Perc =	-9.411376	-8.470624	-7.452106	-6.765584	-6.024422	-45.67994
22	10% Perc =	-8.541853	-7.559639	-6.713468	-5.857709	-5.215231	-39.50723
23	15% Perc =	-7.860382	-6.933333	-6.187143	-5.449895	-4.552212	-33.31434
24	20% Perc =	-7.517902	-6.562781	-5.749441	-5.00773	-4.039846	-28.33883
25	25% Perc =	-7.182192	-6.23794	-5.457998	-4.598377	-3.683832	-23.50751
26	30% Perc =	-6.824297	-5.899373	-5.156869	-4.207958	-3.381366	-18.68776
27	35% Perc =	-6.599123	-5.681827	-4.90829	-3.979935	-3.113896	-14.92111
28	40% Perc =	-6.368097	-5.500281	-4.656072	-3.712862	-2.820898	-11.14794
29	45% Perc =	-6.180004	-5.321341	-4.395678	-3.485848	-2.596487	-7.14002
30	50% Perc =	-5.966582	-5.108392	-4.184331	-3.274668	-2.414001	-2.834792
31	55% Perc =	-5.788366	-4.953723	-4.010651	-3.105671	-2.231174	0.922801
32	60% Perc =	-5.665731	-4.787942	-3.843775	-2.923339	-2.021118	5.175199
33	65% Perc =	-5.532217	-4.612615	-3.679443	-2.763833	-1.8568	11.95491
34	70% Perc =	-5.412705	-4.421892	-3.514884	-2.608267	-1.695573	17.03061
35	75% Perc =	-5.266972	-4.314614	-3.366882	-2.478918	-1.541915	24.15382
36	80% Perc =	-5.134403	-4.184083	-3.238027	-2.318293	-1.397679	30.74301
37	85% Perc =	-5.001848	-4.051627	-3.120807	-2.184902	-1.223392	39.9841
38	90% Perc =	29.50761	21.72475	2.474941	-2.044979	-1.089288	52.33545
39	95% Perc =	55.16515	51.33362	45.08484	35.50145	26.39144	70.78304

Note the Buy and Hold has the highest expected profit, but it has double the risk of the 1% stop loss strategy. Note the risk (standard deviation) is lower with a 1% stop loss, than with a 5% stop loss. VAR is best for 1% strategy. 95 percentile, however is best for Buy and Hold.

Basically, the worth of the stop loss strategy depends on how sure you are about the mean return on the stock. If you are fairly sure about the mean return on the stock, then the stop loss is probably not a great idea. If you are pretty unsure about mean return on stock, stop loss can greatly reduce your risk.

Chapter 14: Modeling a Risk Arbitrage Trade

During merger negotiations the company launching the takeover bid (called the Cannibal) offers to trade r shares of their stock for 1 share of the target (called the Prey). When a merger is in process a **risk arbitrage strategy** involves going long one share of stock of the takeover target (the Prey) and short r shares of the stock of the company launching the takeover (Cannibal). If the deal goes through we lock in an "arbitrage profit" by using the shares of the Cannibal obtained from our long position in the takeover target to cover our short position in the Cannibal. If the deal does not go through, we can lose a ton of money if the Cannibal increases in price and the merger target goes down in price. Here is an example of how to model the risk inherent in a risk arbitrage trade.

Example 14.1

JDS Uniphase (The Cannibal) is considering buying ETECH Dynamics (The Prey). Currently ETECH is selling for $182.75 and JDS is selling for $96.50. The offer is 2.2 shares of JDS for one share of ETECH. To conduct the risk arbitrage trade we go long one share of ETECH and short 2.2 shares of JDS. If the deal goes through we can exchange our ETECH share for 2.2 shares of JDS and cover our short position. Then we have locked in a profit of 2.2(96.5) – 182.75. We estimate an 80% chance that the deal will go through and it will take between 1 and 4 months for the deal to be completed. The historical volatility of ETECH is 108% and JDS is 79%. If the deal does not go through we estimate the annual mean return on ETECH will be 10% and the annual mean return on JDS will be –30%. We assume that if the deal does not go through there will be a negative .50 correlation between the price changes in ETECH and JDS. Model the risk inherent in this transaction.

Solution

Our work is in file **Optics.xls**. See Figure 14.1.

Figure 14.1

	A	B	C	D	E	F	G	H	I	J
1			JDSU buying ETECH			Hurdle rate	0.2			
2			2.2 JDSU for 1 ETECH			Deal Go?	1			
3			Long 1 ETECH Short 2.2 JDSU					Low	Medium	High
4		Current	Volatility	Mean if no deal	Ending price no deal	Prob deal goes?	0.8			
5	Etech	182.75	1.08	0.1	166.3615685	Time to do Deal	0.1944	1	2	4
6	JDSU	96.5	0.79	-0.3	85.67261984					
7						Correlations				
8							1	-0.5		
9							-0.5	1		
10	Profit from deal going through	29.55		spread	7.431804832	mean cap cost	192.59			
11	profit if deal does not go through	0		capital cost	182.75					
12	Total profit	29.55		return	0.78909304					
13										

Step 1: In cell G2 we determine if the deal goes through with the formula

$$= RiskBinomial(1,G4).$$

With probability G4 (.8) this enters a "1" (which means deal goes through) and with probability .2 this enters a "0" (which means deal does not go through).

Step 2: In cell G5 we determine the number of years it takes to complete the deal with the statement

$$= RiskTriang(H5,I5,J5)/12.$$

Step 3: In cells E5 and E6 we compute the prices of ETECH and JDS at the conclusion of the deal period (under the assumption that the deal does not go through) with the following formulas

ETECH PRICE

$$=B5*EXP((D5-0.5*C5^2)*\$G\$5+SQRT(\$G\$5)*RiskNormal(0,1,RiskCorrmat(\$F\$8:\$G\$9,1))*C5)$$

JDS Price

$$=B6*EXP((D6-0.5*C6^2)*\$G\$5+SQRT(\$G\$5)*RiskNormal(0,1,RiskCorrmat(\$F\$8:\$G\$9,2))*C6)$$

Note that the first argument of the RiskCorrmat function indicates the location of the correlation matrix for ETECH and JDS prices while the second argument indicates the column of the correlation matrix that applies to the random variable described in the formula.

Step 4: In cell B10 we compute our "arbitrage" profit that is received if and only if the deal goes through. This profit is 2.2*Current JDS Price – Current ETECH Price.

$$=IF(G2=1,2.2*B6-B5,0).$$

Step 5: In cell B11 we compute our profit if the deal does not go through. Our profit is given by -2.2*(Increase in JDS Price) + (Increase in ETECH price).

$$=IF(G2=0,-2.2*(E6-B6)+(E5-B5),0).$$

Step 6: In cell B12 we compute total profit from trade (here we ignore time value of money) as

$$=B10+B11.$$

Step 7: After making B12 an output cell we obtain the following results

	A	B
19	Name	Total NPV / Current
20	Description	Output
21	Cell	[optics.xls]model!B12
22	Minimum =	-399.6066
23	Maximum =	511.4588
24	Mean =	27.91393
25	Std Deviation =	63.83085
26	Variance =	4074.377
27	Skewness =	0.6452307
28	Kurtosis =	18.94136
29	Errors Calculated =	0
30	Mode =	29.55
31	5% Perc =	-70.95904
32	10% Perc =	14.87933
33	15% Perc =	29.55
34	20% Perc =	29.55
35	25% Perc =	29.55
36	30% Perc =	29.55
37	35% Perc =	29.55
38	40% Perc =	29.55
39	45% Perc =	29.55
40	50% Perc =	29.55
41	55% Perc =	29.55
42	60% Perc =	29.55
43	65% Perc =	29.55
44	70% Perc =	29.55
45	75% Perc =	29.55
46	80% Perc =	29.55
47	85% Perc =	29.55
48	90% Perc =	29.55
49	95% Perc =	96.85315

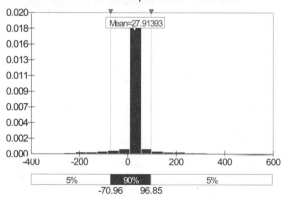

Distribution for Total profit / Current/B12

Although our average profit is $27.91, there is a small chance of a huge loss.

Alternative Methods for Evaluating Trades

We could also evaluate trades in terms of the annual percentage return they generate. We can compute the annual percentage return on a trade as

$$\frac{Profit\ from\ trade(1/duration\ of\ trade)}{mean\ capital\ cost\ of\ trade}$$

Define Spread = Change in ETECH price – 2.2(Change in JDS price). Then our cost of trade may be expressed as follows:

Table 14.1

Situation	Capital Cost
Deal goes through	Today's ETECH price
Deal fails and Spread<0	Today's ETECH price - spread
Deal Fails and Spread>0	Today's ETECH price

In file **Optics.xls** we have computed the percentage return on this transaction and run 4000 iterations to determine the distribution of the percentage return. See Figure 14.2.

Figure 14.2

	A	B	C	D	E	F	G	H	I	J
1			JDSU buying ETECH			Hurdle rate	0.2			
2			2.2 JDSU for 1 ETECH			Deal Go?	1			
3			Long 1 ETECH Short 2.2 JDSU					Low	Medium	High
4		Current	Volatility	Mean if no deal	Ending price no deal	Prob deal goes?	0.8			
5	Etech	182.75	1.08	0.1	158.6612393	Time to do Deal	0.252286	1	2	
6	JDSU	96.5	0.79	-0.3	38.36260737					
7						Correlations				
8							1	-0.5		
9							-0.5	1		
10	Profit from deal going through	29.55		spread	103.8135031	mean cap cost	192.59			
11	profit if deal does not go through	0		capital cost	182.75					
12	Total profit	29.55		return	0.608176718					

Step by Step

Step 1: In cell E10 we determine the spread with the formula

$=(E5-B5)-2.2*(E6-B6).$

Step 2: In cell E11 we compute the capital cost with the formula

$= IF(G2=1,B5,IF(AND(G2=0,E10<0),B5-E10,B5)).$

This formula implements the logic in Table 14.1.

Step 3: After running 1000 iterations with E11 as an output cell we found mean capital cost of 192.59.

Step 4: In cell E12 we compute the annualized portfolio return with the formula

$=B12*(1/G5)/G10.$

Step 5: Making E12 an output cell we obtain the following results.

	J	K	L
		capital cost / Ending price no deal	return / Ending price no deal
18	Name		
19	Description	Output	Output
20	Cell	E11	E12
21	Minimum =	182.75	-12.66593
22	Maximum =	582.3566	15.30896
23	Mean =	191.6024	0.7886351
24	Std Deviation =	36.45128	1.810457
25	Variance =	1328.696	3.277753
26	Skewness =	5.185391	0.1746574
27	Kurtosis =	34.06396	19.06948
28	Errors Calculated =	0	0
29	Mode =	182.75	0.6365494
30	5% Perc =	182.75	-1.914365
31	10% Perc =	182.75	0.4391864
32	15% Perc =	182.75	0.543595
33	20% Perc =	182.75	0.5878232
34	25% Perc =	182.75	0.6254217
35	30% Perc =	182.75	0.6587291
36	35% Perc =	182.75	0.6954782
37	40% Perc =	182.75	0.7317234
38	45% Perc =	182.75	0.767208
39	50% Perc =	182.75	0.8063411
40	55% Perc =	182.75	0.8476524
41	60% Perc =	182.75	0.8858613
42	65% Perc =	182.75	0.9289052
43	70% Perc =	182.75	0.9796745
44	75% Perc =	182.75	1.03964
45	80% Perc =	182.75	1.106373
46	85% Perc =	182.75	1.215732
47	90% Perc =	182.75	1.415528
48	95% Perc =	253.0006	2.585839

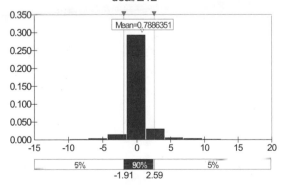

Distribution for return / Ending price no deal/E12

We find an average annualized return of 78.8% with a standard deviation of 181%

We could now compute a **Sharpe Ratio** for this trade. $\dfrac{.786 - .05}{1.81} = .41$

Remarks

1. As pointed out in Chapter 10, many firms allocate capital to traders or investments according to the Sharpe ratio. If a firm had a given amount of capital to invest in Risk Arbitrage deals they could develop a simulation model for each deal and then use Palisade's RISKOptimizer product to determine the combination of Risk Arbitrage deals that would maximize the firm's Sharpe Ratio, subject to the capital availability constraint.

2. Basically the prices of the stocks matter **only in the case when the deal fails**. Many traders find it difficult to model the random variable governing the evolution of the Cannibal and Prey prices in the case of a failed deal. Traders may find it easier to model the SPREAD = Change in ETECH price – 2.2 (Change in JDS price) in the case of a failed deal by a RiskGeneral random variable. Since the spread determines our loss in the case of a failed deal, this makes it unnecessary to model the price of each stock.

Chapter 15: Modeling Stock Prices as Mean Reverting

Folklore has it that periods of high stock returns tend to be followed by low stock returns while periods of low stock returns tend to be followed by periods of high stock returns. This is called **mean** reversion and is common in many economic time series. Our current bootstrapping model does not account for mean reversion. We now show how to model mean reversion. File **Brent.xls** contains our work.[1]

Step by Step

Step 1: Sheet S&P gives annual returns on S&P in column B. In column L we give the compounded average return over last 20 years. For example, in cell L24 we compute the compounded average return for 1926-1945 with the formula

$$= GEOMEAN(F4:F23)-1.$$

Note column F lists 1 + annual return.

	A	B	C	D	E	F	G	H	I	J	K	L
1		S&P 500	S&P 500	S&P 500	S&P 500							
2		ANNUAL	5 YEAR	10 YEAR	20 YEAR							
3						1+Ret	Last 5	Last 10	Last 15	Last6-10	Last 11-15	Last 20
4	1/1/26	11.61%	8.67%	5.85%	7.13%	111.61%						
5	1/1/27	37.48%	-5.11%	7.80%	6.09%	137.48%						
6	1/1/28	43.61%	-12.47%	0.02%	4.71%	143.61%						
7	1/1/29	-8.41%	-11.24%	-0.89%	3.11%	91.59%						
8	1/1/30	-24.90%	-9.93%	-0.05%	4.46%	75.10%						
9	1/1/31	-43.35%	3.11%	1.80%	7.43%	56.65%	8.67%		In regression predict column B from column L			
10	1/1/32	-8.20%	22.47%	6.43%	11.72%	91.80%	-5.11%					
11	1/1/33	53.97%	14.29%	9.35%	13.15%	153.97%	-12.47%					
12	1/1/34	-1.43%	10.68%	7.17%	10.68%	98.57%	-11.24%					
13	1/1/35	47.66%	10.90%	9.28%	13.13%	147.66%	-9.93%					
14	1/1/36	33.92%	0.50%	8.41%	12.48%	133.92%	3.11%	5.85%				
15	1/1/37	-35.02%	-7.51%	4.41%	11.20%	64.98%	22.47%	7.80%				
16	1/1/38	31.14%	4.62%	9.62%	12.97%	131.14%	14.29%	0.02%				
17	1/1/39	-0.42%	3.78%	7.26%	13.48%	99.58%	10.68%	-0.89%				
18	1/1/40	-9.78%	7.67%	9.17%	14.15%	90.22%	10.91%	-0.05%				
19	1/1/41	-11.58%	16.95%	13.38%	14.76%	88.42%	0.50%	1.80%	4.04%	3.11%	8.67%	
20	1/1/42	20.33%	17.87%	17.28%	16.85%	120.33%	-7.51%	6.43%	2.44%	22.47%	-5.11%	
21	1/1/43	25.91%	14.85%	17.09%	15.25%	125.91%	4.62%	9.35%	1.53%	14.29%	-12.47%	
22	1/1/44	19.73%	10.86%	14.31%	15.10%	119.73%	3.77%	7.17%	0.64%	10.68%	-11.24%	
23	1/1/45	36.41%	10.68%	17.12%	14.95%	136.41%	7.67%	9.28%	2.46%	10.91%	-9.93%	
24	1/1/46	-8.07%	9.91%	16.69%	13.84%	91.93%	16.95%	8.41%	6.62%	0.50%	3.11%	7.13%
25	1/1/47	5.70%	16.70%	18.43%	13.72%	105.70%	17.87%	4.41%	10.11%	-7.51%	22.47%	6.09%
26	1/1/48	5.51%	19.37%	16.43%	14.63%	105.51%	14.85%	9.62%	11.15%	4.62%	14.29%	4.71%
27	1/1/49	18.79%	17.86%	20.06%	14.93%	118.79%	10.86%	7.26%	8.39%	3.77%	10.68%	3.11%

Step 2: Next we run a regression to forecast Column B from Column L. The results are given in sheet Annual20.

---

[1] The author is grateful to Brent Kessel, a CFA in Los Angeles, for bringing this problem to the author's attention.

SUMMARY OUTPUT

Regression Statistics	
Multiple R	0.19118266
R Square	0.036550809
Adjusted R Square	0.018372523
Standard Error	0.163692143
Observations	55

ANOVA

	df	SS	MS	F	Significance F
Regression	1	0.053876543	0.053876543	2.01068507	0.16204783
Residual	53	1.420141234	0.026795118		
Total	54	1.474017777			

	Coefficients	Standard Error	t Stat	P-value	Lower 95%	Upper 95%	Lower 95.0%	Upper 95
Intercept	0.189360584	0.042867048	4.417392718	4.96225E-05	0.103380216	0.275340953	0.103380216	0.27534
X Variable 1	-0.45675717	0.32211678	-1.41798627	0.16204783	-1.102841309	0.189326964	-1.102841309	0.18932

The value of .16 is not significant at .05 level, but it does indicate a high probability that the return of stocks during the last 20 years does impact next year's return Therefore we will model next year's return as normally distributed with

Mean = .189 - .456*(Mean return last 20 years)

Standard deviation = .164.

Note that a 1% increase in mean return over last 20 years will knock the mean return for the current year down by .46%.

Step 3: In sheet Model we simulate the market returns for the years 2001-2020.

	A	B	C	D	E	F	G
1							
2		Year	S and P return	Last 20 geometric mean	Return+1		
3		1/1/80	32.41%		132.41%		
4		1/1/81	-4.91%		95.09%		
5		1/1/82	21.41%		121.41%		
6		1/1/83	22.51%		122.51%		
7		1/1/84	6.27%		106.27%		
8		1/1/85	32.17%		132.17%		
9		1/1/86	18.47%		118.47%		
10		1/1/87	5.23%		105.23%		
11		1/1/88	16.81%		116.81%		
12		1/1/89	31.49%		131.49%		
13		1/1/90	-3.17%		96.83%		
14		1/1/91	30.55%		130.55%		
15		1/1/92	7.67%		107.67%		
16		1/1/93	9.99%		109.99%		
17		1/1/94	1.31%		101.31%		
18		1/1/95	37.43%		137.43%		
19		1/1/96	23.07%		123.07%		
20		1/1/97	33.37%		133.37%		
21		1/1/98	28.58%		128.58%		
22		1/1/99	21.03%		121.03%		
23		1/1/00	-9.10%	Last 20 geometric mean	90.90%	no mean reversion	no MR+1
24		1/1/01	-0.059959983	0.16	94.00%	0.152035	1.152035
25		1/1/02	0.398553567	0.16	139.86%	0.065904	1.065904
26		1/1/03	-0.071132665	0.16	92.89%	0.263178	1.263178
27		1/1/04	0.065276952	0.15	106.53%	0.374977	1.374977
28		1/1/05	0.132942037	0.15	113.29%	0.180776	1.180776
29		1/1/06	0.44736911	0.14	144.74%	0.52819	1.52819
30		1/1/07	0.033245753	0.15	103.32%	-0.256061	0.743939
31		1/1/08	-0.039322511	0.15	96.07%	0.079298	1.079298
32		1/1/09	-0.059101254	0.14	94.09%	0.215627	1.215627
33		1/1/10	0.212217136	0.12	121.22%	0.085931	1.085931
34		1/1/11	-0.053165515	0.13	94.68%	-0.084861	0.915139
35		1/1/12	-0.015930372	0.11	98.41%	-0.20294	0.79706
36		1/1/13	0.319108723	0.11	131.91%	0.051976	1.051976
37		1/1/14	0.35866017	0.12	135.87%	0.280484	1.280484
38		1/1/15	0.150306291	0.14	115.03%	-0.128481	0.871519
39		1/1/16	0.054800873	0.13	105.48%	0.377339	1.377339
40		1/1/17	0.249154401	0.12	124.92%	0.55854	1.55854
41		1/1/18	0.260592224	0.11	126.06%	0.245577	1.245577
42		1/1/19	0.075244243	0.11	107.52%	0.21655	1.21655
43		1/1/20	0.043016587	0.11	104.30%	0.21938	1.21938
44							
45		annual return 2001-2020	0.11				0.14046
46							

In D24:D43 we compute the mean return for last 20 years by copying from D24 to D25:D43 the formula

$=GEOMEAN(E4:E23)-1.$

Note that for each year Column E contains 1+ (year's return).

In C24:C43 we generate our simulated stock return for each year by copying from C24 to C25:C43 the formula

$=RiskNormal(0.189-0.4567*D24,0.164).$

After running @RISK we find average annual return for 2001-2020 to be 11.4% with standard deviation of 3.4%. If we simulate each year independently as RiskNormal(.1298,.2017) (the historical mean and sigma) we obtain the standard deviation of our simulated annual return to be much greater (around 4.6%).

Chapter 16: Optimal FX Hedging

All major US companies face significant exchange rate risk. As an example, consider a US company that expects to receive the following in six months: 5,000,000 francs, 2,000,000 pounds and 100,000,000 yen. Suppose today's exchange rates are as follows:

Currency	Today's Exchange Rate ($/unit of currency)
Franc	$0.1649
Pound	$1.6667
Yen	$0.0072

Given today's exchange rates the value of our foreign accounts receivable would be

$$5,000,000(.1649) + 2,000,000(1.6667) + 100,000,000(.0072) = \$4.88 \ million.$$

If the value of the franc, pound, and yen all drop, then the dollar value of our foreign accounts receivable will also drop. For example, if all currencies drop 10% against the dollar, the company has lost $488,000. Exchange rate risk makes it difficult for CFOs who want to ensure that the company meets analyst forecast for Earnings per Share (measured in dollars!). To lessen the risk caused by foreign exchange fluctuations, many treasury departments invest in puts or forward options to reduce risk. In our analysis we will only consider put options. A European put option on a currency having an exercise price x will pay out on the option's expiration date the maximum of $0 and Exercise Price – Currency value (in dollars) on Expiration date. For example, a 6-month put with exercise price of $0.15 on the Franc would pay nothing if the franc was above $0.15 in value in six months and would pay $0.02 if the franc was worth $0.13 in six months. We see that put options pay more money when the value of a currency decreases. Since the dollar value of our foreign accounts receivable decreases as currency value decreases, we see that purchasing puts **hedges** our foreign exchange risk.

The natural question is how many puts to buy on each currency and exercise price to obtain the desired risk profile. We will show you how to attack this problem.

Example 16.1

Consider the FX accounts receivable and current spot rates (June 30, 1998) given above. P and G can purchase on June 30, 1998 the following six-month European put options (prices are given in cents):

Currency	Exercise Price	Option price (in cents)
Franc	$0.15	.0166
Franc	$0.13	.000058
Pound	$1.60	.7396
Pound	$1.50	.094
Yen	$0.006	.00163
Yen	$0.005	.000019

How can we minimize the variability of our six-month profit in dollars subject to the constraint that our average profit is at least $4.80 million?

To meet analysts targets we need to have our six-month profit be at least $4.60 million. How can we minimize the probability of not meeting this target?

Solution

To begin we use Monte Carlo simulation to generate 1000 "scenarios" for the exchange rates of the franc, pound and yen in 6 months. For any possible hedging strategy, we use our scenarios to compute the mean and variance of our dollar profit as well as our probability of not meeting our $4.60 million target Then we formulate parts a and b as optimization problems in which our changing cells are the number purchased of each option.

We use bootstrapping to generate six-month scenarios for the franc, pound, and yen exchange rates[1]. In file **fxdata.xls**, sheet **fx data for hedging**, we are given the daily percentage changes in each currency for the last six months. See Figure 16.1.

---

[1] As discussed in Chapter 9, we may adjust the daily mean change in each FX rate to incorporate analyst forecasts about the directions of future FX movements.

Figure 16.1

	A	E	F	G	H
5	**Date**		**%age ret**		**sigma**
6	1/2/98		% Fr	% Pound	% Yen
7	1/5/98	1	-0.011618	-0.006522	-0.008871
8	1/6/98	2	-0.003592	-0.003374	-0.000401
9	1/7/98	3	0.003109	0.000677	0.013898
10	1/8/98	4	0.003282	-0.008059	-0.006854
11	1/9/98	5	-0.001145	0.00031	0.004512
12	1/12/98	6	-0.000573	0.00527	-0.004756
13	1/13/98	7	0.001556	0.008326	0.008496
14	1/14/98	8	-0.001475	-0.003364	0.005397
15	1/15/98	9	-0.005541	0	0.008641
16	1/16/98	10	-0.00065	0.002884	0.004283
17	1/19/98	11	-0.001216	0.001407	0.00349
18	1/20/98	12	-0.001709	-0.005805	0.002318
19	1/21/98	13	0.010833	0.002581	0.011051
20	1/22/98	14	0.007859	0.010299	-0.001017
21	1/23/98	15	0.015366	0.01517	0.012595
22	1/26/98	16	-0.009234	-0.010161	-0.008292
23	1/27/98	17	0.004429	-0.007065	0.011022
24	1/28/98	18	-0.01498	-0.001095	0.002256
25	1/29/98	19	-0.008084	-0.002131	-0.004876
26	1/30/98	20	-0.00188	-0.003356	-0.010303
27	2/2/98	21	0.006239	0.003367	0.003047
28	2/3/98	22	0.00428	0.004698	0.005316
29	2/4/98	23	0.005548	0.006255	0.01901
30	2/5/98	24	0.008355	-0.001388	-0.000124
31	2/6/98	25	-0.011723	-0.006769	-0.002842
32	2/9/98	26	-0.004925	-0.008381	-0.001859
33	2/10/98	27	0.004536	-0.002593	0.007697
126	6/23/98	120	-0.004386	-0.003407	-0.008686
127	6/24/98	121	-0.000579	0.0006	-0.013524
128	6/25/98	122	0.00282	0.001798	-0.006122
129	6/26/98	123	-0.006592	-0.005864	0.000845
130	6/29/98	124	-0.000165	0.003009	0.002188
131	6/30/98	125	0.001072	0.00072	0.019722

We now use bootstrapping (see Figure 16.2) to generate the daily exchange rate changes. We assume that each of the next 126 trading days (126 trading days = 6 months) is equally likely to have the same percentage changes as one of the trading days from 1/2/98 to 6/30/98.

Figure 16.2

	L	M	N	O	P
5			2	3	4
6		Scenario	Fr	Pound	Yen
7	0		0.164948	1.6677	0.007198
8	1	63	0.164789	1.659718	0.007198
9	2	63	0.164629	1.651775	0.007198
10	3	63	0.16447	1.643869	0.007198
11	4	63	0.16431	1.636001	0.007198
12	5	63	0.164151	1.628171	0.007198
13	6	63	0.163992	1.620379	0.007198
14	7	63	0.163833	1.612623	0.007198
15	8	63	0.163675	1.604905	0.007198
16	9	63	0.163516	1.597224	0.007198
17	10	63	0.163358	1.589579	0.007198
18	11	63	0.163199	1.581971	0.007198
19	12	63	0.163041	1.5744	0.007198
20	13	63	0.162883	1.566865	0.007198
21	14	63	0.162726	1.559365	0.007198
22	15	63	0.162568	1.551902	0.007198
23	16	63	0.16241	1.544474	0.007198
24	17	63	0.162253	1.537082	0.007198
25	18	63	0.162096	1.529726	0.007198
26	19	63	0.161939	1.522404	0.007198
27	20	63	0.161782	1.515118	0.007198
28	21	63	0.161625	1.507866	0.007198
29	22	63	0.161469	1.500649	0.007198
30	23	63	0.161312	1.493467	0.007198
31	24	63	0.161156	1.486319	0.007198
32	25	63	0.161	1.479206	0.007198
33	26	63	0.160844	1.472126	0.007198
126	119	63	0.146981	0.942264	0.007198
127	120	63	0.146839	0.937754	0.007198
128	121	63	0.146697	0.933266	0.007198
129	122	63	0.146554	0.928799	0.007198
130	123	63	0.146412	0.924354	0.007198
131	124	63	0.146271	0.919929	0.007198
132	125	63	0.146129	0.915527	0.007198
133	126	63	0.145987	0.911145	0.007198

To do this we proceed as follows:

Step by
Step

Step 1: In M8 generate the day from 1/02/98-6/30/98 that generates percentage changes for 7/01/98 with the formula

$$=RiskDuniform(\$E\$7:\$E\$131).$$

This formula makes it equally likely that a 1,2, ... 125 is chosen. Copying this formula to M9:M133 generates the scenarios for all other trading days in the next 6 months.

Step 2: By copying from N7 to N7:P133 the formula (range Lookup is E7:H131)

$$=N7*(1+VLOOKUP(\$M8,Lookup,N\$5))$$

we compute the new exchange rate for each day and each currency as

(Yesterday's exchange rate)(Percentage change in exchange rate for chosen scenario).

Step 3: We now run 1000 iterations of @RISK with our output range being N133:P133. This generates 1000 scenarios for exchange rates on December 31, 1998.

The Optimization Model

We copied our 1000 scenarios to the sheet **Fxhedging**. See Figure 16.3.

Figure 16.3

	B	C	D	E	F	G	H	I	J	K	L
2	Mean	4.897033			Francs received	5.00					
3	Sigma	0.199984			Pounds received	2					
4	Prob<=4.6	0.034			Yen received	100					
5					Ex Price	0.15	0.13	1.6	1.5	0.006	0.005
6	Name	Fr	Pound	Yen	cost in cents	0.0166	0.000058	0.7396	0.094	0.00163	0.000019
7	Description	Output	Output	Output	# bought	31.97304	20.21614257	5.683015992	0	436.5398372	4.210699576
8	Iteration#	N133	O133	P133	Total $ value(millions)	$0.15 FR	$0.13 FR	$1.60 Pound	$1.50 Pound	$0.006 Yen	$0.005 yen
9	1	0.170412	1.683064	7.06E-03	4.87E+00	-0.000166	-0.00000058	-0.007396	-0.00094	-0.0000163	-0.00000019
10	2	0.168759	1.678625	7.25E-03	4.87E+00	-0.000166	-0.00000058	-0.007396	-0.00094	-0.0000163	-0.00000019
11	3	0.160371	1.766528	6.37E-03	4.92E+00	-0.000166	-0.00000058	-0.007396	-0.00094	-0.0000163	-0.00000019
12	4	0.145243	1.727003	7.07E-03	4.98E+00	0.004591	-0.00000058	-0.007396	-0.00094	-0.0000163	-0.00000019
13	5	0.1708	1.693594	6.60E-03	4.85E+00	-0.000166	-0.00000058	-0.007396	-0.00094	-0.0000163	-0.00000019
14	6	0.173551	1.82058	7.32E-03	5.19E+00	-0.000166	-0.00000058	-0.007396	-0.00094	-0.0000163	-0.00000019
15	7	0.145603	1.512763	5.93E-03	4.96E+00	0.004231	-0.00000058	0.079841	-0.00094	5.6915E-05	-0.00000019
16	8	0.15276	1.620827	5.88E-03	4.59E+00	-0.000166	-0.00000058	-0.007396	-0.00094	0.000102694	-0.00000019
17	9	0.154288	1.647792	6.59E-03	4.67E+00	-0.000166	-0.00000058	-0.007396	-0.00094	-0.0000163	0.00000019
18	10	0.173659	1.693551	7.16E-03	4.92E+00	0.000100	-0.00000058	-0.007396	-0.00094	-0.0000163	-0.00000019
19	11	0.172747	1.690931	6.84E-03	4.87E+00	-0.000166	-0.00000058	-0.007396	-0.00094	-0.0000163	-0.00000019
20	12	0.16731	1.690735	7.91E-03	4.95E+00	-0.000166	-0.00000058	-0.007396	-0.00094	-0.0000163	-0.00000019
21	13	0.155619	1.597925	6.19E-03	4.55E+00	-0.000166	-0.00000058	-0.005321	-0.00094	-0.0000163	-0.00000019
22	14	0.163917	1.729182	6.72E-03	4.90E+00	-0.000166	-0.00000058	-0.007396	-0.00094	-0.0000163	-0.00000019
23	15	0.17109	1.76739	7.03E-03	5.04E+00	-0.000166	-0.00000058	-0.007396	-0.00094	-0.0000163	-0.00000019
24	16	0.158784	1.545951	6.51E-03	4.79E+00	-0.000166	-0.00000058	0.046653	-0.00094	-0.0000163	-0.00000019
25	17	0.162547	1.726634	8.41E-03	5.05E+00	-0.000166	-0.00000058	-0.007396	-0.00094	-0.0000163	-0.00000019
26	18	0.154672	1.596145	7.20E-03	4.65E+00	-0.000166	-0.00000058	-0.003541	-0.00094	-0.0000163	-0.00000019
27	19	0.163954	1.796618	7.65E-03	5.12E+00	-0.000166	-0.00000058	-0.007396	-0.00094	-0.0000163	-0.00000019
28	20	0.16253	1.502954	5.62E-03	5.04E+00	-0.000166	-0.00000058	0.08965	-0.00094	0.000364822	-0.00000019
29	21	0.166541	1.775459	7.66E-03	5.10E+00	-0.000166	-0.00000058	-0.007396	-0.00094	-0.0000163	-0.00000019
30	22	0.159352	1.688017	6.58E-03	4.78E+00	-0.000166	-0.00000058	-0.007396	-0.00094	-0.0000163	-0.00000019

Step 1: We now compute for each scenario the profit earned on each put option. For example, for the franc $.0.15 put we obtain the profit (in dollars) from one put option for each scenario by copying from G9 to G10:G1008 the formula

$= IF(C9>=G\$5,-G\$6/100,G\$5-C9-g\$6/100).$

If the 12/31/98 franc price exceeds $0.15, we lose the cost of the put. Otherwise our profit equals the payoff from put (G$5-C9) less the cost of the put.

Step 2: We enter trial values for the number (in millions) purchased of each put in G7:L7. We now compute the total dollar value (in millions) of our profits for each scenario by copying from F9:F1008 the formula

$= \$G\$2*C9+\$G\$3*D9+\$G\$4*E9+ SUMPRODUCT(\$G\$7:\$L\$7,G9:L9).$

$SUMPRODUCT(\$G\$7:\$L\$7,G9:L9)$ is the profit from our puts while $\$G\$2*C9+\$G\$3*D9+\$G\$4*E9$ is the dollar value of our accounts receivable.

Step 3: We now compute in cell C2 the average profit for our choice of put purchases with the formula

$= AVERAGE(dollars).$

The range dollars (F9:F1008) contains the returns for each of our 1000 exchange rate scenarios.

In cell C3 we compute the standard deviation of our profit with the formula

$= STDEVP(dollars).$

In cell C4 we compute the fraction of the scenarios for which our profit does not meet our $4.60 million target with the formula

$= PERCENTRANK(dollars,4.6).$

Step 4: To find the portfolio that minimizes our risk (standard deviation of portfolio value) and attains an expected return of at least $4.8 million we use the following Solver window.

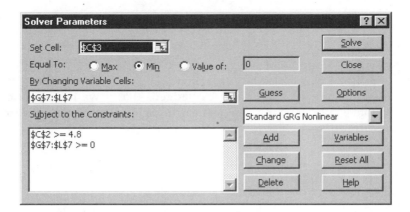

We minimize the standard deviation of our dollar profit (cell C3) by changing the number bought of each put (G7:L7). We rule out shorting puts (G7:L7>=0) and ensure that our mean profit is at least $4.8 million. (C2>=4.8). We find the optimal solution given in Figure 16.3. Note that we buy 32 million $0.15 franc puts, 20 million $0.13 franc puts, 5.7 million $1.60 pound puts, 436.5 million $.006 yen puts and 4.2 million $.005 yen puts. Our standard deviation is around $200,000.

Step 5: To determine the put purchases that minimize the chance of not meeting our $4.6 million goal we use the following Evolver window.

Note we use Evolver because the probability of not meeting a target is not a convex function of losses. Note that we bound the number of puts purchased between 0 and 500. We find (see sheet Min PROB<460) that we can ensure that there is only a 2.4% chance of not meeting Wall Street's $4.6 million target. The number of puts purchased is given in Figure 16.4.

Figure 16.4

	B	C	D	E	F	G	H	I	J	K	L
1						millions					
2	Mean	4.901151			Francs received	5.00					
3	Sigma	0.20223			Pounds received	2					
4	Prob<=4.6	0.024			Yen received	100					
5					Ex Price	0.15	0.13	1.6	1.5	0.006	0.0
6	Name	Fr	Pound	Yen	cost in cents	0.0166	0.000058	0.7396	0.094	0.00163	0.0000
7	Description	Output	Output	Output	# bought	31	404	4	0	410	1

Note (see Figure 16.5 and sheet **Unhedged**) that if we buy no puts our standard deviation is $240,000 and our chance of failing to meet Wall Street's targets is around 10%!

Figure 16.5

	B	C	D	E	F	G	H	I	J	K	L
1						millions					
2	Mean	4.907235			Francs received	5.00					
3	Sigma	0.240275			Pounds received	2					
4	Prob<=4.6	0.098			Yen received	100					
5					Ex Price	0.15	0.13	1.6	1.5	0.006	0.005
6	Name	Fr	Pound	Yen	cost in cents	0.0166	0.000058	0.7396	0.094	0.00163	0.000019
7	Description	Output	Output	Output	# bought	0	0	0	0	0	0
8	Iteration#	N133	O133	P133	Total $ value(millions)	$0.15 FR	$0.13 FR	$1.60 Pound	$1.50 Pound	$0.006 Yen	$0.005 yen

Chapter 17: How Long a Time Horizon for Beta?

As you probably know, the beta of a stock measures the sensitivity of a stock's return to the return of the market. More specifically, the beta of a stock is the slope of a regression in which the dependent variable is the stock's monthly return and the independent variable is the market's monthly return. Most finance texts recommend using 60 months of data to estimate beta. In this chapter we will investigate the optimal number of months of data that should be used to estimate beta. Our goal will be to find the number of months of data that **best estimates a stock's beta for the coming year**. In the file **Beta.xls** column C contains monthly S and P returns while columns I through N contain monthly returns for six stocks during the period 1988-2000 (Cinergy, Dell, Intel, Microsoft, Nortel, and Pfizer).

Figure 17.1

	A	B	C
34	Month#	Date	S and P
35	1	Sep-88	4.20%
36	2	Oct-88	2.70%
37	3	Nov-88	-1.40%
38	4	Dec-88	1.80%
39	5	Jan-89	7.20%
40	6	Feb-89	-2.50%
41	7	Mar-89	2.40%
42	8	Apr-89	5.20%
43	9	May-89	4.00%
44	10	Jun-89	-0.50%
45	11	Jul-89	9.00%

	H	I	J	K	L	M	N
34		Cin	Dell	INTC	MSFT	NT	PFE
35	1	0.009470175	0.282112845	-0.017829	0.045075	0.058011	0.071411
36	2	0.034972764	0.1582397	-0.10007	-0.062147	-0.027437	0.050589
37	3	-0.0370328	-0.08407437	-0.19188	-0.035851	-0.063339	0.002503
38	4	0.009610942	-0.08031774	0.18752	0.127095	0	0.022035
39	5	0.012383132	-0.04990403	0.094718	0.119659	-0.060189	0.003346
40	6	-0.00480484	-0.17171717	-0.0096	-0.002053	-0.007961	-0.0434
41	7	-0.02898118	-0.09512195	0.019386	-0.161786	-0.032253	0.043101
42	8	0.047916917	0.105121294	0.104718	0.120254	0.16664	0.076062
43	9	0.029119155	0.079268293	0.120724	0.082861	-0.007153	-0.005619
44	10	0.042461424	-0.07344633	-0.10772	-0.124003	0.021615	-0.059436

Our goal is to determine how many months of data should be used for each stock in estimating beta. The criterion is to choose the number of months that minimizes the average absolute error in predicting the stock's beta for the next 12 months. The Excel SLOPE function will enable us to compute both the beta estimate and the beta for the next 12 months.

Step by Step

Step 1: Name the range H35:N180 "Lookup". This contains monthly returns on all six stocks.

Step 2: In cell D28 enter the number (1 through 6 with Stock 1 being Cinergy and Stock 6 being Pfizer) of the stock you wish to analyze. In cell E28 enter the number of months (12-60) of data that you want to use to estimate the stock's beta.

Figure 17.2

	D	E
26		
27	Stock #	Beta periods
28	1	12
29		

Step 3: Copying from D35 to D36:D180 the formula

VLOOKUP(A35,Lookup,$D$28+1)

Inserts the monthly returns for the stock in D28 into column D.

Step 4: Copying from D95 to D96:D180 the formula

= SLOPE(OFFSET(D95,-$E$28,0,$E$28,1),OFFSET(C95,-$E$28,0,$E$28,1))

generates all our monthly beta estimates using the number of months given in E28. Note by starting in row 95 we can go back 60 months. The Excel SLOPE function returns the slope of a simple linear regression. OFFSET(D95,-$E$28,0,$E$28,1) begins in D95 and goes up E28 rows and over 0 columns to begin selecting data. Then the formula returns E28 rows and one column of data. This backs out last E28 months of stock returns. OFFSET(C95,-$E$28,0,$E$28,1)) begins in C95 and goes up E28 rows and over 0 columns to begin selecting data. Then the formula returns E28 rows and one column of data. This selects last E28 months of S and P returns. See Figure 17.3.

Figure 17.3

	A	B	C	D	E	F	G
92	58	Jun-93	0.30%	6.86%			
93	59	Jul-93	-0.50%	4.75%	Beta Estimate	Beta for Next Year	Abs Error
94	60	Aug-93	3.80%	0.44%			
95	61	Sep-93	-0.70%	1.77%	-0.485808803	0.761623121	1.247431924
96	62	Oct-93	2.00%	1.07%	-0.450431015	0.717512803	1.167943817
97	63	Nov-93	-0.90%	-6.11%	-0.519998246	0.811605049	1.331603295
98	64	Dec-93	1.20%	2.33%	0.100448175	0.749184909	0.648736734
99	65	Jan-94	3.40%	-2.04%	0.094534632	0.796361043	0.701826412
100	66	Feb-94	-2.70%	-7.55%	-0.106103812	1.067134505	1.173238317
101	67	Mar-94	-4.40%	-2.04%	0.430728281	0.779542344	0.348814063
102	68	Apr-94	1.30%	-2.92%	0.431256172	0.828118905	0.396862733
103	69	May-94	1.60%	-1.09%	0.432057388	0.831283701	0.399226313

Step 5: By copying from F95 to F96:E180 the formula

=SLOPE(D95:D106,C95:C106)

we generate the beta for the next 12 months.

Step 6: By copying from G95 to G96:G180 the formula

= ABS(F95-E95)

we obtain the absolute error in each month's estimate of beta.

Step 7: In cell G33 we compute the mean absolute deviation (MAD) of our monthly absolute errors with the formula

=AVERAGE(G95:G168).

Step 8: In cell I21 we enter the MAD with the formula

=G33.

Then we select the range I21:BF27 for a two-way data table. After selecting Data Table we choose a column input cell of D28 and a row input cell of E28. This ensures that the numbers (1-6) in first column of data table are inserted into D28 and the numbers in the first row of the data table (12-60) are inserted into E28. The resulting table is shown in Figure 17.4. For example, in cell V25 we find that when we estimate MSFT's beta using last 24 months our estimates of the beta for the next 12 months is off by an average of .99. We find, for example, that for Dell estimation of beta based on last 25 months was most accurate. If we had to choose a single number of months to minimize the average MAD over all six stocks we would have found that 44 months minimizes the average of all six MADs.

Figure 17.4

	F	G	H	I	T	U	V	W	AO	AP	AQ	AR	AS	AT	AU	AV	BD	BE	BF
21		Best result		0.394467664	22	23	24	25	43	44	45	46	47	48	49	50	58	59	6
22		0.346379485	Cin	1	**0.35**	0.35	0.35	0.36	0.41	0.41	0.42	0.42	0.42	0.43	0.43	0.44	0.44	0.44	0.4
23		1.474147928	Dell	2	1.63	1.55	1.49	**1.47**	1.53	1.52	1.52	1.51	1.52	1.52	1.52	1.51	1.51	1.5	1.
24		0.828018134	INTC	3	0.99	0.97	0.97	0.95	0.87	0.86	0.85	0.84	0.84	0.84	0.83	**0.83**	0.87	0.87	0.8
25		0.854273073	MSFT	4	1.02	1	0.99	0.98	0.87	0.86	**0.85**	0.86	0.87	0.87	0.87	0.87	0.9	0.9	0
26		0.575493624	NT	5	0.67	0.69	0.69	0.68	**0.58**	0.58	0.6	0.61	0.61	0.63	0.64	0.64	0.7	0.71	0.7
27		0.532525576	PFE	6	0.54	0.54	0.55	0.55	0.65	0.65	0.65	0.64	0.64	0.63	0.62	0.61	**0.53**	0.54	0.5
28		0.813232842	Mean		0.86	0.85	0.84	0.83	0.82	**0.81**	0.81	0.81	0.82	0.82	0.82	0.82	0.82	0.83	0.8
29																			
30																			
31																			
32																			
33	MAD	0.394467664																	

Chapter 18: Matching a Given Market Index

Many trading strategies involve matching a given index such as the Dow, Standard and Poor's, Wiltshire 5000, Bottom 10% in Size Firms, etc. To lower transaction costs, we do not want to own the entire index. As an example, suppose we want to match the Dow (consisting of 30 stocks) as closely as possible with 5 stocks. Our problem becomes one of selecting 5 of 30 stocks (there are over 142,000 ways to do this!) that minimize over, say 24 years, the sum of (annual return on the Dow − annual return on 5 stocks) ^{2}. Let's find the best matching combination of 5 stocks for the period 1973-1996. Annual returns on each stock and the Dow are given in file **Dow.xls**. See Figure 18.1.

Figure 18.1

	A	B	C	D	E	F	AA	AB	AC	AD	AE	AF	AG	AH
1	Pick	0	1	0	0	0	0	0	1	0	0	5		0.046434
2		ALD	AA	AXP	T	BS	TX	UK	UTX	WX	Z		Dow	Portfolio	Diff
3	1973	0.734	0.406	-0.312	..013	0.18	-0.171	-0.276	-0.437	-0.387	-0.374	-0.09431	-0.073	0.000454
4	1974	-0.39	-0.369	-0.397	-0.047	-0.177	-0.218	0.277	0.456	-0.567	-0.424	-0.226633	-0.2154	0.000126
5	1975	0.223	0.338	0.443	0.216	0.432	0.216	0.535	0.483	0.435	1.473	0.4946	0.4926	4E-06
6	1976	0.246	0.518	0.128	0.321	0.289	0.273	0.053	0.727	0.391	0.225	0.2239	0.2654	0.001722
7	1977	0.159	-0.162	-0.0874	0.017	-0.444	0.027	-0.292	-0.035	0.086	-0.22	-0.091847	-0.1322	0.001628
8	1978	-0.32	0.065	-0.146	0.076	-0.024	-0.067	-0.103	0.139	-0.029	0.101	0.137767	0.1328	2.47E-05
9	1979	0.801	0.204	0.086	-0.057	0.153	0.298	0.321	0.163	0.27	0.369	0.101267	0.0812	0.000403
10	1980	0.138	0.145	0.413	0.014	0.324	0.747	0.27	0.47	0.542	0.057	0.2908	0.236	6.4E-07
11	1981	-0.145	-0.08	0.146	0.338	-0.058	-0.264	0.088	-0.276	-0.079	-0.2	0.004	-0.048	0.002704
12	1982	-0.198	0.274	0.506	0.1026	-0.116	0.034	0.093	0.413	0.595	0.538	0.32747	0.3348	5.37E-05
13	1983	0.796	0.486	0.054	0.134	0.512	0.249	0.251	0.326	0.455	0.427	0.237733	0.172	0.004321
14	1984	-0.024	-0.149	0.192	0.158	-0.365	0.035	-0.36	0.038	-0.01	0.105	0.027167	0.0538	0.000709
15	1985	0.407	0.073	0.443	0.344	-0.09	-0.033	1.021	0.246	0.747	0.675	0.353233	0.4188	0.004299
16	1986	-0.035	-0.089	0.094	0.048	-0.6	0.296	0.489	0.083	0.283	0.325	0.2175	0.2408	0.000543
17	1987	-0.251	0.412	-0.57	0.128	1.68	0.059	0.033	-0.233	-0.079	-0.074	0.02466	0.04656	0.00048
18	1988	0.214	0.226	0.197	0.109	0.388	0.433	0.133	0.26	0.097	0.545	0.1817	0.1202	0.003782
19	1989	0.129	0.388	0.342	0.624	-0.201	0.371	-0.054	0.358	0.45	0.274	0.300533	0.4182	0.013845
20	1990	-0.174	-0.192	-0.38	-0.309	-0.1755	0.076	-0.253	-0.008	-0.193	-0.017	-0.044717	-0.0266	0.000328
21	1991	0.684	0.148	0.039	0.343	-0.0237	0.065	0.297	0.171	-0.319	-0.087	0.286177	0.2384	0.002283
22	1992	0.402	0.138	0.262	0.337	0.1429	0.028	-0.135	-0.08	-0.217	0.236	0.08493	0.1294	0.001978
23	1993	0.325	-0.009	0.281	0.055	0.274	0.137	0.391	0.326	0.086	-0.161	0.175933	0.104	0.005174
24	1994	-0.123	0.272	-0.014	-0.018	-0.117	-0.026	0.346	0.045	-0.119	-0.375	0.0241	0.0532	0.000847
25	1995	0.42	0.242	0.433	0.314	-0.229	0.364	0.302	0.542	0.354	-0.123	0.3483	0.3666	0.000335
26	1996	0.43	0.231	0.387	-0.063	-0.36	0.292	0.11	0.443	0.226	0.692	0.261267	0.281	0.000389

Step 1: In cells B1:AE1 we enter trial binary values for the choice of tracking stocks. A "1" indicates we include the stock and a "0" indicates we do not include the stock.

Step 2: In cells AG3:AG26 we compute the annual return on our tracking portfolio by copying from AG3 to AG4:AG26 the formula

$= SUMPRODUCT(\$B\$1:\$AE\$1,B4:AE4)/5.$

Step 3: In AH3:AH26 we compute for each year the squared deviation of the tracking portfolio from the Dow return by copying from AH3 to AH4:AH26 the formula

$=(AG3\text{-}AF3)^2.$

Step 4: In cell AH1 we compute the sum of our squared errors with the formula

$= SUM(AH3:AH26).$

Step 5: In cell AF1 we compute the number of stocks in our tracking portfolio with the formula

$=SUM(B1:AE1).$

Step 6: We now use Evolver to find the best 5 stock tracking portfolio. Our Evolver Window follows:

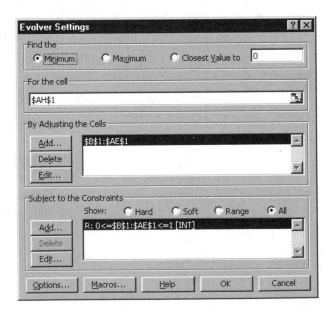

We choose our binary variables (cells B1:AE1) for each member of the Dow ("1" means we select the stock and "0" means we do not select the stock) and ensure that 5 stocks are selected by choosing the Budget method (this requires we start with five stocks selected). Our goal is to minimize the sum of the annual squared differences between the Dow return and the tracking return (Cell AH1). The five stocks selected were as follows:

- Alcoa

- Disney

- JP Morgan

- MMM

- United Technologies

Total squared deviation is .04 and during no year did our tracking portfolio differ by more than 11% from the actual Dow return.

Chapter 19: The Three Stage Valuation Model

Many analysts value firms using the three-stage cash flow (or dividend growth) model. This model assumes that the firm's cash flow will grow as follows:

- Rate G(1) for Y(1) years.

- Rate G(2) for next Y(2) years.

- Rate G(3) for next Y(3) years.

- Grow at terminal rate T rest of time.

Cash flows are then discounted at a rate from CAPM. Of course, G(1)-G(3) and Y(1)-Y(3) are unknown. With @RISK we can ask questions such as what is probability that stock is worth its market value?

Sheet **Valuation.xls** calculates valuation for the three-stage model. We assume during each stage the growth rate declines at a linear rate. For MSFT (current cash flow of around $7 billion/year) let's model T and G(1)-G(3) as triangular random variables. We will assume Y(1)-Y(3) are each equally likely to assume any value between 5 and 15 years. We will assume G(1)-G(3) have a .5 correlation while Y(1)-Y(3) are independent. We also assume from CAPM a 15% discount rate. We will determine cash flows for 69 years and discount them back to today. See Figure 19.1.

Quantity	Lowest	Most Likely	Highest
G(1)	.14	.19	.28
G(2)	.12	.16	.21
G(3)	.08	.15	.20
T	.02	.04	.05

Figure 19.1

	A	B	C	D	E	F	G	H	I	J	K	L
1	Valuation											
2	of MSFT		Low	Most likely	High			%age	Time	Change		
3		Stage 1	0.14	0.19	0.28	1	Stage 1 growth	0.207571774	10	0.005494		
4		Stage 2	0.12	0.16	0.21	2	Stage 2 growth	0.152628087	9	0.006894		
5		Stage 3	0.08	0.15	0.2	3	Stage 3 growth	0.090581308	12	0.003797		
6		Terminal	0.02	0.04	0.05		Term	0.045022716				5
7												6
8				ir	0.15							7
9												8
10			billion	NPV	$244.64							9
11		Year	CF	growth				Correlations				10
12		0	7					1	0.5	0.5		11
13		1	8.453002	0.207571774				0.5	1	0.5		12
14		2	10.16116	0.202077405				0.5	0.5	1		13
15		3	12.15868	0.196583036								14
16		4	14.48206	0.191088668								15
17		5	17.16985	0.185594299								
18		6	20.26214	0.18009993								
19		7	23.80002	0.174605562								

Step by Step

Step 1: In H3: H5 determine the growth rates for Stages 1-3 by copying from H3 to H4:H5 the formula

=RiskTriang(C3,D3,E3,RiskCorrmat(Corr,F3)).

The range Corr H12: J14 contains the correlations between G(1), G(2), and G(3).

In cell H6 we compute the terminal growth rate with the formula

=RiskTriang(C6,D6,E6).

Step 2: In I3:I5 determine the duration of each stage

=ROUND(RiskTriang(6,9,11),0) (Stage 1 duration)

=ROUND(RiskTriang(10,12,15),0) (Stage 2 duration)

=ROUND(RiskTriang(5,8,10),0) (Stage 3 duration)

Note the =ROUND function rounds the =RiskTriang value to the nearest integer.

Step 3: By copying from J3:J5 the formula

=(H3-H4)/I3

we compute the annual decrease in cash flow growth as from Stage I to Stage I + 1.

Step 4: In cell C12 we enter MSFT's current cash flow (7 billion).

Step 5: In D13 we recopy the Stage 1 growth rate from H3. Then by copying from D14 to D15:D81 the formula

=IF(B14<=$I$3+1,D13-$J$3,IF(B14<=$I$3+$I$4+1,D13-$J$4,IF(B14<=$I$3+$I$4+$I$5+1,D13-$J$5,$H$6)))

we compute the cash flow growth rate for each year. Note that during each stage the growth rate gradually adjusts to match the next stage's growth rate.

Step 6: Copying from C13 to C14:C81 the formula

=(1+D13)*C12

computes the cash flow for each year.

Step 7: Assuming each year's entire cash flow is mid-year, the formula entered in cell E10

=NPV(ir,C12:C81)*(SQRT(1+ir))

computes our estimated MSFT value. A histogram and statistical summary follow:

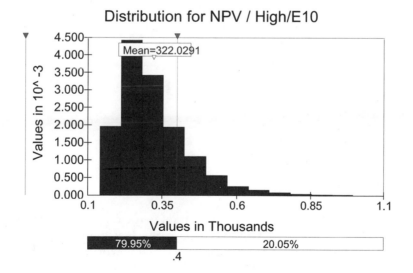

	H	I
		NPV /
20	Name	High
21	Description	Output
22	Cell	E10
23	Minimum	1.41E+02
24	Maximum	1067.703
25	Mean	322.0291
26	Std Deviation	119.9855
27	Variance	14396.53
28	Skewness	1.552979
29	Kurtosis	6.557738
30	Errors Calculated	0
31	Mode	276.265
32	5% Perc	183.7284
33	10% Perc	200.1196
34	15% Perc	214.0804
35	20% Perc	226.1362
36	25% Perc	237.4412
37	30% Perc	248.4382
38	35% Perc	259.7366
39	40% Perc	271.2396
40	45% Perc	281.9801
41	50% Perc	294.3344
42	55% Perc	307.8801
43	60% Perc	321.237
44	65% Perc	337.8132
45	70% Perc	354.9506
46	75% Perc	375.9358
47	80% Perc	400.3435
48	85% Perc	434.4903
49	90% Perc	479.184
50	95% Perc	546.6967

Note our assumptions imply a fair market value for Microsoft equal to the mean of the simulated NPV: $322 billion (this is fairly close to the current value). Our graph indicates that there is an 80% chance Microsoft is worth $400 billion or less.

Remark

Of course, what we really want to know is whether or not a stock is over or undervalued. Suppose a stock has a market capitalization of $320 billion. We can try and "reverse engineer" a set of assumptions for Y(1)-Y(3), G(1)-G(3), and T which yield the current market capitalization. If our set of assumptions seem completely unreasonable, then we realize the stock is overvalued.

Chapter 20: Modeling Key Drivers of Firm Value

In Chapter 23 we will try to create pro-forma statements to help us estimate the value of a company. We will want to use Monte Carlo to model future cash flows because they are uncertain. Today we will discuss simple methods for modeling the uncertainty in key drivers of cash flows such as revenue, COGS/Revenue, NPPE/Revenue.

Modeling Nike Revenue Growth

In file **Nike.xls** (see Figure 20.1), we have listed annual revenue growth for Nike for fiscal years 1995-2000. How would we model future revenue growth? As a naive approach we could assume Nike's annual growth should be normally distributed (mean = 16.9%, sigma = 20.3%). Then we could model Nike's annual growth with the formula

$$=RiskNormal(C11,C12)$$

Figure 20.1

	A	B	C	D	E	F	G	H	I
1									
2	Revenue								
3		Year	Revenue growth			duniform	normal	discrete	
4	1	1995	1.256	1		1.169667	1.16966667	1.0801111	
5	2	1996	1.359	0.6					
6	3	1997	1.419	0.5					
7	4	1998	1.04	2					
8	5	1999	0.919	2					
9	6	2000	1.025	2					
10									
11		Mean	1.169666667						
12		Sigma	0.202999179						
13		skewness	0.070747094						
14		kurtosis	-2.179777204		r	0.751494			
15					RSQ	0.564744			
16					Slope	-0.081543			
17					F	5.189986			
18		less peaked than normal			steyx	0.149734			
10		rv			p-value	0.084959			
20									

To check for normality we compute in cell C13 the skewness (=SKEW(C4:C9)) of the data and kurtosis in cell C14 (=KURT(C4:C9)) of the data. A skewness near 0 indicates symmetry of data (consistent with normal) and a kurtosis near 0 indicates a "shape" like normal random variable. Thus we have symmetric growth rates but the negative kurtosis indicates that revenue growth is less peaked than a normal random variable. If we think Nike will grow at a slower rate in the future, then we could simply reduce the mean of this random variable.

Next we look for a trend in Nike's revenue growth. In F14:F19 we analyze a regression with dependent variable being Nike's annual growth and independent variable being the year. In F154 we compute the RSQ with the formula

=RSQ(C4:C9,B4:B9).

In cell F16 we compute the slope of this regression with the formula

=SLOPE(C4:C9,B4:B9).

In cell F17 we compute the F-statistic ((# observations –2)*(R^2/(1-R^2)) for testing whether there is a significant trend with the formula

=(6-2)*F15/(1-F15).

In cell F18 we compute the p-value for this F-statistic with the formula

=FDIST(F17,1,4).

It appears that there is a significant downward trend in Nike's revenue growth (around .8% per year).

After computing the standard error of the regression in cell F18 with the formula

=STEYX(C4:C9,B4:B9)

we could model next year's revenue as

(This Year's revenue)*RiskNormal(1.025-.008, .15).

Note the standard error of the regression gives an estimate of the accuracy of the forecasts made from a simple linear trend.

We could also model next year's revenue growth to be equally likely to be one of last six years (this is good if we think next six years will be like last six) with formula

=RiskDuniform(C4:C9).

If we thought more recent years were more likely to occur in future than older years then we could model this by function

=RiskDiscrete(C4:C9,D4:D9).

This gives, for example, 1998-2000 twice the likelihood of 1995.

Modeling COGS/Revenue

A key driver of cash flows are a firm's margins. Therefore we now turn attention to modeling the future COGS/Revenue. In Figure 20.2 we see the relevant work.

Figure 20.2

	A	B	C	D	E	F	G
21	COGS/Revenue						
22			Year	COGS/Rev			
23			1995	0.5985	r	0.799065	
24			1996	0.6022	RSQ	0.638504	
25			1997	0.598	Slope	0.00848	
26			1998	0.634	F	5.298854	
27			1999	0.625	p-value	0.104803	Year 2000
28					std err	0.011649	0.63348

It appears that there is a significant upward trend of .8% a year in COGS/Revenue. If we think that is going to continue then we could model Year 2000 COGS/Revenue with the formula

$$=RiskNormal(D27+F25,F28).$$

SGA/Revenue

In a similar fashion (see Figure 20.3) we find that SGA/Revenue appears to be increasing .55% a year.

Figure 20.3

	A	B	C	D	E	F
28					std err	0.011649
29	SGA/Rev		Year	SGA/Rev		
30			1995	0.235	r	
31			1996	0.225	RSQ	0.603551
32			1997	0.232	Slope	0.0055
33			1998	0.25	F	4.567187
34			1999	0.25	p-value	0.122188

NPPE/Revenue

NPPE is often modeled as a fraction of revenue. From Figure 20.4 we find that there is no significant trend in NPPE/Revenue. Thus we might model NPPE/Revenue as

$$= RiskNormal(.116, .018).$$

Figure 20.4

	I	J	K	L
27	NPPE/Rev			
28				
29	Year	NPPE/Rev		
30	1995	0.1165	r	0.662864
31	1996	0.0993	RSQ	0.439389
32	1997	0.1004	Slope	0.00764
33	1998	0.1207	F	2.3513
34	1999	0.144	p-value	0.222719
35				
36			mean	0.11618
37			sigma	0.018224

Forecasting Growth of Grocery Market

Often in a valuation you need to forecast the future size of an industry. For example, if you were going to model Kroger Supermarkets you will probably need to forecast growth of grocery sales in US. See File **Food.xls** and Figure 20.5.

Figure 20. 5

	B	C	D	E	F	G	H	I	J	K
2										
3		Food Sales US								
4										
5			millions	%age growth					Source	
6		1992	377						US Industry and	
7		1993	384	0.018568					Trade Outlook 2000	
8		1994	399	0.039063		rsq	0.414395			
9		1995	410	0.027569		slope	0.003896			
10		1996	415	0.012195		F stat	4.245806			
11		1997	425	0.024096		p-value	0.084993			
12		1998	438	0.030588		steyx	0.012253			
13		1999	460	0.050228						
14		2000	485	0.054348						
15										
16			mean	0.032082						
17			stdev	0.014824						
18			skew	0.375206						
19			kurt	-0.989152						
20										

We find a slight upward trend in the growth rate of grocery sales (.4% per year). Therefore we might model next year's grocery sales as normally distributed with mean of (1.054+.004)*(this year's sales) and standard deviation = (.012*forecast for next year).

Chapter 21: An Eyeball Model of an Internet Company

Nobody really knows if the New Economy business models being floated today will ever make money. By tracking the number of customers a new business has, customer acquisition costs, revenue per customer, and profit margins, we can obtain some idea if a company's business model is viable. Copeland uses this approach in Chapter 15 to value Amazon.com. He only gives a few scenarios for Amazon in 2010. Using @RISK we can generate thousands of scenarios. See file **Eyeballs.xls** and Figure 21.1.

Figure 21.1

	E	F	G	H	I	J	K	L	M
1	Amazon.com								
2									
3	Acquisition cost	50							
4	Current new customers/year	8000000							
5	Current Revenue	1600000000							
6	Current Customers	20000000							
7	Revenue per customer	$ 80.00							
8	Current churn rate	0.2							
9	Current Margin	-0.18							
10									
11		2010 Low	Med	High	Actual	Annual change			
12	Revenue/Customer	150	200	280	210	13			
13	New customers annually	4000000	5000000	7000000	5333333.333	-266666.6667			
14	Margin	0.05	0.08	0.1	0.076666667	0.025666667			
15	Acquisition cost	80	100	110	96.66666667	4.666666667			
16		Beginning customers	New Customers	Churn	Ending customers	Margin	Unit Acquisition cost	Revenue/customer	Profit before taxes
17	2001	20000000	7733333.333		4000000	23733333.33	-0.154333333	54.66666667	$ 93.00	$ (763,400,088.89)
18	2002	23733333.33	7466666.667	4746666.667	26453333.33	-0.128666667	59.33333333	$ 106.00	$ (803,810,417.78)
19	2003	26453333.33	7200000	5290666.667	28362666.67	-0.103	64	$ 119.00	$ (808,441,205.33)
20	2004	28362666.67	6933333.333	5672533.333	29623466.67	-0.077333333	68.66666667	$ 132.00	$ (778,485,236.62)
21	2005	29623466.67	6666666.667	5924693.333	30365440	-0.051666667	73.33333333	$ 145.00	$ (716,376,643.56)
22	2006	30365440	6400000	6073088	30692352	-0.026	78	$ 158.00	$ (625,284,182.02)
23	2007	30692352	6133333.333	6138470.4	30687214.93	-0.000333333	82.66666667	$ 171.00	$ (508,771,393.47)
24	2008	30687214.93	5866666.667	6137442.987	30416438.61	0.025333333	87.33333333	$ 184.00	$ (370,574,396.37)
25	2009	30416438.61	5600000	6083287.723	29933150.89	0.051	92	$ 197.00	$ (214,461,633.00)
26	2010	29933150.89	5333333.333	5986630.178	29279854.05	0.076666667	96.66666667	$ 210.00	$ (44,149,905.42)

In F3:F9 we give current data on Amazon.com. (I guessed at acquisition cost and churn). Note a 20% churn implies a customer stays an average of 6 years; a 5% churn implies a customer stays an average of 21 years, etc. Churn is fraction of customers leaving the business each year (after the first year). In F8 we used a RiskSimtable function to model churn rates of 20%, 15%, 10%, and 5%. In F12:F15 we give a low medium and high estimate for key drivers of profitability in 2010.

We model these values in 2010 using the triangular random variable. Simply copy the formula

=RiskTriang(F15, G15, H15)

from I12 to I13:I15.

Next we assume that each year each key parameter will move 10% of the distance between its 2001 value and its 2010 value. For example, the annual change in Revenue/Customer is computed in cell J12 with the formula

=(I12-F7)/10.

We now generate the profit before taxes of Amazon.com each year.

Step 1: In cell F17 we recopy the number of customers at beginning of 2001.

=F6.

Step 2: In cell G17 we compute the number of new customers obtained in 2001 with the formula

=F4+J13.

Step 3: In cell H17 we compute the (random) number of customers leaving Amazon.com this year. Note that if there is a .20 chance a customer leaves and we have N customers the number leaving is normally distributed with mean .20N and sigma of $\sqrt{.20(1-.20)N}$. Thus number of customers churning during 2001 (we assumed in our churn parameter that new customers spend something or else they would not be customers) is computed with formula

=RiskNormal($F$8*F17,SQRT(F17*$F$8*(1-$F$8))).

Step 4: In cell I17 we compute the number of loyal customers at end of year by adding new customers and subtracting churn.

=F17+G17-H17.

Step 5: In cell J17 we compute our margin for the current year with the formula

=F9+$J$14.

Step 6: In cell K17 we compute the unit acquisition cost per new customer with the formula

=F3+$J$15.

Step 7: In cell L17 we compute our revenue per customer with the formula

=F7+$J$12.

Step 8: In cell M17 we compute our profit with the formula

=L17*I17*J17-K17*G17.

Step 9: In cell F18 we compute our beginning 2002 customers with the formula

=I17.

Step 10: In cell G18 we compute our New 2002 customers with the formula

=G17+$J$13.

Step 11: In cell H18 we compute our Year 2002 churn by copying the churn formula from H17.

Step 12: In cell I18 we compute our Year 2002 ending customers by copying the formula from I17.

Step 13: In cell J18 we compute our Year 2002 margin with the formula

=J17+$J$14.

Step 14: In cell K18 we compute our Year 2002 unit acquisition cost with the formula

=K17+$J$15.

Step 15: In cell L18 we compute our Year 2002 Revenue/customer with the formula

=L17+$J$12.

Step 16: By copying the formula in M17 to M18 we compute our Year 2002 profit.

Step 17: We now copy all 2002 formulas down through Row 26 to compute before tax profit in 2010.

Running 4000 iterations yielded the following statistics:

	E	F	G	H	I
		2010 / Profit before taxes	2010 / Profit before taxes	2010 / Profit before taxes	2010 / Profit before taxes
29	Name				
30	Description	Output (Sim#1)	Output (Sim#2)	Output (Sim#3)	Output (Sim#4)
31	Cell	M26	M26	M26	M26
32	Minimum	-332649900	-245502500	-123908300	39371250
33	Maximum	265881300	468721700	762977100	1178208000
34	**Mean**	**-43910070**	**81797630**	**258347300**	**507375700**
35	Std Deviation	99264680	120120800	151175000	196567300
36	Variance	9.8535E+15	1.443E+16	2.28539E+16	3.8639E+16
37	Skewness	0.1659289	0.2452296	0.3017634	0.3356893
38	Kurtosis	2.940593	2.880448	2.837054	2.811401
39	Errors Calculated	0	0	0	0
40	Mode	5508652	88266980	279635500	553952800
41	5% Perc	-202121000	-105363100	25938040	199500400
42	10% Perc	-169333800	-70183490	71232770	268526500
43	15% Perc	-142220200	-37025420	105793400	302480000
44	20% Perc	-126171800	-20310280	129615700	338324400
45	25% Perc	-111694200	-1486084	150484000	364311800
46	30% Perc	-99197670	13455820	172703600	391874000
47	35% Perc	-87616090	26617720	186716100	416735400
48	40% Perc	-73719880	41956750	206736400	436232500
49	45% Perc	-59594140	60179640	225077400	462981800
50	50% Perc	-45589120	76261590	248607100	493029400
51	55% Perc	-35146590	88888040	267884000	518929100
52	60% Perc	-25962330	106011000	287837800	544746000
53	65% Perc	-10137820	123694200	309260700	571146200
54	70% Perc	6012568	140917600	332911500	606192900
55	75% Perc	20142520	159970700	357322800	635346300
56	80% Perc	37317200	183758300	388024900	671930000
57	85% Perc	61253120	208828800	422129500	716726100
58	90% Perc	87805810	246523200	466240100	780454100
59	95% Perc	130924000	293267300	520093600	841227300
60	Filter Minimum				
61	Filter Maximum				
62	Type (1 or 2)				
63	# Values Filtered	0	0	0	0
64	Scenario #1	>75%	>75%	>75%	>75%
65	Scenario #2	<25%	<25%	<25%	<25%
66	Scenario #3	>90%	>90%	>90%	>90%
67	Target #1 (Value)	**0**	**0**	**0**	**0**
68	Target #1 (Perc%)	**67.31%**	**25.45%**	**4.20%**	**0.18%**
69	Churn rate	**20%**	**15%**	**10%**	**5%**

Note the churn rate makes a big difference in Amazon.com's viability. If you believe in a 5% churn rate they have 100% chance of being profitable by 2010. If you believe in a 20% churn rate they have only a 1/3 chance of being profitable in 2010.

Tornado Graphs

For each churn rate a natural question is which of our random variables' uncertainty has the most influence on the Year 2010 profit. This is easily answered with a **Tornado Graph.** Just right click on the Year 2010 profit output in the Explorer window and select Tornado Graph. You will get the following Tornado graph for a 20% churn rate

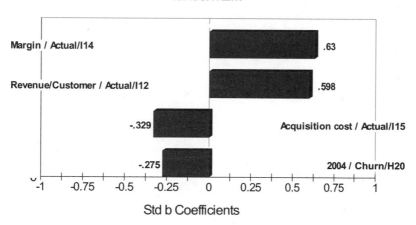

We find (*ceteris paribus*) that a one standard deviation increase in Margin will yield a .63 standard deviation increase in Year 2010 profit. Also a one standard deviation increase in Revenue/customer yields a .60 standard deviation in Year 2010 profit. In short, to accurately determine Amazon.com's viability, we should focus our attention on accurate assessment of the Year 2010 Margin and Revenue/customer for Amazon.com.

Reference

Copeland, T., *Valuation*, John Wiley, 2000.

Chapter 22: Determining Effective Marginal Tax Rates

The tax code allows you to use a loss to offset EBIT (Earnings Before Interest and Taxes) received up to two years earlier or up to 20 years later than the current year. Suppose the tax rate is 50%. Then the **marginal** tax rate for a company that incurs losses during several years may be less than 50%. The marginal tax rate is defined as the change in the PV of taxes caused by a \$1 increase in income. To illustrate this consider a company whose EBIT during each year is a normal random variable with mean 25 and sigma of 50. Such a company has a fairly large chance of a negative EBIT during a year. Assume that two years ago their EBIT was 30 and last year their EBIT was 18. If their current year's EBIT is 0, what is the marginal tax rate? See the file **Tax.xls**. We first compute the PV of all the taxes the company is expected to pay when its Year 0 EBIT is 20. This involves simulating all future EBITs and computing the taxes and discounting these taxes at say, 15%. Then we increase Year 0 EBIT by \$1 and recomputed the expected NPV of all taxes paid (in year 0 dollars). The difference in the expected taxes is the marginal tax rate because it is the extra tax caused by an extra dollar of EBIT.

Our spreadsheet model is tricky. We keep track of how much credit is available to offset taxes paid two years ago, one year ago, and in the future. See Figure 22.1 and file **Tax.xls**

Figure 22.1

	A	B	C	D	E	F	G	H	I	J	K	L	M	N	O
1															
2			Tax Rate												
3			EBIT											NPv taxes	\$161.46
4			mean=25 sigma=50												
5	Year	EBIT	Two year to credit against	One Year to credit against	Current to credit against	Available for 2 yrs	Used for 2 years	Available for 1 ycar	Used for 1 year	Available for current or future	Used for Current	Credit left for future use	Tax paid	Tax credit	Total bill
6	-2	30													15
7	-1	18													9
8	0	20	30	18	20	0	0	0	0	0	0	0	10	0	10
9	1	93	18	20	93	0	0	0	0	0	0	0	46.5	0	46.5
10	2	42	20	93	42	0	0	0	0	0	0	0	21	0	21
11	3	-10	93	42	0	10	10	0	0	0	0	0	0	5	-5
12	4	40	42	0	40	0	0	0	0	0	0	0	20	0	20
13	5	135	0	40	135	0	0	0	0	0	0	0	67.5	0	67.5
14	6	-17	40	135	0	17	17	0	0	0	0	0	0	8.5	-8.5
15	7	82	135	0	82	0	0	0	0	0	0	0	41	0	41
16	8	124	0	82	124	0	0	0	0	0	0	0	62	0	62
17	9	52	82	124	52	0	0	0	0	0	0	0	26	0	26
18	10	63	124	52	65	0	0	0	0	0	0	0	32.5	0	32.5
19	11	90	52	65	90	0	0	0	0	0	0	0	45	0	45
20	12	-60	65	90	0	60	60	0	0	0	0	0	0	30	-30
21	13	28	90	0	28	0	0	0	0	0	0	0	14	0	14
22	14	-50	0	28	0	50	0	50	28	22	0	22	0	14	-14
23	15	17	0	0	17	0	0	0	0	22	17	5	8.5	8.5	0
24	16	94	0	0	94	0	0	0	0	5	5	0	47	2.5	44.5
25	17	-52	0	89	0	52	0	52	52	0	0	0	0	26	-26
26	18	-22	37	0	0	22	22	0	0	0	0	0	0	11	-11
27	19	42	0	0	42	0	0	0	0	0	0	0	21	0	21
28	20	-61	0	42	0	61	0	61	42	19	0	19	0	21	-21

To begin we compute in cells O6 and O7 our total tax bill two years ago and one year ago by copying from O6 to O7 the formula

$= IF(B6<0,0,0.5*B6).$

We also generate random EBIT's for years 1-20 by copying the formula

$=RiskNormal(25,50)$

from cell B9 to B10:B28.

*Step by
Step* **Step 0: In cells B6 and B7 enter the EBIT in year –2 and year –1 respectively.** In cell B8 enter the current year's EBIT + RiskSimtable({0,1}). This will automatically run two simulations for us: one using the current EBIT of 20+0 = 20 and the next with the current EBIT increased by $1.

Step 1: In cell C8 we compute the amount used to generate taxes paid two years ago with the formula

$=IF(B6>0,B6,0).$

Step 2: In cell D8 we compute the amount used to generate taxes one year ago with the formula

$=IF(B7>0,B7,0).$

Step 3: In cell E8 we compute the amount used to generate taxes this year with the formula

$=IF(B8>0,B8,0).$

Step 4: In cell F8 we compute the amount of credit available from the current year to offset taxes from two years ago with the formula

$=IF(B8<0,-B8,0).$

Step 5: In cell G8 we compute the amount of available credit used to offset our tax liability from two years ago with the formula

$=MIN(F8,C8).$

Step 6: In cell H8 we compute the amount of credit available to offset our liability from one year ago or later with the formula

$=F8-G8.$

Step 7: In cell I8 we compute the amount used to offset the one year ago liability with the formula

=IF(H8>0,MIN(H8,D8),0).

Step 8: In cell J8 we compute the amount available to offset a current or future liability with the formula

=IF(B8<0,-B8-G8-I8,0).

Step 9: In cell K8 we compute the amount used to offset our current liability with the formula

=MIN(J8,E8).

Step 10: In cell L8 we compute the amount of credit left for future use with the formula

=J8-K8.

Step 11: In cell M8 we compute the amount of tax paid during the current year with the formula

= IF(B8>0,0.5*B8,0).

Step 12: In cell N8 we compute our total tax credit used during the current year with the formula

=0.5*(SUM(G8,I8,K8)).

Step 13: Finally in cell O8 we compute our total tax paid during year 0 with the formula

=M8-N8.

Step 14: In cell O3 we compute (in Year 0 dollars) our total liability with the formula

=O8+NPV(0.15,O9:O28).

Make this the output cell and run the simulation. Remember to set the number of simulations to 2 in the Iterations tab of the Simulation Settings dialog. Two simulations will be run – one with the actual EBIT in year 0 and another with the year 0 EBIT increased by $1.

Making this our output cell we found a mean tax liability of $89.49. We re-ran the simulation with Year 0 EBIT of $1 and found a mean of $89.96. This means that the tax increased by 47 cents when the income increased by $1 or a marginal tax rate of 47% (not 50%). With Year 0 EBIT = 0 we found a marginal tax rate of 46%.

We changed the annual distribution of EBIT to a normal random variable with a mean of 100 and standard deviation of 30. See file **Taxcoke.xls**. This virtually ensures each year's EBIT is positive. Here we find a marginal tax rate of 50%.

Chapter 23: Incorporating Simulation into Proforma Models

In this chapter we will show you how to generate proforma statements that can be used to estimate a firm's future free cash flow. We will also show how to use @RISK to incorporate uncertainty in our forecasts of future FCF. Our models are based on the Proforma models in Benninga's (1999) wonderful book.

We begin with a brief discussion of circular references.

Often financial spreadsheets have the following type of situation. The value in cell A influences cell B's value. The value in cell B influences cell C's value. The value in cell C influences cell A's value. This type of dependence creates a **circular reference**. By checking on the Excel Tools menu, Options>Calculation, and setting Iterations to say, 100, you can cause Excel to resolve your circular references. Here is an example.

Example   A small company wants to pay out 5% of its after-tax profit to charity. Currently their revenues are $500, costs are $300, and the tax rate is 40%. We want to determine their charitable contribution.

Solution   See file **Circular.xls**.

Step by Step

Step 1: In cell B6 we compute our charitable contribution with the formula

=0.05*B8.

Step 2: In cell C7 we determine our before- tax profit with the formula

=B4-B5-B6.

Step 3: In cell C8 determine our after-tax profit with the formula

=(1-B3)*B7.

We find the following circular reference (indicated by the blue arrows). Before Tax Profit-After Tax Profit-Charitable Contribution-Before Tax Profit.

	A	B
2	Circular References	
3	Tax rate	0.4
4	Revenue	$ 500
5	Costs	$ 300
6	Charitable Cont	0
7	Before tax profit	$ 200
8	After tax profit	$ -

Step 4: To resolve the circular references select Tools>Options>Calculation, and set the dialog box as follows and click OK.

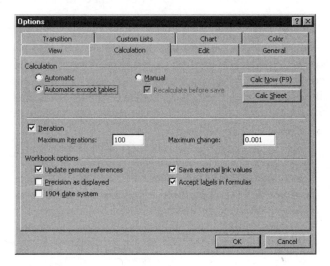

Excel will now try 100 times to resolve the circular references by solving systems of linear equations. As soon as no cell changes by more than .001 Excel will stop. Here is the result:

	A	B
2	Circular References	
3	Tax rate	0.40
4	Revenue	500.00
5	Costs	300.00
6	Charitable Cont	5.83
7	Before tax profit	194.17
8	After tax profit	$ 116.50

Note that our charitable contribution is indeed 5% of after-tax profit.

All our Proformas will contain circular references, so during the rest of this chapter you will need to select Tools>Options>Calculation, and check the Iteration box.

A Deterministic Proforma

In file **Proforma2.xls** we generate the FCF for the next five years for a firm. Our basic assumptions (see Figure 23.1) are as follows:

Figure 23.1

	A	B	C	D	E	F	G	H	I
1		Panel A Inputs					Calculated inputs		
2									
3	0	Sales growth	SG	2%	1	CA/Sales		15%	
4	0	Initial sales	IS	$ 1,000	1	CL/Sales		7%	
5	0	Interest rate on debt	IRD	10%	1	NFA/Sales		60%	
6	0	Dividend Payout	DIV	5%	1	GFA/Sales		90%	
7	0	Tax rate	TR	53%					
8	0	COGS/Sales	COGS	70%					
9	0	Depreciation Rate	DEP	10%					
10		Liquid Asset Interest rate	LAIR	9%					
11		Panel B Balance sheet							
12				0	1	2	3	4	5
13		Cash and mkt. sec.			0.00	0.00	38.50	109.31	177.72
14	6	Current Assets		150	153.00	156.06	159.18	162.36	165.61
15	9	Gross fixed assets		900	1013.33	1139.53	1280.01	1436.39	1610.42
16	8	Acc. dep.		300	401.33	515.29	643.29	786.93	947.97
17	7	Net Fixed Assets		600	612.00	624.24	636.72	649.46	662.45
18	10	Total assets		750.00	765.00	780.30	834.40	921.14	1005.78
19									
20	8	Current liabilities		70	71.40	72.83	74.28	75.77	77.29
21	20	Debt		180	106.99	33.90	0.00	0.00	0.00
22	9	Stock		400	400.00	400.00	400.00	400.00	400.00
23	18	Retained earnings		100	186.61	273.57	360.12	445.37	528.50
24	19	Equity		500	586.61	673.57	760.12	845.37	928.50
25	21	Total liabilities		750.00	765.00	780.30	834.40	921.14	1005.78
26									

- Sales growth is 2% per year.

- Initial sales are $1000.

- Interest rate on debt is 10%.

- Dividend payout is 5%

- Tax rate is 53%.

- COGS are 70% of sales.

- Depreciation is 10% of Gross Fixed Assets.

- Liquid assets earn 9%.

- Current assets are 15% of sales.

- Current Liabilities are 7% of sales.

- Net Fixed Assets are 60% of sales.

Our Income Statement and FCF Statement follow in Figure 23.2.

Figure 23.2

	A	B	C	D	E	F	G	H	I
26									
27	Panel C	Income statement		0	1	2	3	4	5
28	2	Sales		1000	1020	1040	1061	1082	1104
29	3	Cost of goods sold		700	714	728	743	758	773
30	4	Depreciation			101	114	128	144	161
31	5	Operating income			205	198	190	181	170
32		Interest Income			0	0	3	10	16
33	11	Interest expense	32		11	3	0	0	0
34	12	Income before taxes	33		194	195	194	191	186
35	13	Taxes	34		103	103	103	101	99
36	14	Net income	35		91	92	91	90	88
37			36						
38	15	Beg. retained earnings	37		100	187	274	360	445
39	16	Dividends	38		5	5	5	4	4
40	17	Ending retained earnings	39		187	274	360	445	528
41			40						
42			41						
43	Panel D		42						
44	1	Net income	43		91	92	91	90	88
45	2	+Interest expense	44		11	3	0	0	0
46	3	+Income taxes	45		103	103	103	101	99
47		-Interest Income			0	0	-3	-10	-16
48	4	=EBIT	46		205	198	190	181	170
49	5	-Cash Taxes	47		108	105	101	96	90
50	6	=NOPLAT	48		96	93	89	85	80
51	7	+Depreciation	49		101	114	128	144	161
52	8	=Gross cash flow	50		198	207	217	229	241
53	9	-Inc. in NWC	51		-2	-2	-2	-2	-2
54	10	-CAPEX	52		-113	-126	-140	-156	-174
55	11	=FCF	53		83	79	75	71	65

To generate FCF we proceed as follows:

Step by Step

Step 1: Compute sales during each year by copying from E28 to F28:I28 the formula

$$=D28*(1+SG).$$

Step 2: Compute each year's COGS by copying from E29 to F29:I29 the formula

$$=COGS*E28.$$

Step 3: Compute each year's debt in E21:I21 by copying from E21 to F21:I21 the formula

$$= MAX(E18-E20-E24,0).$$

If no debt is needed this formula will enter a debt of 0. Otherwise we set debt to balance assets and liabilities. Later we will record negative debt as liquid assets.

Step 4: In E20:I20 we compute our Current Liabilities for each year by copying from E20 to F20:I20 the formula

$$=\$H\$4*E28.$$

Step 5: In E24:I24 we compute our Equity by copying from E24 to F24:I24 the formula

=SUM(E22:E23).

Step 6: In E13:I13 we compute cash and marketable securities for each year by copying from E13 to F13:I13 the formula

=IF(E21>0,0,MAX(0,E25-E14-E17))

If debt does not balance things, this creates Liquid Assets as the plug that makes assets and liabilities balance.

Step 7: In E33:I33 we compute Interest expense by copying from E33 to F33:I33 the formula

=IRD*E21.

Step 8: In E32:I32 we compute Interest income by copying from E30 to F30:I30 the formula

=$D$10*E13.

Step 9: In E31:I31 we compute Operating Income by copying from E31 to F31:I31 the formula

=E28-E29-E30.

Step 10: In E39:I39 we compute dividends each year by copying from E39 to F39:I39 the formula

=E36*DIV.

Step 11: In F38:I38 we compute Beginning Retained Earnings each year by copying from F38 to G38:I38 the formula

=E40.

Step 12: In E40:I40 we compute each year's ending Retained Earnings by adding Net Income less dividends. To do this we copy from E40 to F40:I40 the formula

=E38+E36-E39.

Step 13: By copying from E34 to F34:I34 the formula

   =E31-E33+E32

we compute Income before Taxes by subtracting interest expense and adding interest income to Operating income.

Step 14: We compute each year's taxes in E35:I35 by copying from E35 to F35:I35 the formula

   =TR*E34.

Step 15: In E36:I36 we compute each year's Net Income by copying from E36 to F36:I36 the formula

   =E34-E35.

Step 16: In E17:I17 we compute each year's Net Fixed Assets by copying from E17 to F17:I17 the formula

   =$H$5*E28.

This forces net fixed assets to equal 60% of sales.

Step 17: In cells E15:I15 we compute Gross Fixed Assets for each year by copying from E15 to F15:I15 the formula

   =E17+E16.

This computes Gross Fixed Assets(t) = NFA(t) + Acc. Dep(t).

Step 18: Each year depreciation is 10% of Gross Fixed Assets. To compute each year's depreciation copy from E30 to F30:I30 the formula

   =DEP*E15.

Step 19: Each year accumulated depreciation is computed by adding the current year's depreciation to the previous year's accumulated depreciation. This is accomplished by copying from E16 to F16:I16 the formula

   =D16+E30

Then in Row 17 we compute Net Fixed Assets by copying from E16 to F16:I16 the formula

   =D15-D16.

Step 20: By adding Liquid Assets, Current Assets, and Net Fixed Assets, we compute our total assets by copying from E18 to F18:I18 the formula

=SUM(E13,E14,E17).

Step 21: By copying from E20 to F20:I20 the formula

=SUM(E20,E21,E24)

we compute total liabilities for each period. Each year will balance because of our debt and liquid asset statements.

Computing Free Cash Flow

To compute FCF proceed as follows:

Step by Step

Step 1: Recopy Net Income, Interest Expense, Taxes, and –Interest Income to cells E44:I47. See Figure 23.3.

Figure 23.3

	A	B	C	D	E	F	G	H	I
42			41						
43	Panel D		42						
44	1	Net income	43		91	92	91	90	88
45	2	+Interest expense	44		11	3	0	0	0
46	3	+Income taxes	45		103	103	103	101	99
47		-Interest Income			0	0	-3	-10	-16
48	4	=EBIT	46		205	198	190	181	170
49	5	-Cash Taxes	47		108	105	101	96	90
50	6	=NOPLAT	48		96	93	89	85	80
51	7	+Depreciation	49		101	114	128	144	161
52	8	=Gross cash flow	50		198	207	217	229	241
53	9	-Inc. in NWC	51		-2	-2	-2	-2	-2
54	10	-CAPEX	52		-113	-126	-140	-156	-174
55	11	=FCF	53		83	79	75	71	65

Step 2: In cells E48:I48 compute EBIT by copying from E48 to F48:I48 the formula

=E44+E45+E35+E47.

Step 3: In cells E49:I49 we compute cash taxes for each year by copying from E49 to F49:I49 the formula

=E48*TR.

Step 4: In E50:I50 we compute NOPLAT (Net Operating Profit Left After Taxes) by copying from E50 to F50:I50 the formula

=E48-E49.

Step 5: In E51:I51 we recopy each year's Depreciation from Row 30.

Step 6: In E52:I52 we compute each year's Gross cash flow by copying from E52 to F52:I52 the formula

=E50+E51.

Step 7: In E53:I53 we compute each year's –(Increase in Working Capital) by copying from E53 to F53:I53 the formula

=-((E14-D14)-(E20-D20)).

Step 8: In E54:I54 we compute each year's –(Capital Expense) by copying from E54 to F54:I54 the formula

=-(E15-D15).

Step 9: In E55:I55 we compute each year's actual cash flow by copying from E55 to F55:I55 the formula

= SUM(E52:E54).

Incorporating a Variable Interest Rate

A company in poor financial health will have to pay higher interest rates. Suppose if EBIT is negative the interest rate is 16%; if Interest expense is more than 10% of EBIT and EBIT is positive, then Interest rate is 13%, otherwise Interest Rate is 10%. This can easily be incorporated into our proforma. See file **Proforma2varintrate.xls**. In row 26 copy from E26 to F26:I26 the formula

= IF(E48<0,0.16,IF(E33/E48>0.1,0.13,0.1)).

Then change Interest Expense formulas in row 33 to key off Row 26. The result follows:

Figure 23.4

	A	B	C	D	E	F	G	H	I
11	**Panel B**	**Balance sheet**							
12				0	1	2	3	4	5
13		Cash and mkt. sec.			0.00	0.00	38.50	109.31	177.72
14	6	Current Assets		150	153.00	156.06	159.18	162.36	165.61
15	9	Gross fixed assets		900	1013.33	1139.53	1280.01	1436.38	1610.42
16	8	Acc. dep.		300	401.33	515.29	643.29	786.93	947.97
17	7	Net Fixed Assets		600	612.00	624.24	636.72	649.46	662.45
18	10	Total assets		750.00	765.00	780.30	834.40	921.14	1005.781
19									
20	8	Current liabilities		70	71.40	72.83	74.28	75.77	77.29
21	20	Debt		180	106.99	33.90	0.00	0.00	0.00
22	9	Stock		400	400.00	400.00	400.00	400.00	400.00
23	18	Retained earnings		100	186.61	273.57	360.12	445.37	528.50
24	19	Equity		500	586.61	673.57	760.12	845.37	928.50
25	21	Total liabilities		750.00	765.00	780.30	834.40	921.14	1005.782
26		Interest rate			0.10	0.10	0.10	0.10	0.10
27	**Panel C**	**Income statement**		0	1	2	3	4	5
28	2	Sales		1000	1020	1040	1061	1082	1104
29	3	Cost of goods sold		700	714	728	743	758	773
30	4	Depreciation			101	114	128	144	161
31	5	Operating income			205	198	190	181	170
32		Interest Income			0	0	3	10	16
33	11	Interest expense	32		11	3	0	0	0
34	12	Income before taxes	33		194	195	194	191	186
35	13	Taxes	34		103	103	103	101	99
36	14	Net income	35		91	92	91	90	88
37			36						
38	15	Beg. retained earnings	37		100	187	274	360	445
39	16	Dividends	38		5	5	5	4	4
40	17	Ending retained earnings	39		187	274	360	445	528
41			40						
42			41						
43	**Panel D**		42						
44	1	Net income	43		91	92	91	90	88
45	2	+Interest expense	44		11	3	0	0	0
46	3	+Income taxes	45		103	103	103	101	99
47		-Interest Income			0	0	-3	-10	-16
48	4	=EBIT	46		205	198	190	181	170

Incorporating a Target Debt/Equity Ratio

Companies often have a desired Debt/Equity ratio. How can we incorporate a desired D/E ratio in our proforma? For example, suppose we want our company to have a 50% D/E ratio for each year. See file **Proforma2targetDE.xls**. Our changes are in rows 13, 21, and 22.

*Step by Step***Step 1: In E21:I21 we compute Debt as the desired percentage of Total Equity by copying from E21 to F21:I21 the formula**

=$H$7*(E22+E23).

Step 2: In E22:I22 we force Stock to be non-negative and balance the Assets and Liabilities by copying the formula

=MAX(0,E18-E20-E21-E23)

from E22 to F22:I22.

Figure 23.5

	A	B	C	D	E	F	G	H	I
1	Panel A	Inputs				Calculated inputs			
2									
3	0	Sales growth	SG	2%	1	CA/Sales		15%	
4	0	Initial sales	IS	$ 1,000	1	CL/Sales		7%	
5	0	Interest rate on debt	IRD	10%	1	NFA/Sales		60%	
6	0	Dividend Payout	DIV	30%	1	GFA/Sales		90%	
7	0	Tax rate	TR	53%		D/E		50%	
8	0	COGS/Sales	COGS	70%					
9	0	Depreciation Rate	DEP	10%					
10		Liquid Asset Interest rate	LAIR	9%					
11	Panel B	Balance sheet							
12					0	1	2	3	4	5
13		Cash and mkt. sec.			213.32	498.50	877.50	1378.90	2039.86
14	6	Current Assets		150	153.00	156.06	159.18	162.36	165.61
15	9	Gross fixed assets		900	1013.33	1139.53	1280.01	1436.38	1610.42
16	8	Acc. dep.		300	401.33	515.29	643.29	786.93	947.97
17	7	Net Fixed Assets		600	612.00	624.24	636.72	649.46	662.45
18	10	Total assets		750.00	978.32	1278.80	1673.41	2190.72	2867.92
19									
20	8	Current liabilities		70	71.40	72.83	74.28	75.77	77.29
21	20	Debt		180	302.31	401.99	533.04	704.98	930.21
22	9	Stock		400	440.91	573.54	764.52	1031.24	1395.91
23	18	Retained earnings		100	163.71	230.44	301.51	378.73	464.51
24	19	Equity		500	604.61	803.98	1066.08	1409.97	1860.42
25	21	Total liabilities		750.00	978.32	1278.80	1673.41	2190.72	2867.92

Step 3: Finally in E13:I13 we compute Cash and Marketable Securities to be non-negative and make Assets and Liabilities balance by copying from E13 to F13:I13 the formula

=MAX(0,I25-I14-I17).

Using Monte Carlo Simulation with Proformas

Clearly parameters such as Sales Growth and COGS/Revenue are unknown. Can we use Monte Carlo simulation to show how the uncertainty in key inputs such as Sales Growth and COGS/Revenue influence future FCF (and therefore firm value)? As an example, suppose we make the following assumptions:

- Annual sale growth is equally likely to be any number between 5%-15%.

- COGS/Revenue is equally likely to be any number between 60%-80%.

- CA/Revenues is equally likely to be any number between 10%-20%.

- CL/Revenues is equally likely to be any number between 3.5%-10.5%.

- NFA/Revenues is equally likely to be any number between 50%-70%.

We may model these uncertain quantities with the =RiskUniform random variable. See file **Proforma2risk.xls**.

For example to model annual sales growth enter the formula

$=RiskUniform(0.05,0.15)$

in E3. In a similar fashion we enter the other uncertain quantities with =RiskUniform in E8 and I3:I5.

Figure 23.6

	A	B	C	D	E	F	G	H	I
1	Panel A	Inputs				Calculated inputs			
2									
3	0	Sales growth	SG	11%	0.122744	CA/Sales		17%	0.1429
4	0	Initial sales	IS	$ 1,000		CL/Sales		9%	0.0421
5	0	Interest rate on debt	IRD	10%		NFA/Sales		60%	0.6888
6	0	Dividend Payout	DIV	5%		GFA/Sales			
7	0	Tax rate	TR	53%					
8	0	COGS/Sales	COGS	80%	0.6634541				
9	0	Depreciation Rate	DEP	10%					
10		Liquid Asset Interest rate	LAIR	9%					
11	Panel B	Balance sheet							
12				0	1	2	3	4	
13		Cash and mkt. sec.			0	0	0	0	
14	6	Current Assets		150	184	204	226	251	
15	9	Gross fixed assets		900	1073	1273	1505	1772	2079
16	8	Acc. dep.		300	407	535	685	862	1070
17	7	Net Fixed Assets		600	666	739	820	909	1
18	10	Total assets			850	943	1046	1160	1
19									
20	8	Current liabilities		70	101	112	124	137	
21	20	Debt		180	205	243	291	349	
22	9	Stock		400	400	400	400	400	400
23	18	Retained earnings		100	144	188	231	274	315
24	19	Equity		500	544	588	631	674	
25	21	Total liabilities			850	943	1046	1160	1
26									
27	Panel C	Income statement		0	1	2	3	4	
28	2	Sales		1000	1110	1231	1366	1516	1
29	3	Cost of goods sold		700	884	981	1088	1207	1
30	4	Depreciation			107	127	150	177	
31	5	Operating income			118	123	127	131	
32		Interest Income			0	0	0	0	
33	11	Interest expense	32		21	24	29	35	
34	12	Income before taxes	33		98	99	98	96	
35	13	Taxes	34		52	52	52	51	
36	14	Net income	35		46	46	46	45	
37			36						
38	15	Beg. retained earnings	37		100	144	188	231	
39	16	Dividends	38		2	2	2	2	
40	17	Ending retained earnings	39		144	188	231	274	
41			40						

	A	B	C	D	E	F	G	H	I
42			41						
43	Panel D		42						
44	1	Net income	43		46	46	46	45	
45	2	+Interest expense	44		21	24	29	35	
46	3	+Income taxes	45		52	52	52	51	
47		-Interest Income			0	0	0	0	
48	4	=EBIT	46		118	123	127	131	
49	5	-Cash Taxes	47		63	65	67	69	
50	6	=NOPLAT	48		56	58	60	62	
51	7	+Depreciation	49		107	127	150	177	
52	8	=Gross cash flow	50		163	185	210	239	
53	9	-Inc. in NWC	51		-3	-9	-10	-11	
54	10	-CAPEX	52		-173	-200	-231	-267	
55	11	=FCF	53		-13	-24	-31	-39	
56			54						
57				NPV	($84.87)				
58									

Using Monte Carlo Simulation with Proforma

Next we create a macro to paste the random input parameters into the cells that drive the Proforma. Finally we link the macro to @RISK and simulate the Five Year NPV (calculated in E57 at 20% WACC) 400 times.

Step by Step

Step 1: Choose Tools>Macros>Create New Macro (we named it Macro 4). Then Edit>Copy>Paste Special>Values E3 to D3, E8 to D8, and I3:I5 to H3:H5. Then choose the Stop Recording button.

Step 2: Click the Simulation Settings icon and select Macros.

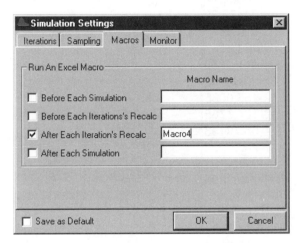

Enter Macro 4 in After Each Iteration's Recalc. After computing random input Excel will compute our 5 Year NPV. This will be done 400 times if we choose Iterations = 400.

After running the simulation we get the following output.

	L	M
17	Name	NPV
18	Description	Output
19	Cell	E57
20	Minimum	-300.7749
21	Maximum	**468.0117**
22	Mean	104.1153
23	Std Deviation	146.5278
24	Variance	21470.39
25	Skewness	-0.129471
26	Kurtosis	2.61537
27	Errors Calculated	0
28	Mode	90.04263
29	5% Perc	-155.0035
30	10% Perc	-104.3765
31	15% Perc	-56.76193
32	20% Perc	-24.16902
33	25% Perc	6.414292
34	30% Perc	29.32365
35	35% Perc	53.72442
36	40% Perc	76.38326
37	45% Perc	90.27739
38	50% Perc	116.5613
39	55% Perc	128.3766
40	60% Perc	144.5091
41	65% Perc	162.2007
42	70% Perc	182.1432
43	75% Perc	206.4009
44	80% Perc	227.8774
45	85% Perc	258.8322
46	90% Perc	291.041
47	95% Perc	342.2016

Mean NPV **is around $104**, but Five Year NPV can range as low as -$301 or as high as $468. There is around a 24% chance of a negative FCF in the next 5 Years! Of course, our Year 5 FCF is the lynchpin used to generate the firm's terminal value.

Monte Carlo Simulation with Scenarios

Consider an uncertain input parameter (such as Annual Sales Growth). Our previous model assumed that Annual Sales Growth would be the same (but uncertain) each year. Following Chapter 15 of Copeland we now show how to create scenarios for the next five years and have @RISK randomly choose a scenario. As an example, let's suppose that we believe Sales Growth/Year and COGS/Revenue are uncertain for each of the next five years. Assume we believe the following four scenarios will occur with the given probabilities for the next five years:

	J	K	L	M	N	O	P
1	Prob		**COGS**				
2	0.2	1	0.7	0.68	0.66	0.64	0.62
3	0.3	2	0.7	0.72	0.74	0.76	0.78
4	0.4	3	0.7	0.7	0.7	0.7	0.7
5	0.1	4	0.7	0.69	0.68	0.67	0.66
6							
7			Scenario	3			
8		Scenario	**Sales growth**				
9	0.2	1	0.05	0.1	0.15	0.2	0.25
10	0.3	2	0.1	0.08	0.06	0.04	0.02
11	0.4	3	0.1	0.1	0.1	0.1	0.1
12	0.1	4	0.1	0.11	0.12	0.13	0.14

Can we model the distribution of discounted FCF over the next five years?

Our work is in file **Proforma2riskscenarios.xls**.

Step by Step

Step 1: In cell M7 we randomly generate a scenario with the formula

$=RiskDiscrete(K2:K5,J2:J5)$.

Step 2: In cells O28:S29 we generate the actual Sales growth and COGS/Revenue for each year. Copying from O28 to P28:S28 the formula

$= VLOOKUP(\$M\$7,\$K\$9:\$P\$12,O26)$

generates actual Sales growth that keys off our scenario.

Copying from O29 to P29:S29 the formula

$= VLOOKUP(\$M\$7,\$K\$2.\$P\$5,O26)$

generates actual COGS/Revenue for each year that keys off the scenario.

Step 3: We now set up a macro to Edit>Copy>Paste Special>Values our actual Sales Growth and COGS from O28:S29 to J28:N29.

	J	K	L	M	N	O	P	Q	R	S
27	Copied 1	Copied 2	Copied 3	Copied 4	Copied 5	Actual 1	Actual 2	Actual 3	Actual 4	Actual 5
28	0.1	0.11	0.12	0.13	0.14	0.1	0.1	0.1	0.1	0.1
29	0.7	0.69	0.68	0.67	0.66	7.00E-01	7.00E-01	7.00E-01	7.00E-01	7.00E-01

Step 4: We now compute our revenue in Row 28 by copying from column E to columns F: I the formula

$=D28*(1+J28).$

Step 5: We now compute our COGS in row 29 by copying from column E to columns F:I the formula

$=E28*J29.$

Step 6: We now track our Five Year discounted NPV in cell E57 and link our macro (as before) to @RISK. After running 400 iterations we find the following results:

	P	Q
33	Name	NPV
34	Description	Output
35	Cell	E57
36	Minimum	9.36E+01
37	Maximum	1.11E+02
38	Mean	1.05E+02
39	Std Deviation	6.26E+00
40	Variance	3.92E+01
41	Skewness	-1.12E+00
42	Kurtosis	2.81E+00
43	Errors Calculated	0.00E+00
44	Mode	106.7279
45	5% Perc	93.61276
46	10% Perc	93.61279
47	15% Perc	93.61279
48	20% Perc	93.61282
49	25% Perc	106.7279
50	30% Perc	106.7279
51	35% Perc	106.7279
52	40% Perc	106.7279
53	45% Perc	106.7279
54	50% Perc	106.7279
55	55% Perc	106.728
56	60% Perc	106.7876
57	65% Perc	106.7877
58	70% Perc	111.2835
59	75% Perc	111.2835
60	80% Perc	111.2835
61	85% Perc	111.2835
62	90% Perc	111.2836
63	95% Perc	111.2836

Simulating an Unfavorable Future

Suppose we believe next year's revenue growth will average 10% (with a standard deviation of 5%) and each successive year revenue growth will drop on average by 2% a year. Also suppose we believe that next year's COGS/Sales will average 70% (with a standard deviation of 4%) and each successive year COGS/Sales will increase on average by 1% a year. Under these assumptions how would we simulate the NPV (at 10%) of the FCF for the next five years? See File **Proformadown.xls**.

	J	K	L	M	N	O	P	Q	R	S
28	Copied @RISK Functions J:N					@RISK Functions O-S				
29	1	2	3	4	5	1	2	3	4	5
30	0.1174967	0.15536	0.094634	0.151054	0.261957	0.049352	-0.069485	-0.151048	-0.175534	-0.188346
31	0.758839	0.74349	0.710981	0.677706	0.734927	0.692639	0.653003	0.679857	0.70938	0.668688

Step by Step

Step 1: In cell O30 generate growth rate in sales next year with the formula

=*RiskNormal(0.1,0.05)*.

Step 2: In cell P30:S30 generate growth rate in sales for Years 2-5 by copying from P30 to Q30:S30 the formula

=*RiskNormal(O30-0.02,0.05)*.

Step 3: In cell O31 generate COGS/Sales for the next year with the formula

=*RiskNormal(0.7,0.04)*.

Step 4: In cells P31:S31 generate COGS/Sales for remaining years by copying from P31 to Q31:S31 the formula

=*RiskNormal(O31+0.01,0.04)*.

Step 5: Now create a macro (called Pasteit) to Edit>Copy>Paste Special>Values the numbers created by @RISK in cells O30:S31 to J30:N31.

Step 6: In cells E30:I30 we generate Actual Sales for next five years which key off columns J:N. Next year's sales are computed in I30 with the formula

=*Sales_0*(1+J30)*.

Sales for the subsequent four years are computed by copying from F30 to F30:I30 the formula

=*E30*(1+K30)*.

Step 7: In cells E31:I31 we generate COGS for each year by copying from E31 to F31:I31 the formula

=E30*J31.

Step 8: In cell E68 we compute the NPV of our FCF's (at 10%) with the formula

=RiskOutput() + NPV(0.1,E66:I66).

	A	B	C	D	E	F	G	H	I	J
58	Panel E		58							
59	1	Cash flow from operations	59		104	126	166	211	200	
60	2	-Change in required cash bal	60		0	0	0	0	0	
61	3	=Adjusted cash balance	61		104	126	166	211	200	
62	4	+Interest expense	62		29	33	35	39	46	
63	5	-Interest tax shield	63		-15	-17	-18	-21	-24	
64	6	=Cash flow from ops (unlev)	64		117	142	182	229	222	
65	7	-CAPEX	65		-82	-122	-86	-149	-298	
66	8	=FCF	66		35	20	97	80	-77	
67										
68					$128.18					
69										

Step 9: After running 400 iterations we obtain the following output:

	L	M
34		
35	Name	
36	Description	Output
37	Cell	E68
38	Minimum	-774.3707
39	Maximum	915.1918
40	Mean	381.4703
41	Std Deviati	227.7903
42	Variance	51888.4
43	Skewness	-1.063607
44	Kurtosis	5.281482
45	Errors Calc	0
46	Mode	463.3838
47	5% Perc	-24.20016
48	10% Perc	84.35219
49	15% Perc	176.9274
50	20% Perc	221.1749
51	25% Perc	267.8144
52	30% Perc	293.5208
53	35% Perc	323.4169
54	40% Perc	359.2709
55	45% Perc	387.462
56	50% Perc	408.9908
57	55% Perc	435.7859
58	60% Perc	462.2071
59	65% Perc	483.158
60	70% Perc	509.575
61	75% Perc	536.7392
62	80% Perc	569.1741
63	85% Perc	600.4235
64	90% Perc	629.1509
65	95% Perc	677.6864

	A	B	C	D	E	F	G	H	I
28			28						
29	Panel C	Income statement	29	0	1	2	3	4	5
30	2	Sales	30		1117	1291	1413	1627	2053
31	3	Cost of goods sold	31		848	960	1005	1102	1509
32		Depreciation	32		0	0	0	0	0
33	4	Operating income	33		269	331	408	524	544
34	10	Interest expense	34		29	33	35	39	46
35	11	Income before taxes	35		240	299	374	486	498
36	12	Taxes	36		127	158	100	257	264
37	13	Net income	37		113	140	176	228	234
38			38						
39	14	Beg. retained earnings	39		100	145	201	272	363
40	15	Dividends	40		68	84	105	137	141
41	16	Ending retained earnings	41		145	201	272	363	457

Chapter 24: Forecasting Income of a Major Corporation

In many large corporations (GM is one example) different parts of a company makes forecasts for quarterly net income and an analyst in the CEO's office pulls together the individual forecasts to create a forecast for the entire company's net income. In this section we show an easy way to pool forecasts from different portions of a company and create a probabilistic forecast for the entire company. With such a forecast it is easy to answer questions such as, "What is the probability our quarterly net income will exceed $4 billion?"

So far we have usually assumed that @RISK functions in different cells are independent. For example, the value of a RiskNormal(0,1) in cell A6 has no effect on value of a RiskNormal(0,1) in any other cell. In many situations, however, variables of interest might be correlated. For example, a weak yen will lower the US price of a Japanese car and hurt GM's market share. Since higher price incentives increase market share, GM's market share may also be negatively correlated with car price. As another example, it is clear that net income of NAO (North American Operations) is correlated with net income in Europe. The following example shows how to model correlations with @RISK. Recall that the correlation between two random variables must lie between -1 and +1 with

- Correlation near +1 implies strong positive linear relationship.

- Correlation near -1 implies strong negative linear relationship.

- Correlation near +.5 implies a moderate positive linear relationship.

- Correlation near -.5 implies a moderate negative linear relationship.

- Correlation near 0 implies a weak linear relationship.

The following example shows how to model correlations with @RISK.

Example 24.1   Suppose GM CEO Rick Waggoner has received the following forecast (all numbers are fictitious!) for quarterly net income (in billions) for Europe, NAO, Latin America and Asia. See Figure 24.1 and sheet **Corrinc.xls**.

Figure 24.1

	A	B	C	D	E	F	G
1	**Net Income Consolidation**						
2	**with correlation**					Goal is 4 billion!	
3			Mean	Std. Dev	Actual		
4	1	LA	0.4	0.1	0.449011	0.521472	
5	2	NAO	2	0.4	1.256578	1.264837	
6	3	Europe	1.1	0.3	1.14203	0.994558	
7	4	Asia	0.8	0.3	0.685143	0.707549	
8				Total!!	3.532761	3.488417	
9							
10		Correlations	LA	NAO	Europe	Asia	
11		LA	1	0.6	0.7	0.5	
12		NAO	0.6	1	0.6	0.4	
13		Europe	0.7	0.6	1	0.5	
14		Asia	0.5	0.4	0.5	1	
15							
16							

For example, we believe Latin American income will be on average $0.4 billion. Based on past forecast records, we believe the standard deviation of our forecast errors is 25%, so our standard deviation of net income is $0.1 billion. We assume that actual income will follow a normal distribution. Historically net income in different parts of the world has been correlated. Suppose the correlations are as given in B10:F13. Thus Latin America and Europe are most correlated and Asia and NAO are least correlated. What is the probability that total net income will exceed $4 billion?

Solution   To correlate the net incomes of the different regions we use the RiskCorrmat function. The syntax is as follows:

> = *Actual @RISK formula ,riskcorrmat(Correlation matrix, relevant column of matrix))*

Here

- Correlation Matrix : Cells where correlations between variables are located

- Relevant Column : Column of correlation matrix which gives correlations for this cell.

- Actual @RISK formula: distribution of random variable

Step 1: We generate actual Latin America income in cell E4 with the formula

   =RiskNormal(C4,D4,RiskCorrmat($C$11:$F$14,A4))

This ensures the correlation of Latin America income with other incomes is created according to the first column of C11:F14. Also Latin America income will be normally distributed with a mean of $0.4 billion and standard deviation of $0.1 billion.

Step 2: Copying the formula in E4 to E5:E7 respectively generates the net income in each region and tells @RISK to use the correlations in C11:F14.

Step 3: In cell E8 we compute total income with the formula

   =SUM(E4:E7).

Step 4: We made cell E8 our output cell. We find from Targets (value of 4) that there is a 36% chance of not meeting of $4 billion target. Also standard deviation of Net income is $895 million.

Figure 24.2

	B	C	D	E	F
54	Scenario #3 =	>90%		36% chance we fail	
55	Target #1 (Value)=	4		to meet target	
56	Target #1 (Perc%)	35.72%	▲		
57					

	B	C	D
17	Name	Total!! / Actual	
18	Description	Output	
19	Cell	E8	
20	Minimum =	1.858541	
21	Maximum =	6.71191	
22	Mean =	4.300031	
23	Std Deviation =	0.895158	
24	Variance =	0.801308	
25	Skewness =	-5.82E-02	
26	Kurtosis =	2.894021	
27	Errors Calculated =	0	
28	Mode =	4.470891	
29	5% Perc =	2.756473	
30	10% Perc =	3.186955	
31	15% Perc =	3.364678	
32	20% Perc =	3.554199	
33	25% Perc =	3.715597	
34	30% Perc =	3.854618	
35	35% Perc =	3.96633	
36	40% Perc =	4.080534	
37	45% Perc =	4.173182	
38	50% Perc =	4.306374	
39	55% Perc =	4.413318	
40	60% Perc =	4.530555	
41	65% Perc =	4.632649	
42	70% Perc =	4.7776	
43	75% Perc =	4.907873	
44	80% Perc =	5.04496	
45	85% Perc =	5.216321	
46	90% Perc =	5.456462	
47	95% Perc =	5.758535	

What If Net Incomes Are Not Correlated?

In workbook **Nocorrinc.xls** we ran the simulation assuming that the net incomes in different regions were independent (that is had 0 correlation). The results follow:

Figure 24.3

	B	C	D
15	Name	Total!! / Actual	
16	Description	Output	
17	Cell	E8	
18	Minimum =	2.174825	
19	Maximum =	6.290998	
20	Mean =	4.299921	
21	Std Deviation =	0.605397	
22	Variance =	0.366506	

	B	C	D	E	F
53	Target #1 (Value)=	4			
54	Target #1 (Perc%)=	30.76%		31% chance we fail	
55				to meet target	
56					
57					
58					

Note the absence of correlation has reduced the standard deviation to $600 million and our chance of failing to meet our $4 billion income target. This is because if the incomes of all the regions are independent, then it is likely that a high income in one region will be cancelled out by a low income in another region. If the incomes of the regions are positively correlated, these correlations reduce the diversification or hedging effect.

Checking the Correlations

We can check that @RISK actually did correctly correlate our net incomes. Make sure you check Collect Distribution Samples when you run the simulation. Once you have run the simulation select the Data option from the Results menu. The results of each iteration will appear in the bottom half of your screen. You can Edit>Copy>Paste this data to a blank worksheet. See Figure 24.4. We can now check the correlations between each region's Net Income with Data>Analysis Tools>Correlations. Select Data>Analysis Tools>Correlations, and fill in your dialog box as in Figure 24.5. Note the correlations between the Net Incomes are virtually identical to what we entered in our spreadsheet!

Figure 24.4

	B	C	D	E	F	G	H	I	J	K	L
5											
6	Name	Total!! / Ac	LA / Actual	NAO / Actu	Europe / A	Asia / Actual					
7	Description	Output	Normal(C4	Normal(C5	Normal(C6	Normal(C7,D7)					
8	Iteration#	E8	E4	E5	E6	E7		LA	NAO	Europe	Asia
9	1	4.804644	0.478546	2.196594	1.351783	0.777721	LA	1			
10	2	4.132098	0.441263	1.699526	1.184871	0.806438	NAO	0.591262	1		
11	3	6.129157	0.496915	2.453791	1.91255	1.265901	Europe	0.702735	0.587704	1	
12	4	6.54744	0.57896	2.424948	1.968532	1.574999	Asia	0.498132	0.399115	0.496651	1
13	5	3.057065	0.319965	1.517732	0.968105	0.251263					
14	6	5.324339	0.488499	2.292126	1.084479	1.459235					
907	899	4.735623	0.469691	2.19903	1.466369	0.600534					
908	900	4.901974	0.507751	2.242637	1.004801	1.146786					

Figure 24.5

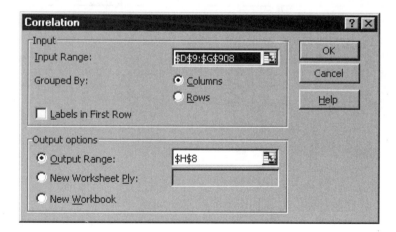

Chapter 25: Forecasting Structural Costs

Structural Costs Problem

@RISK is well suited to forecast the timing of major structural costs. The major sources of uncertainty are the time to complete a project, the time after project when the cost is incurred, and the size of the cost. The following example shows how @RISK can be used to forecast structural costs. See file **Costs.xls**.

Example 25.1

A major problem at manufacturing companies is predicting structural or capital costs. Suppose you are assigned to forecast the timing and amount of the structural costs associated with a new vehicle: the Knightrider. Costs in developing this vehicle are associated with three events:

- Building a prototype.

- Building a plant.

- Purchasing machinery

We cannot build a plant until a prototype has been built and we cannot purchase machinery until we build a plant. Even when an event occurs, the time that the expenditures take place is usually several quarters after the event occurs. You are given the following information about building a prototype and building a plant:

Building Prototype	Time (in quarters) needed for activity	Quarters after event When cash flows occur	Size of expenditure (in billions)
Smallest	3	1	2
Most Likely	5	2	2.5
Largest	10	4	3.5
Building Plant			
Smallest	4	1	3
Most Likely	6	2	4
Largest	9	3	8

Payments must be classified into a particular quarter. Therefore we need to ensure that the times when payments occur are in integers. Use Excel's INT function to do that.

The time needed to buy machinery will be 2, 4, or 5 quarters, with probabilities .3, .6, .1, respectively. The number of quarters after the machinery is bought until we have to pay for the machinery will be 1, 2, or 3 quarters with probabilities .5 , .4, .1 respectively. The amount we have to pay for machinery will be (in billions) .5, 1, or 2 with probability .6 , .3, and .1, respectively.

a. You are 95% sure actual structural costs incurred during the next four years will be between ____ and ____.

b. You are 95% sure the mean of the structural costs incurred during the next four years will be between ____ and ____.

c. Construct a histogram of actual structural costs for Year 2.

Our work is in the file **Costs.xls**. See Figure 25.1.

Figure 25.1

	G	H	I	J	K	L	M
2							
3				Spending		Spending	
4	Event	Time	Amount	Quarter	Amount	Year	Amount
5	Prototype Built	5.906681		1	0	1	0
6	Plant built	11.72791		2	0	2	2.292472
7	Machinery bought	15.72791		3	0	3	0
8	Paid for prototype	7	2.292472	4	0	4	6.833059
9	Paid for plant	14	6.833059	5	0	Total	9.125531
10	Paid for Machinery	19	1	6	0		
11				7	2.292472		
12				8	0		
13				9	0		
14				10	0		
15				11	0		
16				12	0		
17				13	0		
18				14	6.833059		
19				15	0		
20				16	0		
21				Total	9.125531		

	A	B	C	D
1	**Forecasting Structural Costs**			
2		Time needed for activity	Quarters after event where cash outflow occurs	Size of expenditure (in billions)
3	**Build Prototype**	5.906681	1.169954	2.29247241
4	Smallest	3	1	2
5	Most likely	5	2	2.5
6	Largest	10	4	3.5
7	**Build plant**	5.82123	1.987996	6.83305861
8	Smallest	4	1	3
9	Most likely	6	2	4
10	Largest	9	3	8
11	**Buy Machinery**	4	3	1
12	Time needed	Prob		
13	2	0.3		
14	4	0.6		
15	5	0.1		
16	Quarters after	Prob		
17	1	0.5		
18	2	0.4		
19	3	0.1		
20	Size of expenditure	Prob		
21	0.5	0.6		
22	1	0.3		
23	2	0.1		

Modeling the Uncertainty

We begin by generating the duration of important events (parts of projects and delays in payment) as well as size of payments. Then we keep track of the quarter in which each cost is incurred.

Step by Step

Step 1: In cells B3:D3 we enter triangular random variables to generate the time needed to build prototype, time payments are delayed, and size of payments for prototype. Simply copy from B3 to C3:D3 the formula

$$=RiskTriang(B4,B5,B6).$$

Step 2: Similarly, in B7:D7 we generate the time needed to build a plant, time plant payments are delayed and amount of plant building costs by copying from B7 to C7:D7 the formula

$$=RiskTriang(B8,B9,B10).$$

Step 3: In cell B11 we generate the number of quarters needed to buy machinery with the formula

$$=RiskDiscrete(A13:A15,B13:B15).$$

Step 4: In cell C11 we generate number of quarters by which machinery payments are delayed with the formula

$$=RiskDiscrete(A17:A19,B17:B19).$$

Step 5: In cell D11 we generate size of machinery payments (in billions) with the formula

$$=RiskDiscrete(A21:A23,B21:B23).$$

Timing of Costs

In H5:H10 we determine the time at which key events occur. Note we cannot build the plant until prototype is developed and we cannot buy machinery until the plant is built. Also, we use the Excel INT function to determine the actual quarter during which a payment is incurred. The INT function rounds a number down. For example, INT(7.3) and INT(7.9) both = 7.

Step 6: In cell H5 we determine when prototype is completed with formula

=B3.

Step 7: In cell H6 we determine when plant is completed with the formula

=H5+B7.

Step 8: In cell H7 we determine when machinery is built with formula

=H6+B11.

Step 9: In cell H8 we determine quarter when we pay for prototype with formula

= INT(H5+C3) + 1.

For example, if the time the prototype was paid for was 7.2, this formula yields 7 + 1 = 8, indicating prototype was paid for during 8th quarter.

Step 10: In cell H9 we determine the quarter when we pay for the plant with the formula

= INT(H6+C7) + 1.

Step 11: In cell H10 we determine the quarter when we pay for machinery with the formula

=INT(H7+C11)+1.

Bookkeeping Each Quarter's Costs

In I8:I10 we recopy the cost of building the prototype, plant and machine. Then we use IF statements to compute the cost incurred during each quarter.

Step 13: In K5:K20 we use IF statements to determine the payments during each quarter. Simply copy from K5 to K6:K20 the formula

=IF($H$8=J5,$I$8,0)+IF($H$9=J5,$I$9,0)+IF($H$10=J5,$I$10,0).

The first IF statement picks up prototype cost that occurs during the quarter. The second IF statement picks up plant building cost during the quarter during which it occurs. The third IF statement places machinery cost in proper quarter.

Step 14: In M5:M8 we determine total cost during each year. In M5 we compute Year 1 cost with the formula

=SUM(K5:K8).

In a similar fashion we compute Years 2, 3, and 4 cost in cells M6, M7 and M8.

Step 15:In cell M9 we compute total cost for the first four years with the formula

=SUM(M5:M8).

Running and Interpreting the Simulation

Step 16:We now select M9 (total four year costs) and M6 (Year 2 Costs) as output cells.

Our @RISK output (for 900 iterations) is below:

Figure 25.2

	M	N	O
12	Name	Plant built /	Total / Amount
13	Description	Output	Output
14	Cell	M6	M9
15	Minimum	0	2.017615
16	Maximum	3.438132	11.9392
17	Mean	1.191158	6.938519
18	Std Deviation	1.348754	2.362357
19	Variance	1.819137	5.580729
20	Skewness	0.296308	-0.783481
21	Kurtosis	1.184026	2.693133
22	Errors Calculated	0	0
23	Mode	0	6.827249
24	5% Perc	0	2.391562
25	10% Perc	0	2.586415
26	15% Perc	0	2.893714
27	20% Perc	0	5.7936
28	**25% Perc**	0	6.317718
29	**30% Perc**	0	6.585204
30	35% Perc	0	6.807868
31	40% Perc	0	7.005313
32	**45% Perc**	0	7.19495
33	**50% Perc**	0	7.396423
34	**55% Perc**	**0**	7.634341
35	**60% Perc**	**2.289373**	7.806849
36	65% Perc	2.411709	8.027048
37	70% Perc	2.505503	8.289688
38	75% Perc	2.598614	8.537424
39	80% Perc	2.691367	8.794687
40	85% Perc	2.796296	9.213993
41	90% Perc	2.93347	9.478641
42	95% Perc	3.107286	9.914397
43	Filter Minimum		
44	Filter Maximum		
45	Type (1 or 2)		
46	# Values Filtered	0	0.00%
47	Scenario #1	>75%	>75%
48	Scenario #2	<25%	<25%
49	Scenario #3	>90%	>90%
50	Target #1 (Value)	-423897.9	2.262823582
51	Target #1 (Perc%)	2.50%	2.50%
52	**Target #2 (Value)**	**2361415**	**10.32535553**
53	**Target #2 (Perc%)**	**97.50%**	**97.50%**
54	Target #3 (Value)	0	
55	Target #3 (Perc%)	9.35%	

Part (a)
Solution

By entering Target Percentages 2.5% and 97.5% for cell M9 (four year costs) we find that we are 95% sure total costs for the four years will be between $2.26 billion and $10.32 billion.

Part (b)
Solution

We are 95% sure mean costs for the four years are between $7.16 and $7.43 billion.

	O	P
5	Lower	6.781029
6	Upper	7.096009

We computed this as

$$6.94 \pm \frac{2.36 * 2}{\sqrt{900}} = 6.94 \pm .16 \, billion \cdot$$

Part (c)
Solution

Our histogram for Year 2 costs shows us the spread in Year 2 costs.

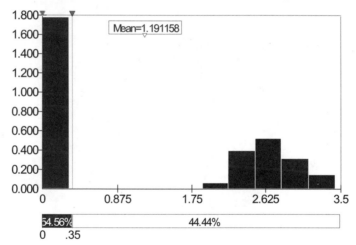

Distribution for Plant built / Amount/M6

The large spike at 0 indicates a 55% chance of no Year 2 costs. Otherwise costs cluster around $2.5 billion.

Chapter 26: Modeling the Profitability of a New Product: Batmobile Sales

The following example illustrates many of the issues involved in modeling profitability of a new product. We show how @RISK can be used to estimate both the average profitability and riskiness of a new product.

Example 26.1

GM is thinking of marketing a new car: the Batmobile. Here is relevant information:

Product Development Time

It is equally likely that the car will take 1, 2, or 3 years to develop.

Development Cost

Development cost is assumed equally split over development time. Best case is development cost of $300 million, most likely case is development cost of $800 million, worst case is development cost of $1.7 billion.

Sales Life

The product will begin sales during the year after development concludes. The number of years the car will be sold for is assumed to be governed by the following probability distribution:

Years	Probability
4	.1
5	.3
6	.4
7	.2

Market Size

The size of the market during the first year of sales is unknown, but the worst case is a market size of 100,000, most likely case is a market size of 145,000, and best case of 165,000. Over the next ten years the average annual growth in market size is unknown, but is assume to have a worst case of 1% per year, most likely case of 6% a year, and best case of 8% per year.

Market Share

First year market share is unknown, but our worst case is a 30% market share, our most likely case is 45% market share, and our best case is 50%. After the first year of sales market share will fluctuate. On average next year's share will equal this year's share. We are 95% sure that next year's market share will be within 40% of this year's market share.

Price

During the first year of sales price is unknown, with a worst case price of $16,000, most likely price of $17,500, and best case price of $18,000. Each year price increases by 5%.

Variable Cost

During the first year of sales our best case estimate for the cost of producing a car is $11,000, most likely cost is $13,000, and worst case cost is $14,500. Each year variable cost increases by 5%.

Our discount rate for this project is 15%.

    a.   We are 95% sure that mean NPV from this project is between ___ and ___.

    b.   What is probability that project will make its hurdle rate?

    c.   What are the key drivers of the project's success?

    d.   Construct a graph that illustrates the range of possible NPV's that might be generated from this project.

Solution   The key random variable used in this model will be the **triangular** random variable. The triangular random variable is an easy generalization of the best case, worst case, and most likely scenarios. The triangular random variable allows any value between the best and worst case to occur, with values near the most likely value of the random variable having the largest chance of occurring. The syntax used by @RISK is:

    =RiskTriang(lowest value, most likely value, largest value).

For example, market share during the first year of sales may be modeled by the formula

    =RiskTriang(.3,.45,.5).

This formula generates observations from a random variable having the following density function.

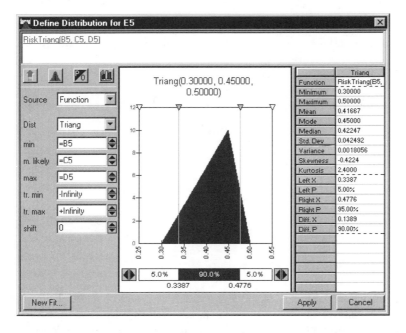

Note that first year market share must be between .3 (worst case) and .5 (best case). Since density is largest near .45, 45% market share is most likely. Note that height of density equals 10, because this makes area under density equal to 1. A 37.5% market share is half as likely as a 45% market share (why?).

Another key to our model will be clever use of IF statements to make sure that costs and revenues occur during the proper years. IF statements will also be used to model growth in market size and changes in market share. Our work is in file **bat.xls**. See Figure 26.1.

Figure 26.1

	A	B	C	D	E	I	J	K
1	Batmobile	Low	Medium	High	Actual			
2	Development Time				3			
3	Sales Life				5			
4	First Year Market Size	100000	145000	165000	148797.411			
5	First year market share	0.3	0.45	0.5	0.42001510			
6	Development cost	300000000	8.00E+08	1.70E+09	1465513257			
7	Year 1 price	16000	17500	18000	17601.9228			
8	Year 1 vc	11000	13000	14500	12824.7166			
9	Annual market growth	0.01	0.06	0.08	0.05090662			
10	First year sales	4						
11	Last year sales	8						
12	annual developmen cost	488504419.1						
13	Years	1	2	3	4	8	9	10
14	Development cost	488504419.1	488504419	488504419	0	0	0	0
15	Market Size	0	0	0	148797.411	181489.7	0	0
16	Market share	0	0	0	0.42001518	0.496886	0	0
17	Unit sales	0	0	0	62497.171	90179.67	0	0
18	unit price	0	0	0	17601.9228	21395.25	0	0
19	unit vc	0	0	0	12824.7166	15588.52	0	0
20	sales revenue	0	0	0	1100070381	1.93E+09	0	0
21	total variable cost	0	0	0	801508509	1.41E+09	0	0
22	profit	-488504419.1	-488504419	-488504419	298561872	5.24E+08	0	0
23								
24	discount rate	0.15						
25	NPV	($234,443,744.68)		Name	NPV / Low			

We proceed as follows:

Step 1: In cell E2 Development Time is generated with the formula

> =RiskDuniform({1,2,3}).

This ensures that Development time is equally likely to be 1, 2, or 3 years.

Step 2: In cell E3 we generate number of years of sales life with the formula

> =RiskDiscrete({4,5,6,7},{0.1,0.3,0.4,0.2}).

This ensures that 4 years of sales has a 10% probability, 5 years of sales has a 30% probability, etc.

Step 3: By copying from E4 to E5:E9 the formula

> =RiskTriang(B4,C4,D4)

we model First Year Market Size, First Year Market Share, Development Cost, First Year Price, First Year Variable Cost, and Annual Market Size Growth as triangular random variables with the appropriate parameters. For example, First Year price will have a worst case of $16,000, most likely price of $17,500 and best case of $18,000.

Step 4: First year of sales will be year after development is completed. We model this in cell B10 with the formula

> =E2+1.

Step 5: Last year of sales will equal (Year Development is Completed) + (Number of Years of Sales). We model this in cell B11 with the formula

> =E2+E3.

Step 6: In B12 we use the formula

> =E6/E2

to compute annual development cost by dividing the total cost by number of years needed for development. Then in B14:K14 we compute development cost for each year. Recall that Development Cost is spread equally over each year of development process. We model this idea by copying from B14 to C14:K14 the formula

> =IF(B13<=$E$2,$B$12,0).

This formula records the correct fraction of development cost during the years in which development occurs, and incurs no cost during other years.

Step 7: Next we model the Market Size. There is no market in years the product is not sold. During the first year of sales the Market Size is computed in E4. During later years, the market size grows by a fraction given in E9. To model these complex relationships, copy from B15 to C15:K15 the formula

=IF(OR(B13<$B$10,B13>$B$11),0,IF(B13=$B$10,$E$4,A15*(1+$E$9))).

The first part of the formula (IF(OR(B13<$B$10,B13>$B$11),0) ensures that there is no market before product comes to market or after it leaves the market. The second part of the formula IF(B13=$B$10,$E$4) ensures that during the first year of development, market size is given by the triangular random variable computed in Row 4. The last part of the formula (A15*(1+$E$9)) ensures that during the second and later years in the market, market size grows by the percentage derived from the triangular random variable in Row 9.

Step 8: Next we model the changes in Market Share. When product is not sold, there is no market share. During first year product is sold, Market Share is given by triangular random variable in Row 5. In later years we are 95% sure market growth will change by 40% or less. Assuming percentage change in annual market share follows a normal random variable, this means standard deviation (call it σ) for percentage change in market share should satisfy 2σ= 40% or σ = 20%. Therefore I would model annual percentage change in market share as a normal random variable with mean 1 and standard deviation of 20%. These complex dynamics can be modeled by copying from B16 to C16:K16 the formula

=IF(B15=0,0,IF(B13=$B$10,$E$5,A16*(RiskNormal(1,0.2)))).

The first part of the formula (IF(B15=0,0,) ensures that our market share is 0 during years in which product is not sold. The second part of the formula IF(B13=$B$10,$E$5,) ensures that during first year of sales market share is given by the triangular random variable computed in E5. The final part of the formula (A16*(RiskNormal(1,0.2)) ensures that during later years market share for the current year has a mean equal to the previous year and a standard deviation equal to 20% of the current market share.

Step 9: In B17:K17 we compute unit sales for each year by multiplying market size times market share. To do this copy from B17 to C17:K17 the formula

=B15*B16.

Step 10: In B18:K18 we compute the unit price for each year. We insert $0 for years in which the product is not sold. During first year of sales unit price is given by triangular random variable in cell E7. During later years of sales price is simply increased by 5% over the previous year. To accomplish this modeling we copy from B18 to C18:K18 the formula

$=IF(B17=0,0,IF(B\$13=\$B\$10,\$E7,A18*1.05))$.

The first part of the formula $IF(B17=0,0)$ ensures that unit price is $0 in years where no sales occur. The second part of the formula $IF(B\$13=\$B\$10,\$E7)$ ensures that during first year of sales unit price is given by triangular random variable in E7. Last part of formula $,A18*1.05)$ ensures that during later years unit price is 5% more than price during previous year.

Step 11: Copying the formulas in B18:K18 to B19:K19 ensures that unit cost is correctly computed during each year.

Step 12: In B20:K20 we compute total revenue for each year by multiplying unit sales times unit price. To do this copy from B20 to C20:K20 the formula

$=B18*B17$.

Step 13: In B21:K21 we compute total variable cost for each year by multiplying unit sales times unit variable cost. To do this copy from B21 to C21:K21 the formula

$=B19*B17$.

Step 14: In B22:K22 we compute profit for each year as (Total Revenue) - (Development Cost) - (Total Variable Cost). To do this simply copy from B22 to C22:K22 the formula

$=-B14+B20-B21$.

Step 15: Assuming cash flows occur at end of year, we compute NPV of cash flows in cell B25 with the formula

$=NPV(B24,B22:K22)$.

Step 16: We now select B25 (NPV) as an output cell. To do this choose the Add Outputs icon.

Then we choose to run 1600 iterations. To run 1600 iterations we select the Simulation Settings icon and then click on iterations tab and fill it out as follows:

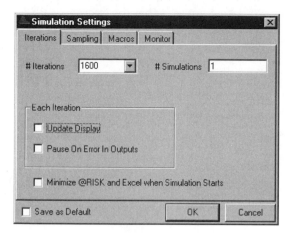

We obtained the @RISK output in Figure 26.2.

Figure 26.2

	D	E	I	J	K
27	Cell	B25			
28	Minimum =	-1.06E+09		95% CI for mean NPV	
29	Maximum =	2.59E+09		Lower	6.06E+07
30	Mean =	**8.10E+07**		Upper	1.01E+08
31	Std Deviation =	**4.09E+08**			
32	Variance =	1.67E+17			
33	Skewness =	0.5482193			
34	Kurtosis =	4.166639			
35	Errors Calculated =	0			
36	Mode =	1.84E+08	2		
37	5% Perc =	-5.34E+08			
38	10% Perc =	-4.23E+08			
39	15% Perc =	-3.39E+08			
40	20% Perc =	-2.64E+08			
41	25% Perc =	-2.06E+08			
42	30% Perc =	-1.54E+08			
43	35% Perc =	-9.61E+07			
44	40% Perc =	-3.97E+07			
45	45% Perc =	1.08E+07			
46	50% Perc =	5.93E+07			
47	55% Perc =	1.07E+08			
48	60% Perc =	1.62E+08			
49	65% Perc =	2.06E+08			
50	70% Perc =	2.65E+08			
51	75% Perc =	3.36E+08			
52	80% Perc =	4.02E+08			
53	85% Perc =	4.79E+08			
54	90% Perc =	6.15E+08			
55	95% Perc =	7.73E+08			
56	Target #1 (Perc%)=	**44.25%**			

Key things are

1) mean NPV appears to be $81.0 million. This means if the project could be done many times our best guess is that the average NPV is $81.0 million.
2) Standard deviation of $409 million indicates there is a lot of spread in the NPV about its mean.

We are now ready to answer questions (a)-(d)

Question (a): We are 95% sure that mean NPV from this project is between ___ and ____.

To find a 95% confidence interval for mean NPV we use the formula

$$\bar{x} \pm \frac{2s}{\sqrt{n}}.$$

Here

x = sample mean

s = sample standard deviation

n = number of iterations.

Thus we are 95% sure mean NPV is between (see cells K29 and K30)

$$8.10E7 \pm \frac{2*(4.09E8)}{\sqrt{1600}} = 60.5 \text{ to } 101.5 \text{ million} \cdot$$

Thus our best estimate of mean NPV from this project is $81 million.

Suppose we feel this interval is too wide. Suppose we want to be 95% sure that we have estimated mean NPV within $10 million. How many iterations do we need? Here we can use Excel's Goal Seek feature. See Figure 26.3

Figure 26.3

	J	K
24	iterations	6575.147
25	Halfwidth of interval	10000000

Step by Step

Step 1: Insert a trial number of iterations (say 1600) in cell K24.

Step 2: Using sample standard deviation from our 1600 iterations compute half the width of the confidence interval in cell K25 with the formula

=2*E31/SQRT(K24).

160

Step 3: Use Excel's Goal Seek to change cell K24 until cell K25 equals $10 million. The Goal Seek window is as follows:

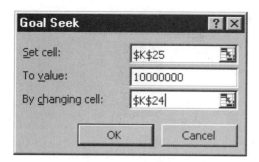

We find that with 6575 iterations the half-width of our confidence interval would be $10,000,000. Then we would be 95% sure that we have estimated mean NPV within $10 million.

Question (b): What is the probability that project will make its hurdle rate?

A project makes the hurdle rate if its NPV under that hurdle rate is >=0. Thus we go to the Detailed Statistics window and insert a Target of 0. We find there is a 44.25% chance that NPV is <=0. Thus there is a 1- .4425 = 55.75% chance that project makes its hurdle rate. See Figure 26.4.

Figure 26.4

	D	E
56	Target #1 (Perc%)=	**44.25%**
57	Value	0

Question (c): What are the key drivers of the project's success?

Here we use a **tornado graph**. Make sure that in the Simulations Settings dialog box Sampling Tab you select Collect Distribution Samples. Then, after simulating, right click on Output cell B25 from the Explorer list in the @RISK-Results window, and select Tornado Graph and then choose the Correlation option.

You will obtain the Correlation tornado graph in Figure 26.5.

Figure 26.5

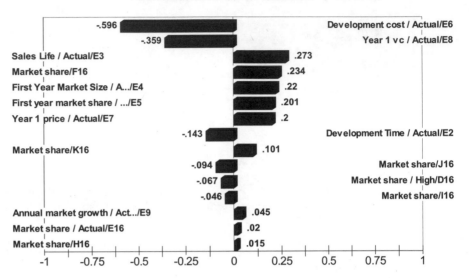

Correlations for NPV / Low/B25

The largest bars indicate the key drivers of the project. To construct a tornado graph @RISK correlates each random cell in spreadsheet with output cell (NPV). We find the key drivers of the project to be Fixed Cost, First Year Variable Cost, and Product Life. More specifically,

- There is a -.596 correlation between fixed Development Cost and NPV. Essentially a one standard deviation increase in Development Cost reduces NPV by .596 standard deviations.

- There is a -.359 correlation between First Year Variable Cost and NPV, Essentially a one standard deviation increase in First Year Variable Cost reduces NPV by .359 standard deviations.

- There is a .273 correlation between number of years product is sold ("Sales Life") and NPV. Thus a one standard deviation increase in Product Life will result in a .273 standard deviation increase in NPV.

We could also (by choosing regression) obtain a Regression Tornado Graph. See Figure 26.6

Figure 26.6

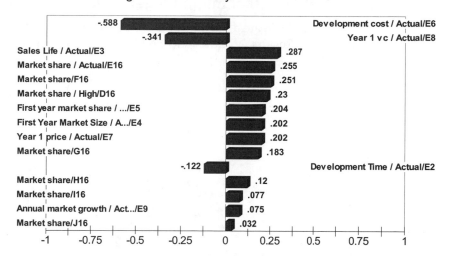

Regression Sensitivity for NPV / Low/B25

Each bar here gives (after adjusting for all other random variables in the spreadsheet) the number of standard deviations by which NPV will increase if we increase the given random variable in the spreadsheet by one standard deviation.

For example:

After adjusting for all other random variables, a one standard deviation increase in Development Cost will decrease NPV by -.588 standard deviations.

After adjusting for all other random variables, a one standard deviation in Sales Life will increase NPV by .287 standard deviations.

Question (d): Construct a graph that illustrates the range of possible NPVs that might be generated from this project.

Here we simply create a histogram of NPVs (see Figure 26.7). From the Explorer list in the @RISK-Results window, select NPV, right click and select Graph Histogram.

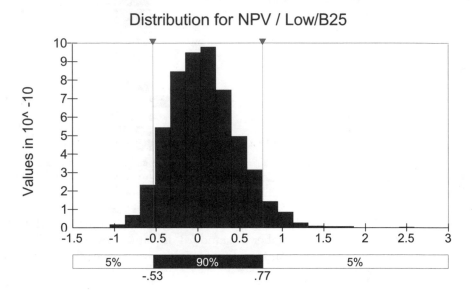

Figure 26.7

Distribution for NPV / Low/B25

NPVs ranging from -$1 billion to +$2 billion are possible. Distribution of NPVs is skewed to the right.

In making decisions we look at both mean NPV and spread about the mean. Obviously, we prefer a larger mean and less spread about mean. Spread about mean is also measured by standard deviation of NPV ($409 million).

Scenarios

If you check Collect Distribution Samples in the Simulation Settings dialog, then by clicking on the Scenario icon you can obtain a Scenario Analysis. For a given scenario, such as all iterations where NPV is in top 10% of all iterations the Scenario Analysis identifies random variables whose values differ significantly from their median values.[1]

As an example, we find that in the iterations yielding the bottom 25% of all NPVs the following variables differ significantly from their overall medians:

- Sales Life (median is 5, 1.11 sigma below average). The median Sales Life when NPV was in bottom 25% of all iterations was the 40 percentile of Sales Life in all iterations

- Development Cost (median is $1.2 billion, 1.03 sigma above average). The median Development Cost in iterations yielding the bottom 25% of all NPVs is the 81st percentile of all iterations.

Note we selected the All-Percentiles Actuals and Ratios option. This Scenario option shows the most information.

Figure 26.8

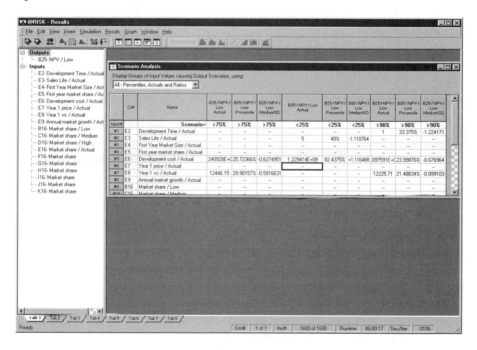

---

[1] @RISK will identify any random variable whose median value in iterations satisfying the scenario condition differs by more than .5 standard deviations from the median value of the random variable in all iterations.

Chapter 27: The XNPV and XIRR Functions

Often cash flows occur at irregular intervals. This makes it difficult to compute the NPV or IRR of these cash flows. Fortunately, the Excel XNPV and XIRR functions make computing NPVs and/or IRRs of irregularly timed cash flows a snap! To use the XNPV and XIRR function you must first have added-in the Analysis Toolpak. To do this select Add-Ins from Excel's Tools menu, and check the Analysis Toolpak and Analysis Toolpak VBA boxes. Here is an example of XNPV in action.

Example 27.1

Suppose on 4/08/01 we pay out $900. Then we receive

- $300 on 8/15/01
- $400 on 1/15/02
- $200 on 6/25/02
- $100 on 7/03/03.

If the annual discount rate is 10%, what is the NPV of these cash flows?

Solution

We enter the dates (in Excel date format) in D3:D7 and the cash flows in E3:E7. Entering the formula

$$=XNPV(A9,E3:E7,D3:D7)$$

in cell D11 computes the project's NPV in terms of 4/08/01 dollars. This is because 4/08/01 is the first date chronologically.

	A	B	C	D	E	F	G	H
1								
2	XNPV Function		Code	Date	Cash Flow	Time	df	
3			36989.00	4/8/01	-900		1	
4			37118.00	8/15/01	300	0.353425	0.966876	
5			37271.00	1/15/02	400	0.772603	0.929009	
6			37432.00	6/25/02	200	1.213699	0.890762	
7			37805.00	7/3/03	100	2.235616	0.808094	
8	Rate							
9		0.1						
10				XNPV	Direct			
11				20.62822	20.628217			
12								
13				XIRR				
14				12.97%				

What Excel did was as follows:

Compute the number of years after April 8, 2001 each date occurred. (We did this in column F). For example 8/15/01 is .3534 years after 04/08/01.

Then discount cash flows at a rate $\left(\dfrac{1}{1+rate}\right)^{years\,after}$. For example, the August 15, 2001 cash flow is discounted by $\left(\dfrac{1}{1+.1}\right)^{.3534} = .967$.

We obtained Excel Dates in serial number form by changing format to GENERAL.

Similarly, entering in cell D14 the formula

$= XIRR(A9,E3:E7,D3:D7)$

yields the project's IRR (12.97%).

Remark

Note that the NPV returned by the XNPV function is measured in dollars as of the first chronological date listed. If you want the NPV to be measured in today's dollars, then simply insert a row above your cash flows containing today's date and $0 cash flow! Now your NPV will be in today's dollars!

Chapter 28: Option Definitions

We begin our study of options with some basic definitions:

- A **call option** gives the owner the right to buy a share of stock for a price called the **exercise price**.

- A **put option** gives the owner the right to sell a share of stock for the exercise price.

- An **American option** can be exercised on or before a time known as the **exercise date**.

- A **European option** can be exercised only at the exercise date.

Example 28.1

Let's look at cash flows from a 6-month European call option on Microsoft with an exercise price of $110. Let P = price of Microsoft in six months. Then payoff from call option is $0 if P≤110 and P-110 if P≥110. This is because for P below $110 we would not exercise the option while if P is larger than $110 we would exercise our option to buy stock for $110 and immediately sell stock for $P, thereby earning a profit of P –110. Figure 28.1 displays the payoff from this put option. Note that call payoff may be written as max(0, P –110).

Figure 28.1

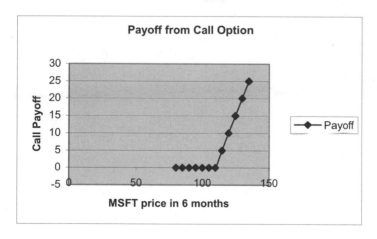

Note the call option graph has slope 0 for P smaller than exercise price and has slope 1 for P greater than exercise price.

Example
28.2

By the way, it can be shown that if a stock pays no dividends, then it's never optimal to exercise an American call option early. See Chapter 34 for a proof of this result. Therefore for a non-dividend paying stock an American and European call have the same value.

Let's look at cash flows from a 6-month European put option on Microsoft with an exercise price of $110. Let P = price of Microsoft. Then payoff from put option is $0 if P≥110 and 110 - P if P≤110. This is because for P below $110 we would buy a share of stock for $P and immediately sell the stock for $110. This yields a profit of 110 – P. If P is larger than $110 it would not pay to buy the stock for $P and sell it for $110, so we would not exercise our option to sell the stock for $110. Figure 28.2 displays the payoff from this put option. Note that put payoff may be written as Max(0, 110 – P).

Figure 28.2

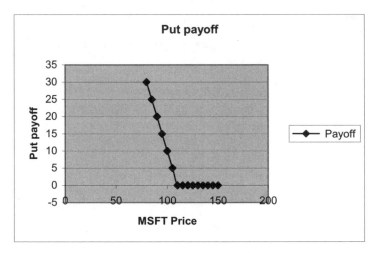

Note that slope of put payoff is –1 for P less than exercise price and slope of put payoff is 0 for P greater than exercise price.

We note that an American put option may be exercised early, so the cash flows from an American put cannot be determined without knowledge of the stock price at times before the expiration date.

Chapter 29: Types of Real Options

The key observation that led to the field of real options was the observation that many **actual** investment opportunities (not just those involving stocks) may be viewed as combinations of puts and calls. Therefore, if we know how to value puts and calls we can value many actual investment opportunities. Here are some examples of **real options**.

Option to Purchase an Airplane

Suppose we have the option to purchase an airplane 3 years from now for $20 million. Let P = value of an airplane three years from now. P is uncertain and would depend on the economic cycle, fuel prices etc. Then the cash flows in 3 years from the option to purchase would equal MAX(P-20,0). This is the same equation that would define the cash flows from a call option with exercise price $20 million. This implies that the option to purchase an airplane is equivalent to a call option. Thus if we can value a call option we can value an option to purchase an airplane.

Abandonment Option

Suppose we are undertaking an R and D project and five years from now we can sell what we have accomplished so far for $80 million. If we let P = value of ideas we have developed after 5 years, then the value of our abandonment option would equal MAX(80 − P,0). This is the same equation that would define the cash flows from a put option with exercise price $80 million. This implies that the option to abandon a project is equivalent to a put option. Thus if we can value a put option we can value an abandonment option.

Other Real Option Opportunities

There are many other real investment opportunities that can (with some effort) be represented as combinations of puts and calls. As we proceed we will learn how to value these types of options. Here are some examples:

Expansion Option

Suppose that three years from now we have an option to double the size of a project. What is this option worth?

Contraction Option

Suppose that three years from now we have the option to cut the scale of a project in half. What is this option worth?

Postponement Option

We are thinking of developing a new SUV-minivan hybrid. In two years we will know more about the size of the market. We have the option to wait two years before deciding to develop the car. What is this option worth?

Pioneer Option

Microsoft decided to buy Web TV even though the deal had a negative NPV. Perhaps this was because Web TV was a "pioneer option" that gave Microsoft the opportunity to, in several years, enter new markets that may or may not be profitable. Without having purchased Web TV, Microsoft would not have been able to enter these new markets. If the value of the option to enter new markets later exceeds the negative NPV of Web TV, then the purchase would be a good idea.

Flexibility Option

An auto company is thinking of building a plant that can produce three types of cars. The cost per unit of capacity for such a flexible plant far exceeds the unit capacity cost for a plant that can produce only one type of car. Is the increased flexibility worthwhile?

Licensing Option

Suppose that during any year in which profit from drug exceeds $50 million, we pay 20% of all profits to developer of drug? What is a fair price for such a licensing agreement?

Chapter 30: Valuing Options by Arbitrage Methods

The famous Black-Scholes option pricing formula is based on arbitrage pricing methods. Arbitrage pricing (for our purposes) implies that if an investment **has no risk it should yield the risk-free rate of return**. If this is not the case then we can create a money-making machine or **arbitrage opportunity.** By an arbitrage opportunity we mean a situation in which we can spend $0 today and ensure we have no chance of losing money and a positive chance of making money. We can use this simple insight to price very complex financial derivatives. Here is an example.

Example 30.1

A stock is currently selling for $40. One period from now the stock will either increase to $50 or decrease in price to $32. The risk free rate of interest is 11 1/9%. What is a fair price for a European call option with an exercise price of $40?

Solution

The key to our problem is the realization that if we create a portfolio consisting of x shares of stock and short one call option, then for some value of x the portfolio will have no risk. This is reasonable because an increase in the stock price benefits the stock owned but hurts the value of our shorted call while a decrease in the stock price hurts the stock owned but helps the value of our shorted call. Then this portfolio must earn the risk-free rate. Our work is in file **Arbvalue.xls**. See Figure 30.1. Any model in which a stock price can only increase or decrease by a certain amount during a period is called a **binomial model**.

Figure 30.1

	A	B	C	D	E	F	G	H	I	J	K
1					Step 1						
2	Arbitrage value				x shares of stock						
3	of call option				1 call						
4					risk-free if						
5					50x-10=32x						
6					x=5/9						
7					Step 2						
8					risk-free portfolio			c = call price today			
9					must earn risk-free rate			value in one period=32(5/9)=160/9			
10					so value today= (1/(1+r)*value in one period						
11					(5/9)*40-c=(1/(1+(1/9))*(160/9)						
12					200/9-c =16						
13					c = 56/9						
14								Using Arbitrage method			
15								to Value a			
16								Call with exercise price of $40			
17								11 1/9% risk free rate			
18										1 period later	
19										Stock value	Call Value
20							today		up	$50	$10
21											
22							$40		down	$32	$0
23											
24											

We begin by computing the value of our portfolio if the stock increases or decreases in value:

Stock Price	Portfolio Value
$50	50x - 10
$32	32x - 0

To create a portfolio with no risk we simply set the portfolio value to be the same for both stock prices. That is

$50x - 10 = 32x$

or $18x = 10$

or $x = 5/9$.

Thus a portfolio consisting of 5/9 shares of stock and short one call **has no risk**. Therefore this portfolio must yield the risk-free rate. This means that

Value of portfolio in one period$/(1 + r)$ = initial value of portfolio.

Here r = risk free rate. Therefore

$$\frac{5}{9}(40) - c = \frac{1}{1 + \frac{1}{9}}\left(\frac{160}{9}\right)$$

or $\dfrac{200}{9} - c = 16$

or $c = \dfrac{56}{9}$

Creating a Money-Making Machine if Call Option is Incorrectly Priced

To gain greater insight on why the call price must equal 56/9, let's show that if the call price is any value other than 56/9 then we can make guaranteed positive profits at Time 1 **with an investment today of $0.** In the real world such an **arbitrage opportunity** would never exist. If the call price today (call it c) is less than 56/9 the call is "underpriced" and shorting our risk-free portfolio can yield an arbitrage opportunity. We will show that if today we buy one call, short 5/9 shares of stock, and lend out 200/9 - c dollars we have a $0 cash outlay today and a guaranteed positive cash position at Time 1. These investments yield the following cash flows:

Action	Time 0 Outflow	Time 1 Inflow in Up State	Time 1 Inflow in Down State
Buy call	c	10	0
Short stock	-200/9= -(5/9)(40)	-(5/9)(50)= -250/9	(-5/9)(32) = -160/9
Lend money	200/9 - c	(10/9)(200/9 – c)	10/9(200/9 - c)

Our Time 0 cash outflow is $0 (we chose the size of the loan to make this work!)

If stock goes up to $50 our Time 1 cash inflow is positive if and only if

$$\frac{-250}{9} + 10 + \frac{2000}{81} - \frac{10c}{9} \succ 0$$

$$or\ \frac{560}{81} - \frac{10c}{9} \succ 0$$

or c < 56/9. If the stock price drops our Time 1 cash inflow is positive if and only if

$$\frac{2000}{81} - \frac{10c}{9} - \frac{160}{9} \succ 0$$

$$or\ \frac{560}{9} - \frac{10c}{9} \succ 0$$

or c< 56/9. Thus if the call is underpriced, we have created a money-making machine!

Now suppose that the call is overpriced (c>56/9). Now at Time 0 we short the call, buy 5/9 share of stock, and borrow 200/9 - c dollars. This investment strategy yields the following cash flows:

Action	Time 0 Outflow	Time 1 Inflow in Up State	Time 1 Inflow in Down State
Short call	-c	-10	-0
Buy stock	200/9= (5/9)(40)	(5/9)(50)= 250/9	(5/9)(32) = 160/9
Borrow money	c –200/9	-(10/9)(200/9 - c)	-(10/9)(200/9 – c)

Our Time 0 cash outflow is $0 (we chose the amount of the borrowing to make this work!)

If stock goes up to $50 our Time 1 cash inflow is positive if and only if

$$\frac{250}{9} - 10 - \frac{2000}{81} + \frac{10c}{9} > 0$$

$$\frac{-560}{81} + \frac{10c}{9} > 0$$

or c > 56/9. If the stock price drops our Time 1 cash inflow is positive if and only if

$$\frac{-2000}{81} + \frac{10c}{9} + \frac{160}{9} > 0$$

$$or \ \frac{-560}{9} + \frac{10c}{9} > 0$$

or c> 56/9. Thus if the call is overpriced, we have created a money-making machine!

In short if we do not price the call according to arbitrage pricing a money-making "Philosopher's Stone" exists. This argument should convince you that arbitrage-pricing techniques do indeed yield valid prices.

Why Doesn't the Stock's Growth Rate Influence the Call Price?

From our analysis the key factor that influences the option price are the two values of the stock price. The further spread out the up and down prices are, the more value the call has. Note that the **probability that the stock goes up or down** does not influence the option value. In effect this says that the **average growth rate** of the stock does not affect the call's value. At first glance this doesn't make sense. If stock has more chance of increasing in value, then shouldn't the call sell for more because the call pays off for high stock prices? The answer to this conundrum is that **the current price of the stock incorporates information about the stock's growth rate.** In effect the probabilities of the stock increasing or decreasing in value are included in today's price, so they do not affect the value of the call option.

Chapter 31: Modeling Stock Price or Project Value with Lognormal

In reality, stock prices can assume any non-negative value. In a binomial tree, of course, only a finite number of stock prices are possible. The **lognormal or Geometric Brownian Motion** random variable is often used to model the evolution of stock prices.

The lognormal model for asset value (or stock price) assumes that in a small time Δt the stock price changes by an amount that is normally distributed with

$Standard\ Deviation = \sigma S \sqrt{\Delta t}$

$Mean = \mu S \Delta t$

Here S = *current stock price.*

μ may be thought of as the instantaneous rate of return on the stock. By the way, this model leads to really "jumpy" changes in stock prices (like real life). This is because during a small period of time the standard deviation of the stock's movement will greatly exceed the mean of a stock's movement. This follows because for small Δt, $\sqrt{\Delta t}$ will be much larger than Δt. This is consistent with reality. For example, per day Microsoft has in the recent past had mean growth per day = .40/252 = .0016 and σ per day = $\sqrt{1/252}*(.47) = .03$. (note .03>.016!). σ is roughly speaking, a measure of the percentage volatility in the annual return of a stock. As we will see later, Microsoft has a volatility of 47%, AOL 65%, and Amazon.COM in 1999 had a volatility of 120%! The **volatility of a stock or project is crucial to a real options calculation**.

We use the following equation to simulate future stock prices in Excel.

$$S_t = S_0 e^{(\mu - .5\sigma^2)t + \sigma \sqrt{t} RISKNORMAL\,(0,1))} \quad (1)$$

Here S_0 = Today's stock price, μ = instantaneous rate of return on stock, and σ = Annual volatility of stock (standard deviation of stock price changes over a small unit of time on an annualized basis). The =*RiskNormal(0,1)* generates a sample from a standard normal (mean 0 and sigma 1) random variable.

Remarks

Taking the logarithm of both sides of (1) shows us that we could simulate Ln(S_t))using the fact that

$$Ln(S_t) = Ln(S_0) + (\mu - .5\sigma^2)t + \sigma\sqrt{t}RISKNORMAL(0,1))\ (2)$$

This shows than Ln (S_t) is normally distributed. This explains the name **lognormal distribution.**

If our stock is growing instantaneously at rate μ, then why do (1) and (2) seem to indicate that we are growing at a rate of μ - .5σ²? The reason for this is that over time **increased volatility reduces the mean growth rate of a stock**. To see this consider two stocks:

- Stock 1 always yields 10% a year.

- Stock 2 doubles during half of all years and loses 50% of its value during half of all years.

On average Stock 1 grows by 10% per year and Stock 2 grows by 25% per year. Yet over time Stock 2 will certainly end up lower than Stock 1 due to its large volatility or variability.

Simulating the Lognormal Random Variable

In file **lognormal.xls** we simulate for 5 years quarterly Microsoft stock prices under the assumption that $\mu = .30$ and $\sigma = .38$ and that today's stock price is $100. See Figure 31.1.

Figure 31.1

	C	D	E	F	G
1					
2		mu	0.3		
3		sigma	0.38		
4					
5		Date	Price	RN	
6		Today	100		
7		0.25	78.24848	0.05584	
8		0.5	87.4427	0.612166	
9		0.75	83.55709	0.294955	
10		1	124.0535	0.962476	
11		1.25	144.4007	0.691332	
12		1.5	177.1342	0.78101	
13		1.75	188.4546	0.510497	
14		2	233.7532	0.797858	
15		2.25	354.9943	0.971244	
16		2.5	440.8483	0.799619	
17		2.75	414.2939	0.265424	
18		3	590.0955	0.940843	
19		3.25	542.4397	0.228761	
20		3.5	711.7793	0.870807	
21		3.75	720.6463	0.407269	
22		4	437.7635	0.001732	
23		4.25	400.2455	0.220259	
24		4.5	398.2597	0.372245	
25		4.75	292.9255	0.027651	
26		5	356.3406	0.767818	
27					

Step by Step

Step 1: In F7:F26 we generate standard normal random variables used in (1) to create each period's stock price. We copy from F7 to F8:F26 the formula

> *=RiskNormal(0,1).*

Step 2: In E7:E26 we generate the Microsoft stock price for each of the next 20 quarters using (1). We copy from E7 to E8:E26 the formula

> *=E6*EXP((mu-0.5*sigma^2)*0.25+sigma*SQRT(0.25)*(F7)).*

Step 3: Selecting E26 as an output cell and running 10,000 iterations yields the following statistical output:

	I	J
11	Name	Price
12	Description	Output
13	Cell	E26
14	Minimum	15.60499
15	Maximum	8147.99
16	Mean	449.1588
17	Std Deviation	464.8013
18	Variance	216040.3
19	Skewness	3.847023
20	Kurtosis	30.14282
21	Errors Calculated	0
22	Mode	151.5773
23	5% Perc	76.66622
24	10% Perc	103.9005
25	15% Perc	128.9063
26	20% Perc	153.5016
27	25% Perc	176.7954
28	30% Perc	200.4245
29	35% Perc	225.7186
30	40% Perc	251.9839
31	45% Perc	281.8614
32	50% Perc	314.3795
33	55% Perc	350.1238
34	60% Perc	389.1598
35	65% Perc	432.472
36	70% Perc	486.2347
37	75% Perc	554.0205
38	80% Perc	633.3387
39	85% Perc	745.8146
40	90% Perc	922.2651
41	95% Perc	1275.003

Thus we find our best estimate of the average MSFT price in 5 years to equal $449 and our best estimate of the standard deviation is $465. There is a 5% chance that in five years MSFT will sell for $76.67 or less. There is also a 5% chance that MSFT will sell for $1275 or more!

Simulating the Lognormal Random Variable

Chapter 32: The Black-Scholes Option Pricing Model

In 1973 the brilliant trio of Fisher Black, Robert Merton and Myron Scholes developed the Black-Scholes option pricing formula. They were justly awarded the Noble Prize in economics for their work. Assuming that the price of the underlying stock follows a lognormal random variable, they found a closed form solution for the price of a European call and European put. Essentially their method was to extend the arbitrage pricing approach developed in Chapter 31 by letting the length of a period in the binomial model go to zero. They were able to find the following formulas for pricing European puts and calls. Let:

- S = Today's stock price.

- t = Duration of the option.

- X = Exercise or strike price.

- r = risk-free rate. This rate is assumed to be continuously compounded. Thus if r = .05, this means that in one year $1 will grow to $e^{.05}$ dollars.

- σ = Annual volatility of stock (we will explain how to estimate σ in Chapter 34).

- y = percentage of stock value paid annually in dividends.

For a European call option the price is computed as follows:

Define $d_1 = \dfrac{Ln(\dfrac{S}{X}) + (r - y + \dfrac{\sigma^2}{2})t}{\sigma\sqrt{t}}$ and $d_2 = d_1 - \sigma\sqrt{t}$. Then the call price C is given by $C = Se^{-yt}N(d_1) - Xe^{-rt}N(d_2)$. Here N(x) is the cumulative normal probability for a normal random variable having mean 0 and σ = 1. For example, N(-1) = .16, N(0) = .5, N(1) = .84 N(1.96) =.975. The cumulative normal probability may be computed in Excel with the NORMSDIST( ) function.

The price of a European put P may be written as

$$P = Se^{-yt}(N(d_1) - 1) - Xe^{-rt}(N(d_2) - 1).$$

American options are usually modeled using binomial trees (see Chapter 39).

In file **Bstemp.xls** we have set up a template that let's you enter S, X, r, t, σ, and y and read off the European call and put prices. Here are some examples:

Example 32.1

Suppose the current stock price of MSFT is $100, and we own a 7-year European call option with an exercise price of $95. Assume r = .05 and σ = 47% (we will see where this comes from in the next chapter). From Figure 32.1 we see that this call option is worth $57.15. Thus if MSFT gave you 1000 of these options, there worth would be around $57,150. We note that an American call on a stock that does not pay dividends should be exercised early, so this is also the value of an American call option.

Example 32.2

Assuming the same situation as Example 32.1, Figure 32.1 shows that a European put with exercise price $95 would be worth $24.10. An American put might be exercised early, so it could be worth more that $24.10.

Figure 32.1

	A	B	C	D	E
1	**Call with dividends**				
2					
3					
4	**Input data**				
5	Stock price	$100			
6	Exercise price	$95			
7	Duration	7			
8	Interest rate	5.00%			
9	dividend rate	0			
10	volatility	47.00%			
11					
12				Predicted	
13	Call price		=	$57.15	
14	put			$24.10	
15					
16					
17	Other quantities for option price				
18	d1	0.944463		N(d1)	0.827534
19	d2	-0.29904		N(d2)	0.382455
20					

Comparative Statics Results

It is natural to ask how changes in key inputs will change the value of an option. An Excel one-way data table makes it easy to answer these questions. For example, in Figure 32.2 we show how changing the duration of a European call option from 1-10 years changes the value of the call option.

Figure 32.2

	J	K
7		
8	Duration	
9		$57.15
10	1	22.90206
11	2	31.82951
12	3	38.65993
13	4	44.31017
14	5	49.15378
15	6	53.39188
16	7	57.14977
17	8	60.51304
18	9	63.5439
19	10	66.28968

To obtain this Data Table we proceeded as follows:

Step 1 Enter possible durations in J10:J19.

Step 2: In cell K9 enter the formula you want calculated (the call price) for different durations

  =D13.

Step 3: Select the table range J9:K19.

Step 4: Choose from the Data menu the Table option. Then select cell B7 as Column Input Cell. This will ensure that the possible durations in J10:J19 are input to cell B7.

We see that lengthening the duration of the call option increases its value. If the option paid dividends this might not be the case (why?).

In Figure 32.3 we construct another data table to show how a change in stock volatility from 10%-100% affects the value of a call option.

Figure 32.3

	N	O
8	Volatility	
9		$57.15
10	0.1	33.66137
11	0.2	38.53958
12	0.3	45.28839
13	0.4	52.33248
14	0.47	57.14977
15	0.5	59.15782
16	0.6	65.53342
17	0.7	71.33781
18	0.8	76.50927
19	0.9	81.02667
20	1	84.89906

Note an increase in volatility always **increases the value of any kind of option**.

In general, the comparative statics results for puts and calls (*ceteris paribus*) are given in the following table.

Parameter	European Call	European Put	American Call	American Put
Stock Price	+	-	+	-
Exercise Price	-	+	-	+
Time to Expiration	?	?	+	+
Volatility	+	+	+	+
Risk-free rate	+	-	+	-
Dividends	-	+	-	+

- An increase in today's stock price always increases the value of a call and decreases the value of a put.

- An increase in the exercise price always increases the value of a put and decreases the value of a call.

- An increase in the duration of an option always increases the value of an American option. In the presence of dividends, an increase in the duration of an option can either increase or decrease the value of a European option.

- An increase in volatility always increases option value.

- An increase in the risk-free rate increases the value of a call. This is because higher rates tend to increase the growth rate of the stock price (this is good for the call). This more than cancels out the fact that option payoff is worth less due to the higher interest rate. An increase in the risk-free rate always decreases the value of a put because the higher growth rate in stocks tends to hurt puts as does the fact that future payoffs from puts are worth less. Again this assumes that interest rates do not affect current stock prices and they do!

- Dividends tend to reduce the growth rate of a stock price so increased dividends reduce the value of a call and increase the value of a put.

Valuing Warrants

Companies often issue **warrants**. A warrant is basically a call option issued by a company on its own stock. A simple modification of Black-Scholes lets us value warrants. The trick is to note that if the warrants are exercised, the per share value to original shareholders is diluted. Hull discusses this on pages 252-253. We have included a template (**Warrant.xls**) to enable you to price a warrant. All you need to do is enter the ordinary Black-Scholes inputs as well as the current number of shares and warrants outstanding. Then invoke the Solver (this solves for the warrant price by using the circular relationship between warrant price and per share value). Just remember that the volatility measure is the volatility of the company's total equity and not just its share price. Here is an example.

Example 32.3

HAL Computer has 1 million shares of stock outstanding at a current price of $50. To raise money they are going to issue 500,000 five-year warrants with an exercise price of $60.00. The risk-free rate is 10% and the current dividend yield is 2%. The volatility of equity is 20%. What is a fair price for the warrant?

Solution

In Figure 32.4 we have entered the relevant parameters and run Solver. We find a fair price for the warrant to equal $2.39. Note that inputs are entered into shaded cells.

Figure 32.4

	A	B	C	D	E	F
1	**Warrant**			C*Sh/(Sh+W)		
2	**Warrant value**	2.3904791	=	2.39E+00		
3	Actual Stock price	50				
4	**Shares**	1.00E+06				
5	**Warrants**	5.00E+05				
6	DillutedStock price	34.13016				
7	Exercise price	60				
8	Duration	5				
9	Interest rate	0.1				
10	dividend rate	0.02				
11	volatility	0.2				
12						
13				Predicted		
14	Call price		=	$3.59		
15						
16						
17						
18	Other quantities for option price					
19	d1	-0.143473		N(d1)	0.442958	
20	d2	-0.590687		N(d2)	0.277365	

Reference

By far the best reference on options (although not real options!) is Hull's classic work. Luenberger's book is also great and he talks more about real options.

Hull J., *Options and Other Derivatives,* 4th edition, 2000, Prentice-Hall Publishing.

Luenberger, D., *Investment Science,* 1997, Oxford Press.

Chapter 33: Estimating Volatility

In a real options analysis the value of the option will depend crucially on the volatility of the underlying project or asset. Under the assumption that a stock follows a lognormal random variable, the volatility is the σ characterizing the stock's lognormal price random variable. Most experts believe that the best way to estimate volatility of say, an Internet startup or a biotech drug is to look at the volatility the market has placed on companies in a similar line of business. It is therefore important to understand how to estimate the volatility of a stock. Basically there are two approaches to estimating volatility:

1. Estimate volatility based on historical data.
2. Look at a traded option and estimate volatility as the value of sigma that makes the actual option price match the predicted Black-Scholes price. This approach is called **implied volatility estimation**.

Most experts prefer to estimate volatility via the implied volatility approach. The reason is, of course, that the implied volatility approach is forward-looking and the historical approach is based on the past. We illustrate both approaches.

Historical Approach to Volatility Estimation

In the sheet labeled Historical of the file **volest.xls** we are given quarterly prices of Microsoft stock. We may therefore estimate quarterly volatility as follows:

Step by Step

Step 1: Compute $S(t)/S(t-1)$**, where** $S(t)$ **is quarter t stock price.**

Step 2: Compute $Ln\dfrac{S(t)}{S(t-1)}$,

Step 3: Find the Standard deviation of the $Ln\dfrac{S(t)}{S(t-1)}$.

This estimates the quarterly volatility.

Step 4: If the volatility is v for one unit of time, then the volatility for t units of time is $v\sqrt{t}$ **.** Thus we go from quarterly volatility to annual volatility by multiplying by 2 and we go from annual volatility to daily volatility by multiplying by $\sqrt{\dfrac{1}{252}}$. This assumes 252 trading days per year. Here is an example of the historical volatility calculations. See Figure 33.1.

Figure 33.1

	A	B	C	D	E	F	G	H
1								
2		Historical Volatility Calculation						
3								
4								
5								
6								
7				Period #	Date	Value	P(t)/P(t-1)	ln(P(t)/P(t-1))
8				1	Jul-95	90.5		
9				2	Oct-95	100	1.104972376	0.099820335
10				3	Jan-96	92.5	0.925	-0.077961541
11				4	Apr-96	113.25	1.224324324	0.20238912
12				5	Jul-96	117.875	1.040838852	0.040026977
13				6	Oct-96	137.25	1.164369035	0.152179339
14				7	Jan-97	204	1.486338798	0.396315913
15				8	Apr-97	243	1.191176471	0.174941449
16				9	Jul-97	282.75	1.163580247	0.151501672
17				10	Oct-97	260	0.91954023	-0.083881484
18				11	Jan-98	298.375	1.147596154	0.137669454
19				12	Apr-98	360.25	1.207373272	0.18844715
20				13	Jul-98	427.75	1.187369882	0.171740678
21				14	Oct-98	423.5	0.99006429	-0.009985399
22				15	Jan-99	700	1.652892562	0.502526821
23				16	Apr-99	650.5	0.929285714	-0.073339037
24								
25							sigma(quarterly)	0.165192579
26							sigma(annually)	0.330385159

Step 1: Compute the ratio of successive stock prices by copying from G9 to G10:G23 the formula

   =F9/F8.

Step 2: Compute the logarithm of each of these ratios by copying from H9 to H10:H23 the formula

   = LN(G9).

Step 3: In H25 compute the quarterly sigma with the formula

   = STDEV(H9:H23).

Step 4: In cell H26 annualize the quarterly volatility by multiplying by 2.

Thus on a historical basis we estimate Microsoft's volatility to be around 33%.

The Implied Volatility Approach

At the end of trading on February 8, 2000 MSFT sold for $106.61. A March put option (expiring on March 25, 2000) with exercise price $100 sold for $3.75. Risk-free rate on 90 day T-bills was 5.5%. How can we estimate Microsoft's implied volatility at this point in time?

Figure 33.2

	A	B	C	D	E
1					
2	**Microsoft Implied Volatility**			February 9 ,2000	
3				March $100 put	
4	Input data			expires	
5	Stock price	$106.61		25-Mar	
6	Exercise price	$100			
7	Duration	0.1229508			
8	Interest rate	5.33%			
9	dividend rate	0			
10	volatility	47.07%			
11					
12		Actual		Predicted	
13	Call price		=	$11.01	
14	put	$3.75		$3.75	
15					
16					
17	Other quantities for option price				
18	d1	0.5099518		N(d1)	0.694957
19	d2	0.3448948		N(d2)	0.634913

Step by Step

Step 1: Our work is in sheet option of file volest.xls. We enter all parameters (stock price, duration, risk-free rate, actual put price, and exercise price) into our Black-Scholes template. Note we enter Ln (1 + .055) as our risk-free rate because Black Scholes assumed risk-free rate is compounded continuously. Duration of option is 45/366 days.

Step 2: We now use Goal Seek to determine the value of sigma that makes predicted Black-Scholes price (in D14) equal actual price (in B14). We fill out our Goal Seek window to set cell D14 to the value B14 by changing volatility (B10). We find the implied volatility of MSFT to be 47.07%.

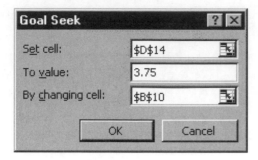

A similar analysis for Amazon.com in Figure 33.3 shows that Amazon.com's implied volatility is around 75%.

Figure 33.3

	A	B	C	D	E	F
1						
2	**Amazon Implied Volatility**			February 9 ,2000		
3				March $75 put		
4	**Input data**			expires		
5	Stock price	$74.94		25-Mar		
6	Exercise price	$75				
7	Duration	0.1229508				
8	Interest rate	5.33%				
9	dividend rate	0				
10	volatility	75.24%				
11						
12		Actual		Predicted		
13	Call price		=	$8.06		
14	put	$7.63		$7.63		
15						
16						
17	Other quantities for option price					
18	d1	0.1535665		N(d1)	0.561024	
19	d2	-0.1102461		N(d2)	0.456107	

Remarks

Of course, different puts (or calls) will yield slightly different implied volatilities. You can use Solver to combine several options into a single volatility estimate. See Chapter 49 for an explanation of this approach.

In a real options model, you should estimate implied volatility for a time horizon that is as close as possible to the duration of the real option.

The Implied Volatility Approach

Chapter 34: The Risk Neutral Approach to Option Pricing

The arbitrage pricing approach we previously developed can be difficult to implement. The reason is that it can often be hard to determine the risk-free portfolio that yields an arbitrage opportunity. Cox Ingersoll and Ross came up with a brilliant alternative method of pricing options called the **risk neutral pricing approach**. As we will see, the risk neutral approach often greatly simplifies the process of pricing options.

Logic Behind the Risk Neutral Approach

Recall that the arbitrage argument works independent of a person's risk preferences. For example, whether a decision-maker is risk averse, risk seeking or risk neutral[1] she would accept the option price obtained by the arbitrage pricing argument.

This observation leads to the following conclusions:

1. In a world where everyone is risk neutral arbitrage pricing is valid.
2. In a risk neutral world all assets must yield a return equal to the risk free rate.
3. In a risk neutral world any asset (including an option) is worth the expected value of its discounted cash flows.
4. Set up a risk neutral world in which all stocks yield risk free rate and use Monte Carlo simulation (or a binomial tree) to determine expected discounted cash flows from an option.
5. Let p = price of an option in our world (Earth!). Then the price of the option in a risk neutral world must also be p. By using steps 1-4 we may find the price in the risk-neutral world (call it p'). But since the option price in all worlds is the same our p' must equal the price p in our complex non-risk neutral world!

---

[1] A risk averse decision-maker values an uncertain situation at less than the situation's expected value. For example, a risk averse decision-maker would prefer $1000 for certain to a coin toss lottery where heads yields $10,000 and tails loses $8000. A risk seeking decision-maker values an uncertain situation at more than the situation's expected value. Thus in our previous situation the risk seeking decision maker would choose the coin toss lottery. Finally, a risk neutral decision-maker always ranks uncertain situations according to their expected value (irregardless of the risk involved). Thus a risk averse decision-maker would be indifferent between $1000 for certain and the coin toss lottery.

Essentially we use Step 2 to "adjust" the probabilities of various states of the world. Then we use Step 3 to value the derivative.

Example of Risk Neutral Pricing

Let's price our call option of Chapter 31 via risk neutral pricing. Recall the situation was as follows:

Example 34.1

A stock is currently selling for $40. One period from now the stock will either increase to $50 or decrease in price to $32. The risk free rate of interest is 11 1/9%. What is a fair price for a European call option with an exercise price of $40?

Solution

We now value our call option in a risk neutral world. Let p = the risk neutral probability that the stock increases to $50. Then $1 - p$ = the risk neutral probability that the stock decreases to $32. From Step 2 we know that in a risk neutral world our stock (and any other asset) must yield on average the risk-free rate of return. This requires

$$50p + 32(1-p) = 40(1+\frac{1}{9}) \text{ or } 18p + 32 = \frac{400}{9} \text{ or } 18p = \frac{112}{9} \text{ or } p = \frac{56}{81}.$$

Thus in a risk neutral world the stock has a 56/81 chance of increasing to $50 and a 25/81 chance of decreasing to $32.

In the $50 state the option is worth $10 while in the $32 state the option is worth $0. In a risk neutral world any asset is worth the expected discounted value of its cash flows. Therefore in a risk neutral world our call option is worth

$$\frac{1}{1+\frac{1}{9}}((\frac{56}{81})(10)+\frac{25}{81}(0)) = \frac{56}{9}.$$

Since in the risk neutral world the arbitrage-pricing price must be correct, we know that the real world price for this call equals the risk neutral price $\frac{56}{9}$!

The beauty of the risk neutral approach is that it is usually easy to get the risk neutral probabilities. **Then we may value our derivative as the expected discounted value of its cash flows.** This is very intuitive and much more satisfying than the original Black-Scholes derivation.

Proof that American Call is Never Exercised Early

As an example of the power of the risk neutral approach, we give an easy proof that early exercise is never optimal for a non dividend-paying American call option. Assume we are using the risk neutral approach to value an American call with a binomial model. Assume exercise price is c and per period risk free rate is r. Assume up move is by a factor u and down move is by factor d. Let p be the probability of an up move. Then we know that for a non-dividend paying stock

$$(1)\, pu + (1-p)d = 1+r.$$

Also assume there are N total periods in our binomial tree approach.

Let $V_n(x)$ be value of American call at time n when price is x. Then

$$V_n(x) = max(x - c, \frac{1}{1+r}(pV_{n+1}(ux) + (1-p)V_{n+1}(dx)).$$

We need to show this maximum is always attained by

$$\frac{1}{1+r}(pV_{n+1}(ux) + (1-p)V_{n+1}(dx) \cdot$$

We will have shown it is always optimal to continue if

$$\frac{1}{1+r}(pV_{n+1}(ux) + (1-p)V_{n+1}(dx)) \geq x - c.$$

Now $V_{n+1}(ux) \geq ux - c$ and $V_{n+1}(dx) \geq dx - c$. This implies that

$$\frac{1}{1+r}(pV_{n+1}(ux) + (1-p)V_{n+1}(dx)) \geq \frac{1}{1+r}(p(ux - c) + (1-p)(dx - c)) =$$

$$\frac{1}{1+r}((1+r)x - c) = x - \frac{c}{1+r} \succ x - c.$$

The first equality follows from (1). This shows that continuing is at least as good as exercising the option. Therefore an American call (on a non-dividend paying stock) will never be exercised early.

Chapter 35: The State Price Approach to Asset Valuation

Another way to look at asset valuation is the **state price approach**. This approach turns out to be equivalent in most situations to the arbitrage pricing and risk neutral approaches. For every possible state k that can occur we define the **state price** P(k) to be the fair value associated with a situation in which we receive $1 whenever state k occurs. If state prices exist, then we can simply value any security yielding d(k) dollars in state k as

$$(1) \sum_k d(k)P(k) \cdot$$

We will use our simple binomial example to illustrate the computation and use of state prices. Essentially, we compute state prices to be consistent with our security (stock and call) prices. Given we have already computed risk neutral probabilities for this example, it is probably easiest to compute state prices by going to a risk neutral world. Recall the risk neutral probabilities for our simple example were 56/81 for $50 and 25/81 for $32. Since in the risk neutral world the stock price is $50 with probability 56/81 we find $P(50) = \frac{9}{10}(\frac{56}{81}) = \frac{504}{810}$. Since in the risk neutral world a $32 price occurs with probability 25/81 we find

$$P(32) = \frac{9}{10}(\frac{25}{81}) = \frac{225}{810}.$$

Now we can use (1) to value the option as

$$10(\frac{504}{810}) + 0(\frac{225}{810}) = \frac{56}{9} \cdot$$

We can also value our share of stock as

$$50(\frac{504}{810}) + 32(\frac{225}{810}) = 40 \cdot$$

By the way, we could have also found the state prices by solving the following equations (can you see why?)

$$P(50) + P(32) = \frac{9}{10}$$
$$50P(50) + 32P(32) = 40$$

The following theorem is proven in Section 9.9 of Luenberger.

Theorem: A set of positive state prices exists if and only if there are no arbitrage opportunities.

By the way an arbitrage opportunity is simply a money-making machine that can take an investment of $0 (or a negative investment) today and turn (with positive probability) a profit.

The Theorem doesn't say that the state prices are unique. If there are more states than traded securities, then there may exist multiple sets of state prices that are consistent with our security prices and prices of derivatives may not be unique.

Chapter 36: Valuing an Internet Start-up with Black-Scholes Formula

We now show how the option way of thinking can be applied to make the correct business decision in two situations:

- Valuing an investment in an Internet start-up.

- Valuing the opportunity to purchase a company with negative NPV projections.

In both situations we will find that the option way of thinking leads to a different (and more satisfying) decision than the traditional DCF approach.

Valuing an Internet Start-up

We are thinking (see file **Netstart.xls**) of investing in a potential Internet start-up. We are quite sure that today and every three months for the next 21 months we will have to invest $0.5 million to keep the project going. Our present estimate of the NPV of revenues (less future operating costs) to be received from this project (revenues begin 2 years from now) is $22 million. We will have to spend $12 million two years from now to complete the start-up. Assume a risk-free rate of 5%. Should we go ahead with this project? We will assume the revenue stream has an annual volatility of 40%.

Figure 36.1

	B	C	D	E	F	G	H	I	J	K	L	M
2	Internet Startup											
3	Classic NPV					Cost through Q7		Option value				
4	Analysis					3.834325		$5.02				
5												
6						NPV with option		$1.19				
7												
8												
9												
10			rf rate	0.05								
11			int rate	0.23								
12			Static NPV									
13												
14			time	0	0.25	0.5	0.75	1	1.25	1.5	1.75	2
15			investment	0.5	0.5	0.5	0.5	0.5	0.5	0.5	0.5	12
16			revenue									22
17			dfcosts	1	0.987877	0.9759	0.964069	0.952381	0.940835	0.929429	0.918161	0.907029
18			PV costs	0.5	0.493938	0.48795	0.482034	0.47619	0.470417	0.464714	0.45908	10.88435
19			NPV rev	14.54161								0.660982
20			NPV costs	14.71868								
21			NPV inv	-0.17707								

Solution   Figure 36.1 contains a traditional DCF analysis of the project. We are sure about the project costs so we discount them at 5%. This yields an NPV (cell E20) of $14.72 million. By the way, the costs excluding the $12 million expense have an NPV of $3.83 million. The revenue stream is, of course, risky so we discount the revenue stream at the appropriate risk-adjusted rate (let's assume that it equals 23%). Then the NPV of the revenue is $14.54 million. Thus on a traditional DCF basis we should not do the project.

What are we missing here? The traditional DCF argument has at least two flaws

- The riskiness of the project changes over time. Do we really know the appropriate discount rate for all our cash flows?

- The revenue stream is highly uncertain. In two years we will have a much better idea of the value of our revenue stream. If things look bad, we will probably not invest $12 million. If things look good we will. In short we have an **option** to invest in this project that we may or may not exercise.

How can we apply Black-Scholes to this situation? The uncertain quantity here is the NPV of the future operating profits from the start-up. Our best current estimate is $14.54 million. In two years we have the option to spend $12 million to obtain the operating profits from the start-up. The operating profits (at Time 2) from the start-up are the analog of the stock price at expiration. To model the operating profits at Time 2 we need to estimate volatility. Suppose similar projects have a volatility of 40%. Then our option to invest in two years is equivalent to a two-year call option with exercise price of $12 million. Plugging the relevant parameters

- Current Stock Price: $14.54 million

- Duration = 2 years

- Volatility = 40%

- Dividend rate = 0 (no profits are earned before year 2)

- Exercise Price = $12 million

- Risk-free rate= 5%

into our Black-Scholes template yields the result in Figure 36.2.

We find that our option opportunity is worth $5.02 million. Since NPV of costs prior to Time 2 is only $3.83 million we now see that our opportunity to pursue the Internet startup is worth $5.02 - $3.83 = $1.19 million. The use of option thinking has turned our no-go decision into a GO! Later we will learn how to value this opportunity if we can abandon the project at any time in the next two years.

Sensitivity Analysis

Of course, we are not really sure about the volatility value. Therefore, we used a one-way Data Table to determine how the value of our option varies as volatility varies between 10% and 40%. We see that our option value outweighs the costs for the next 1.75 years as long as the volatility is at least 17%. Of course, any high-tech project will have volatility at least this large, so we feel pretty good about going ahead with the project!

Figure 36.2

	A	B	C	D	E	F	G	H
1	**Call with dividends**							
2								
3								
4	**Input data**							
5	Stock price	$14.54						
6	Exercise price	$12					Cost through quarter 7	$ 3.83
7	Duration	2						
8	Interest rate	5.00%						
9	dividend rate	0					Volatility	$5.02
10	volatility	40.00%					0.1	3.694589
11							0.11	3.704829
12				Predicted			0.12	3.718931
13	Call price		=	$5.02			0.13	3.736975
14	put			$1.34			0.14	3.758878
15							0.15	3.784453
16							0.16	3.813459
17	Other quantities for option price						0.17	3.845628
18	d1	0.799025		N(d1)	0.787862		0.18	3.880691
19	d2	0.23334		N(d2)	0.592251		0.19	3.918384
20							0.2	3.958461
21							0.21	4.000694
22							0.22	4.044874
23							0.23	4.090811
24							0.24	4.138334
25							0.25	4.187288
26							0.26	4.237536
27							0.27	4.288952
28							0.28	4.341425
29							0.29	4.394852
30							0.3	4.449144
31							0.31	4.504218
32							0.32	4.56
33							0.33	4.616423
34							0.34	4.673426
35							0.35	4.730952
36							0.36	4.788953
37							0.37	4.847381
38							0.38	4.906194
39							0.39	4.965353
40							0.4	5.024824

Valuing a "Pioneer Option": Web TV

In April 1997 Microsoft purchased Web TV for $425 million. Let's assume that Microsoft felt that the true value of Web TV at this point in time was $300 million. Could the purchase of Web TV still be worthwhile? If the purchase of Web TV gives Microsoft the "option" to enter another business in the future, then the value of this option might outweigh the -$125 million NPV of the Web TV deal. More concretely, let's suppose that buying Web TV gives us the opportunity (for $2 billion) to enter (in three years) another Internet related business that has a current value of $1 billion. Assume a risk-free rate of 5%. Assume an annual volatility of 50% for the value of the Internet related business. Does the "pioneer" option created by Web TV exceed our Web TV NPV of -$125 million?

Solution

Again our Pioneer option is a European call option with the following parameters:

- Current Stock Price = $1 billion

- Exercise Price = $2 billion

- Risk free rate = 5%

- Duration = 3 years

- Volatility = 50%

- Dividend rate = 0% (we assume none of value of Internet related business is paid out prior to exercise date)

Figure 36.3

	A	B	C	D	E	F	G	H	I	J	K	L	M
1	**Call with dividends**												
2													
3													
4	**Input data**												
5	Stock price	$1											
6	Exercise price	$2											
7	Duration	3											
8	Interest rate	5.00%											
9	dividend rate	0											
10	volatility	50.00%											
11													
12				Predicted									
13	Call price		=	$0.17									
14	put			$0.90									
15												Volatility	
16													$0.17
17	Other quantities for option price											0.3	0.05095
18	d1	-0.19416		N(d1)	0.423025							0.31	0.05611
19	d2	-1.060185		N(d2)	0.14453							0.32	0.061432
20												0.33	0.066902
21												0.34	0.07251
22												0.35	0.078246
23												0.36	0.0841
24												0.37	0.090062
25												0.38	0.096124
26												0.39	0.102279
27												0.4	0.108518
28												0.41	0.114835
29												0.42	0.121223
30												0.43	0.127676
31												0.44	0.134188
32												0.45	0.140754
33												0.46	0.147369
34												0.47	0.154029
35												0.48	0.160728
36												0.49	0.167463
37												0.5	0.174229
38												0.51	0.181023
39												0.52	0.187842
40												0.53	0.194681
41												0.54	0.201539
42												0.55	0.208412
43												0.56	0.215297
44												0.57	0.222192
45												0.58	0.229094
46												0.59	0.236001
47												0.6	0.24291

From Figure 36.3 (see file **Weboptions.xls**) we find that the value of our option to enter the Internet related business is $.17 billion = $170 million. This more than compensates for the negative NPV of the Web TV deal.

Sensitivity Analysis

Of course, the actual volatility of the Internet related business is unknown. In Figure 36.3 we used a one-way data table to see how the value of our Pioneer option varies as the volatility changes between 30% and 60%. We find that as long as the volatility exceeds 43%, the Pioneer option is worth more than our negative NPV of $125 million.

Chapter 37: Valuing an R and D Project

In today's world accurate valuation of R and D projects is critical to a firm's success. The real option approach is very useful for valuation of R and D projects. The following example is based on Jagle's article in *R and D Management*.

Example 37.1

Development of a new drug requires that the drug go through the following stages of development:

- Preclinical development.

- Phase I Trials

- Phase II Trials

- Phase III Trials

Failure at any stage results in termination of the project. From published industry data we have estimates of the probability of success at each stage and the duration of each stage. Information on the revenue due from success or failure at each state and the cost of each stage is also given in Figure 37.1 (see file **Pharmrd.xls**.)

Figure 37.1

	A	B	C	D	E	F	G	H	I	J
1	New Drug									
2	R and D		WACC	0.1						
3			rf	0.06						
4						all in millions of $s				
5		Decision	Time	Actual estimated Prob of Success	Duration of Activity	Revenue from success	Revenue from Failure	Value of Being at this point	Risk neutral prob of success	Cost of stage
6		Phase III	3.5	0.8	2.5	2000	0	1260.777	0.729244	200
7		Phase II	2	0.44	1.5	0	450	699.2711	0.386222	100
8		Phase I	1	0.43	1	0	250	402.8969	0.394129	50
9		Preclinical	0	0.47	1	0	200	268.5105	0.417065	200

The company's WACC for this type of project is 10% and the risk-free rate is 6%. What is the value of this development project?

Solution

We begin by determining the value at each decision point of future revenues. Then we can use these revenue values to compute risk neutral probabilities and conduct a risk neutral valuation of the situation.

Step 1: The expected discounted value of the future revenue if we are at the beginning of Phase III is computed as

$$\frac{1}{(1+.10)^{2.5}}(.8(2000)+.2(0)) = \$1260.77.$$

Step 2: The expected discounted value of all future revenue if we are at the beginning of Phase II is computed as

$$\frac{1}{(1+.10)^{1.5}}(.44(0+1260.77)+.56(450)) = \$699.27.$$

Step 3: The expected discounted value of all future revenues if we are at the beginning of Phase I is computed as

$$\frac{1}{(1+.10)^{1}}(.43(699.27+0)+.57(250)) = \$402.90.$$

Step 4: Finally if we at the beginning of Preclinical trials the expected discounted value of all future revenues is computed as

$$\frac{1}{(1+.1)^{1}}(.47(0+402.90)+.53(200)) = \$268.51.$$

All these values were computed in cells H6:H9 by copying from H6 to H7:H9 the formula

    =D6*F6/(1+$D$2)^E6+(1-D6)*G6/(1+$D$2)^E6.

Determination of Risk Neutral Probabilities

We may now determine the risk neutral probabilities of success for each stage of the project. For example, suppose we are at the beginning of Phase III and we want to compute a risk neutralized probability of Phase III success. The value of the revenues at this point are $1260.77. In 2.5 years the value of these revenues will change to either $2000 or $0. Using the risk-free rate of 6% we may solve for p = Probability of Phase III success using the following equation:

$$1260.77 = \frac{1}{(1+.06)^{2.5}}(2000p+0(1-p)) \quad or \quad p=.729.$$

More generally suppose expected discounted (at WACC) value of future revenues is S and in time t value of future revenues can change to either u or d (u>d). If we let p = the risk neutralized probability of an up move and r = risk-free rate we know that in a risk neutral world the following must hold:

$$S = \frac{pu}{(1+r)^t} + \frac{(1-p)d}{(1+r)^t} \ \ or$$

$$pu + (1-p)d = S(1+r)^t \ \ or$$

$$p(u-d) = S(1+r)^t - d \ \ or$$

$$p = \frac{S(1+r)^t - d}{u-d}.$$

In I6 we can compute the risk neutral probability for Phase III success with the formula

=((1+$D$3)^E6*H6-G6)/(F6-G6).

Note that for other stages S comes from column H, u comes from Column F (moving up one row), and d comes from Column G (same row). Therefore copying from I7 to I7:I9 the following formula yields the correct risk neutral probabilities for the remaining stages:

=(H7*(1+$D$3)^E7-G7)/(H6-G7).

Working Backwards to Determine Project Value

We can now use our risk neutral probabilities (and incorporate project costs) to determine the initial value of the project. See Figure 37.2 and Figure 37.4.

Figure 37.2

	A	B	C	D	E	F	G	H	I	J
11		Option valuation								
12										
13		Decision	Time	Actual estimated Prob of Success	Duration of Activity	Revenue from success	Revenue from Failure	Value of Being at this point	Risk neutral prob of success	Cost of stage
14		Phase III	3.5	0.8	2.5	2000	0	1060.777	0.729244	200
15		Phase II	2	0.44	1.5	0	450	528.4914	0.386222	100
16		Phase I	1	0.43	1	0	250	289.3976	0.394129	50
17		Preclinical	0	0.47	1	0	200	23.85330	0.417005	200
10										

Step 1: If we get to the beginning of Phase III the project value at this point is given by

$$max(0,-200+\frac{1}{(1+.06)^{2.5}}(.729(2000)+(1-.729)(0))=\$1060.77.$$

Step 2: If we get to the beginning of Phase II the project value at this point is given by

$$max(0,-100+\frac{1}{(1+.06)^{1.5}}(.386(1060.77)+(1-.386)(450))=\$528.49.$$

Step 3: If we get to the beginning of Phase I the project value at this point is given by

$$max(0,-50+\frac{1}{(1+.06)^{1}}(.394(528.49)+(1-.394)(250))=\$289.39.$$

Step 4: Finally at the beginning of the Preclinical trials the project value is

$$max(0,-200+\frac{1}{(1+.06)^{1}}(.417(289.39)+(1-.417)(200))=\$23.85.$$

Thus we arrive at an estimate of $23.85 million for the project value!

We note that we computed the project value at Phase III in H14 with the formula

=MAX(0,(1+$D$3)^-E15*(I15*H14+(1-I15)*G15)-J15) .

We computed the value at all other stages in H15:H17 by copying from H15 to H16:H17 the formula

=MAX(0,(1+$D$3)^-E15*(I15*H14+(1-I15)*G15)-J15).

Sensitivity Analysis

Clearly many of the parameters in our model are unknown. There we may want to change them in a range within 10% of our estimated value to determine impact on project NPV. This is easily done with a one-way data table. For example, Figure 37.3 shows how project value is changed by a change in the revenue from complete success or the probability of Preclinical success.

Figure 37.3

	D	E	F	G	H	I
19						Project value
20			%age	New CF	23.85339	%age change
21	Base	2000	0.9	1800	16.51228	-30.7759637
22			0.92	1840	17.96782	-24.6739162
23			0.94	1880	19.43016	-18.5434023
24			0.96	1920	20.89881	-12.3864094
25			0.98	1960	22.37335	-6.20473293
26			1	2000	23.85339	0
27			1.02	2040	25.33857	6.22631
28			1.04	2080	26.82858	12.4728481
29			1.06	2120	28.32313	18.73838092
30			1.08	2160	29.82193	25.02177792
31			1.1	2200	31.32474	31.3220004
32						Project value
33	Preclinical Prob					%age change
34	Base	0.47	%age	New Prob	23.85339	
35			0.9	0.423	20.03367	-16.0133105
36			0.92	0.4324	20.79761	-12.8106484
37			0.94	0.4418	21.56156	-9.60798628
38			0.96	0.4512	22.3255	-6.40532419
39			0.98	0.4606	23.08944	-3.20266209
40			1	0.47	23.85339	0
41			1.02	0.4794	24.61733	3.202662093
42			1.04	0.4888	25.38127	6.405324186
43			1.06	0.4982	26.14522	9.607986279
44			1.08	0.5076	26.90916	12.81064837
45			1.1	0.517	27.6731	16.01331046

For example, to compute the effect of a change of ±10% in Project cash flows from the base of $2000 we create the percentage changes (from 90% to 110%) in cash flows from the base value in G21:G31. We see that project cash flows are varying from $1800 to $2200. Then we put the project value in cell H20. By running a one-way Data Table with Column Input cell F6 we place the corresponding project values in H21:H31. Note that a 10% decrease in Cash Flow reduces project value by 31%.

A similar analysis of the effect of a change in the probability of Preclinical success on project value shows that a 10% decrease in the probability of Preclinical success has much less effect on project value (only a 16% reduction) than a 10% decrease in project cash flows.

Remark

For our data table analysis to work we need columns C-G and I-J in rows 13-17 to be copies of the corresponding numbers in rows 5-9. This is to ensure that when a number changes in rows 5-9 it also changes in rows 13-17.

Reference

Jagle, A. "Shareholder Value, Real options, and Innovation in Technology Intensive Companies," *R&D Management*, Volume 29, No. 3, 1999.

Figure37.4

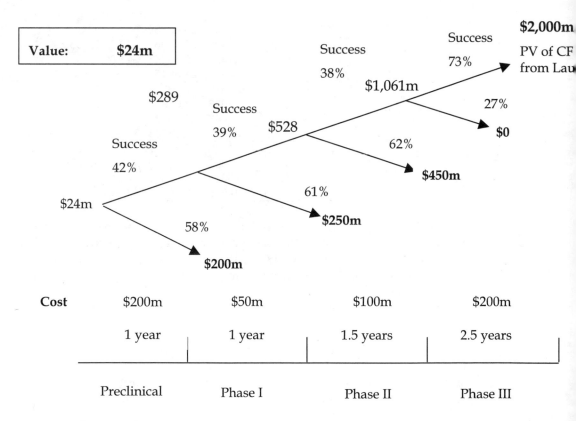

Assumptions:
- Risk-free interest rate = 6%
- Discount rate = 10% (for PV of CFs from launch)

Chapter 38: Relationship Between Binomial and Lognormal Models

The Black-Scholes option pricing formula for pricing European puts and calls was derived under the assumption that future stock prices follow a lognormal random variable. To price American options, however, we often need to approximate stock prices in discrete time and work backwards from the option's expiration date. It therefore becomes crucial to know how to approximate a lognormal random variable by a discrete random variable. The usual method is to utilize a **binomial tree**. In a binomial tree we assume that each period of length Δt one of the following occurs:

- With probability p the stock price is multiplied by a factor u>1

- With probability q = 1 – p the stock price is multiplied by a factor d = 1/u<1.

In short, the stock either increases or decreases each period. For a given lognormal random variable having a mean return of μΔt and a standard deviation of $\sigma \sqrt{\Delta t}$ in a length of time Δt the file **binlognorm.xls** computes values of p, u and d that closely approximate the lognormal. The way this works is we use Solver to choose values of p, u , and d for which the binomial model yields a mean growth by a factor of $e^{\mu \Delta t}$ and a standard deviation of $\sigma \sqrt{\Delta t}$ in one time period. Figure 38.1 illustrates the idea. Reconsider our Microsoft example. If we choose a period of 1 month = 1/12 year with μ = .30 and σ = .38 we insert those values into our spreadsheet. Then we run Solver and obtain the results in Figure 38.1.

Figure 38.1

	A	B	C	D	E
1	Given mu and sigma				
2	find p and u				
3	**Exact**				
4				mu	0.3
5	p	0.585919		sigma	0.38
6	u	1.117534			
7	d	0.894828			
8	time	0.083333			
9		Prob	Value	Sq Dev	
10	up	0.585919	1.117534	0.008504	
11	down	0.414081	0.894828	0.017027	
12		binomial		lognormal	
13	mean growth	1.025315	=	1.025315	
14	var growth	0.012033	=	0.012033	
15					
16	**Approximate**				
17	a	1.025315			
18	up move	1.115939			
19	down move	0.896106			
20	prob up	0.587759			
21	prob down	0.412241			

We find that the best binomial approximation to model Microsoft's growth is to assume that each period Microsoft's stock price increases (with probability .586) by 11.8% or Microsoft's stock price decreases by 10.5% (with probability .414).

Using Simulation to Show the Binomial Approximation Works

In the spreadsheet **binomsim.xls** (see Figure 38.2) we show how the approximation works. Our goal is to simulate the price of MSFT stock in 60 months given $\sigma = 38\%$ and $\mu = .30$ and a current price of $100. We use time intervals of 1 month (1/12 year) and apply the values of u, d, and p given in Figure 38.1.

Figure 38.2

	A	B	C	D	E	F	G	H	I	J	K
1					p	0.585919		76.67	5th %ile		80.07337
2	Microsoft simulation				u	1.117534		1275	95th %ile		1152.769
3	discrete time				d	0.894828		449.16	Mean		445.769
4								464.8	Sigma		437.712
5								Lognormal			Binomial
6				Date	Price	RN					
7				Today	100						
8				1	89.4828	0.653927					
9				2	100.0001	0.476678					
10				3	111.7535	0.500347					
11				4	124.8883	0.203208					
12				5	111.7536	0.655102					
13				6	124.8884	0.154175					
14				7	111.7536	0.936949					

Step 1: In cells F8:F67 we enter = RiskUniform(0,1) to generate random numbers between 0 and 1.

Step 2: In cells E8:E67 we use the binomial model to generate monthly changes in stock prices by copying from E8:E67

$=IF(F8<p,u*E7,d*E7).$

With probability p this formula increases stock price by u and with probability 1 – p this formula increases stock price by d.

Step 3: To track the results of the simulation we use @RISK's statistical functions. We enter

$=RiskPercentile(E67,.05)$ *(cell K2 to compute 5th percentile)*

$=RiskPercentile\ (E67,.95)$ *(cell K3 to compute 95th percentile*

$=RiskMean(E67)$ *(cell K4 to compute mean)*

$=RiskStdDev(E67)$ *(cell K5 to compute standard deviation)*

Figure 38.3

	H	I	J	K
1	76.67	5th %ile		80.07337
2	1275	95th %ile		1152.769
3	449.16	Mean		445.769
4	464.8	Sigma		437.712
5	Lognormal			Binomial
6				

From Figure 38.3 we find the simulated results from the binomial approximation are close to the lognormal simulation results. If we had let the length of a time period be smaller and run more iterations our approximation would have even been better.

An Approximation to the Approximation!

Most real options geeks and geekettes do not know about Solver so they use an approximation to the values of u, d, and p we found with Solver. For Δt small these approximations are extremely accurate. The formulas used in most books are as follows:

$$u = 1/d$$

$$p = \frac{a-d}{u-d}$$

$$u = e^{\sigma\sqrt{\Delta t}}$$

$$a = e^{\mu\Delta t}$$

We have entered the formulas for these approximations in our spreadsheet in cells B17:B21. As you can see from Figure 38.1 the difference between the exact values of p, u and d and the approximate values are very small. To be consistent with other authors, we will always use these approximations in our binomial tree analyses.

Chapter 39: Pricing an American Option with Binomial Trees

We cannot use the Black-Scholes model to price many American options because to determine the cash flows from the option we need to account for the possibility of early exercise. American options are usually priced with **binomial trees**. We divide the duration of the option into smaller time periods (usually weeks or months). During each time period the stock price either increases by a factor u or decreases by a factor d. We assume d = 1/u. Let Δt equal length of period in tree. The probability of an increase each period (p) is chosen in conjunction with u and d so the stock price grows on average at the risk-free rate r and has an annual volatility of sigma. We let q = 1- p equals the probability of a decrease during each period. To perform risk neutral valuation we assume (given that the stock pays no dividends)[1] that the underlying asset grows according a lognormal random variable having μ = the risk free rate (r). If σ is the volatility parameter for the underlying stock's lognormal random variable then we know from Chapter 38 that the lognormal movement of prices can be approximated by a binomial model with parameters given by

$$u = 1/d$$
$$p = \frac{a-d}{u-d}$$
$$u = e^{\sigma\sqrt{\Delta t}}$$
$$a = e^{\mu\Delta t}$$
$$q = 1-p.$$

In one part of our spreadsheet we model the evolution of the stock price. Then we value the option by working backwards from the last time period. At each node (a combination of stock price and time) we recursively determine value of option from that point on. By the time we have reached today's node, we have well approximated the value of the option today. Note that our approximation will improve as Δt is reduced. To begin we value an American put option. Recall that an American call option on a non-dividend paying stock will never be exercised early. As we will soon see, an American put option may be exercised early. Our work is in file **American.xls**.

---

[1] In a later section we will show that if a stock pays dividends at rate q (or project pays out a percentage q of its value each year) then we assume asset grows in risk neutral world at rate r – q.

| **Example** | Let's price a 5-month American put having |
| **39.1** | |

- Current stock price = $50

- Exercise price = $50

- Risk-free rate = 10%

- Annual volatility = 40%

- Δt = 1 month = .083 years.

All this data plus the previous definitions of u, d, a, q, and p are input in the range A1:B13 of the spreadsheet. We have used range names to make the tree easier to explain.

The Stock Price Tree

We begin by determining the possible stock prices during the next 5 months. Column B has today's (Month 0) price, Column C Month 1, etc.

Step 1: Enter today's stock price ($50) in B16 with the formula

=B3.

Step 2: By copying the formula

=u*B16

from C16 to D16:G16 we obtain the price each month when there have been no down moves.

Step 3: To compute all other prices note that in each column as we move down a row the price is multiplied by a factor (d/u). Also note that during Month i there are i + 1 possible prices. This allows us to compute all prices by copying from C17 to C17:G21 the formula

=IF($A17<=C$15,(d/u)*C16,"-").

As we move down each column, the prices are successively multiplied by d/u Also, our formula places a "-" where a price does not exist.

The Optimal Decision Strategy

We now work backwards to find the value of the American put. Remember at each node the value of the put equals the **expected discounted value of future cash flows from the put**.

Step 1: At month 5 the option is just worth

maximum (0,exercise price – current stock price). Thus we enter

> =MAX(0,$B$4-G16)

in cell G24 and copy this formula down to G29.

Step 4: In Month 4 (and all previous months) the value of the option at any node is

Maximum (value from exercising now, $\left(\dfrac{1}{1+\dfrac{.1}{12}}\right)$ *(p*(value of option for up move),

+ q(value of option for down move)).

For example, in F28 the value of option is

> $max(50 – 31.50, (1/1.0083)*(.507*(\$14.64) + .493*(\$21.93)) = \$18.50.$

Since this maximum is attained by exercising now, if this node occurs we would exercise the option now. At the node in F26 the maximum is attained by not exercising. To implement this decision-making procedure we enter in cell F24 the formula

> =IF($A24<=F$23,MAX($B$4-F16,(1/(1+r_*deltat))*(p*G24+(1-p)*G25)),"-").

Copying this formula to B24:F29 generates value of the option for all possible prices during Months 1-4 and places a "-" in any cell where there is no actual stock price. In cell B24 we find the estimated value of the put to equal $4.49. Of course, $4.49 is an approximation to the put value. As Δt grows small, however, our price will converge to the actual price of the put if the stock grew according to a lognormal random variable.

Using Conditional Formatting to Describe the Optimal Exercise Policy

Assuming the stock grows at the risk free rate, how would we react to actual price changes? Suppose the first three months have down moves. We do not exercise during first two months but we exercise after third down move. Suppose the first four months are down up down down. Then we exercise after the fourth month. To make this clearer, we use Excel's Conditional Format Option to format the spreadsheet so that cells for which option would be exercised are in bold face. We begin by noting that **it is optimal to exercise the option at a Month and price if and only if the value of the cell corresponding to the month and price equals (exercise price) - (stock price).**

To indicate the cells where exercising the option is optimal begin in cell G24 by selecting Format>Conditional Formatting and enter the following:

Then click on the Format button and select Bold from the Font Style drop-down menu. This dialog box ensures that if the option is exercised in the state with 5 up moves in period 5 then a bold font is used. The interpretation of

$$=(\$B\$4-G16)=G24$$

is the format takes hold only if $(\$B\$4-G16)=G24$ which is equivalent to the option being exercised. If we Edit>Copy cell G24 and Paste Special>Formats (or use the Format Painter) to the range B24:G29 we ensure that any period and number of up moves for which exercise of the option is optimal will be indicated in bold font.

Figure 39.1

	A	B	C	D	E	F	G
1	**American Option**						
2	**Put**						
3	Current price	$ 50.00					
4	Exercise price	$ 50.00					
5	r	0.1					
6	sigma	0.4					
7	t	0.416667					
8	deltat	0.083333					
9	u	1.122401					
10	d	0.890947					
11	a	1.008368					
12	p	0.507319					
13	q	0.492681					
14		Time					
15	**Stock Prices**	0	1	2	3	4	5
16	0	$ 50.00	$ 56.12	$ 62.99	$ 70.70	$ 79.35	$ 89.07
17	1		$ 44.55	$ 50.00	$ 56.12	$ 62.99	$ 70.70
18	2		-	$ 39.69	$ 44.55	$ 50.00	$ 56.12
19	3		-	-	$ 35.36	$ 39.69	$ 44.55
20	4		-	-	-	$ 31.50	$ 35.36
21	5		-	-	-	-	$ 28.07
22	**Down Moves**						
23	**Put Value**	0	1	2	3	4	5
24	0	$ 4.49	$ 2.16	$ 0.64	$ -	$ -	$ -
25	1	-	$ 6.96	$ 3.77	$ 1.30	$ -	$ -
26	2	-	-	$ 10.36	$ 6.38	$ 2.66	$ -
27	3	-	-	-	$ 14.64	$ 10.31	$ 5.45
28	4	-	-	-	-	$ 18.50	$ 14.64
29	5	-	-	-	-	-	$ 21.93

Sensitivity Analysis

Using one-way data tables it is easy to see how changes in various input parameters change the price of the put. We varied the annual volatility of the stock from 10%-70%. Figure 39.2 (a one-way data table with Input Cell sigma) shows how an increase in volatility greatly increases the value of the put. Increased volatility gives us a larger chance of a big price drop, which increases the value of the put.

Figure 39.2

	H	I
7	**Volatility**	4.489053
8	0.1	0.680146
9	0.2	1.91777
10	0.3	3.197364
11	0.4	4.489053
12	0.5	5.799995
13	0.6	7.104648
14	0.7	8.400682

Figure 39.3 shows how a change in the exercise price of the stock changes the value of the put. We used a one-way data table with input cell B4.

Figure 39.3

	K	L
7	Ex Price	4.489053
8	$ 45.00	2.139609
9	$ 46.00	2.609498
10	$ 47.00	3.079387
11	$ 48.00	3.549275
12	$ 49.00	4.019164
13	$ 50.00	4.489053
14	$ 51.00	4.980604
15	$ 52.00	5.484364
16	$ 53.00	5.988124
17	$ 54.00	6.52469
18	$ 55.00	7.092245
19	$ 56.00	7.733071

As the exercise price increases, the value of the put increases because an increased exercise price increases the number of values for which the put is "in the money."

Finally, Figure 39.4 shows that an increase in the risk-free rate decreases the value of the put.

Figure 39.4

	N	O
7	r	4.489053
8	0.01	5.300677
9	0.02	5.207424
10	0.03	5.114923
11	0.04	5.023183
12	0.05	4.932208
13	0.06	4.842007
14	0.07	4.752584
15	0.08	4.663947
16	0.09	4.576102
17	0.1	4.489053
18	0.11	4.405002
19	0.12	4.333566

This is because an increase in the risk-free rate makes the payoff from the put (which occurs in the future) less valuable.

Using Conditional Formatting to Describe the Optimal Exercise Polic

Relationship to an Abandonment Option

Often an option to abandon a project may be thought of as a put. To see this in the current context, suppose the current value of a project is $50 million, the risk-free rate is 10%, and the project has a 40% annual volatility. Any time in the next five months we may abandon the project and receive $50 million. To determine the value of this abandonment option we would proceed exactly as we proceeded to value the put. We would have found the value of the abandonment option to be $4.49 million.

Computing the Early Exercise Boundary

Given the price of the stock today is $50 it would be nice to know, in advance what we would do (exercise or not exercise) for any given price during a future period. For example, would we exercise if the Month 1 price were $42? If we have not exercised during the first three months would we exercise during Month 4 if the price were $40? Answering this question requires that we compute the **early exercise boundary** for each period. It turns out for each month there exists a "boundary price" p(t) such that we will exercise during Month t (assuming option has not been exercised) if and only if the Month t price is less than or equal to p(t). Together p(1), p(2), p(3), p(4), and p(5) define the early exercise boundary for the put. To find the early exercise boundary it is convenient to make four copies of our original sheet. To copy a sheet put the cursor on the sheet name, hold down the left mouse button, and drag the sheet to another tab. We have renamed our four copies Ex Bound 1, Ex Bound 2, etc. In sheet Ex Bound 1 we determine p(1) as follows. The value p(1) for which we exercise during Month 1 if and only if p≤p(1) can be found by observing that **p(1) is the largest Month 1 price for which Exercise price - p(1) equals the Month 1 value of the option.** To find p(1) (see Figure 39.5) we proceed as follows:

Figure 39.5

	A	B	C	D	E	F	G
1	American Option						
2	Put						
3	Current price	$ 50.00					
4	Exercise price	$ 50.00					
5	r	0.1					
6	sigma	0.4					
7	t	0.416667					
8	deltat	0.083333					
9	u	1.122401					
10	d	0.890947					
11	a	1.008368					
12	p	0.507319					
13	q	0.492681					
14		Time					
15	down moves	0	1	2	3	4	5
16	0	$ 50.00	$ 39.19	$ 43.98	$ 49.37	$ 55.41	$ 62.19
17	1		$ 31.11	$ 34.91	$ 39.19	$ 43.98	$ 49.37
18	2		-	$ 27.71	$ 31.11	$ 34.91	$ 39.19
19	3		-	-	$ 24.69	$ 27.71	$ 31.11
20	4		-	-	-	$ 22.00	$ 24.69
21	5		-	-	-	-	$ 19.60
22		ex-price	$ 10.81				
23	Put Value	0	1	2	3	4	5
24	0	14.6728	10.81387	6.84145	3.096029	0.309755	0.00
25	1		18.89456	15.08723	10.81387	6.017455	0.63
26	2		-	22.28669	18.89456	15.08723	10.81
27	3		-	-	25.30891	22.28669	$ 18.89
28	4		-	-	-	28.00154	$ 25.31
29	5		-	-	-	-	$ 30.40

Step by Step

Step 1: In cell C16 insert a trial value for p(1). Note that the way we have set up the price tree ensures that the prices in B16 and C17 have no effect on the value of the put computed in C24.

Step 2: Assuming that the Month 1 price equals the value in C16, we compute in C22 the value if the put is exercised in Month 1 with the formula

=B4-C16.

Step 3: We can now use Solver to determine p(1). To find p(1) note that p(1) is the largest price (entered in C16) for which the value of exercising now (in cell C22) equals the Month 1 value of the option (computed in C24). Therefore the following Solver settings enable us to compute p(1).

Computing the Early Exercise Boundar

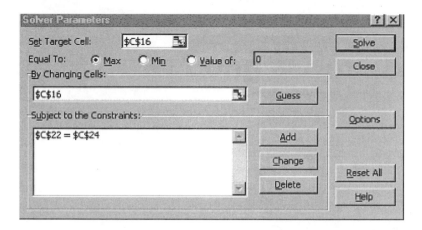

We find that p(1) = $39.19. Thus if the Month 1 price is below $39.19 we should exercise, otherwise go on. The reader should try a variety of Month 1 prices in B16 to convince herself that it is optimal to exercise for any price below $39.19 and continue for any price above $39.19. Of course, we are assuming that exercise can only occur at time =1, 2, … 5, but it turns out that even if many more points of exercise were allowed, p(1) would be fairly close to $39.19. In a similar fashion we find the rest of the early exercise boundary to be the following:

Time	Exercise if price <=
1	$39.19
2	$39.41
3	$41.64
4	$45.28
5	$50.00

Chapter 40: Using Real Options to Value a Lease on a Gold Mine

Many investment opportunities involve decisions that are made at different points in time. If the value of the investment opportunities depend on the price of a commodity (such as gold price) then the risk neutral approach we used to value stock options can be used to value real investment opportunities. Our current example is due to Luenberger.

Example 40.1

Goldco is trying to value a 10-year lease on a gold mine. Each year up to 10,000 ounces of gold can be extracted at a cost of $200 per ounce. The risk free rate is assumed to remain constant at 10%. The price received for all gold extracted during a year is assumed to equal the price of gold at the beginning of the year, but the all cash flows occur at the end of the year. The current price of gold is $400 and the future price of gold is uncertain. We model the future price of gold with a **binomial tree**. Each year we assume that gold will (with probability .75) increase by 20% and (with probability .25) decrease by 10%. The annual interest rate is 10%. What is the value of the lease?

Solution

Again we use the risk neutral approach. We need to find the probability (p) of an up move in gold prices, which makes gold yield the risk free rate. Then we use the gold price tree we create to find the expected discounted value of all the cash flows associated with the option. See Figure 40.1 and file **Gold.xls**.

Figure 40.1

	A	B	C	D	E	F	G	H	I	J	K	L
1	Simplico Gold mine			r		0.1 p	0.66666667					
2				u		1.2 Cost	200					
3		Gold Prices		d		0.9						
4	Down moves	0	1	2	3	4	5	6	7	8	9	10
5	0	400	480	576	691.2	829.44	995.328	1194.3936	1433.272	1719.927	2063.9121	2476.694569
6	1		360	432	618.4	622.08	746.496	895.7952	1074.954	1289.945	1547.9341	1857.520927
7	2		-	324	388.8	466.56	559.872	671.8464	806.2157	967.4588	1160.9506	1393.140695
8	3		-	-	291.6	349.92	419.904	503.8848	604.6618	725.5941	870.71293	1044.855521
9	4		-	-	-	262.44	314.928	377.9136	453.4963	544.1956	653.0347	783.641641
10	5		-	-	-	-	236.196	283.4352	340.1222	408.1467	489.77603	587.7312307
11	6		-	-	-	-	-	212.5764	255.0917	306.11	367.33202	440.798423
12	7		-	-	-	-	-	-	191.3188	229.5825	275.49901	330.5988173
13	8		-	-	-	-	-	-	-	172.1869	206.62426	247.949113
14	9		-	-	-	-	-	-	-	-	154.9682	185.9618347
15	10		-	-	-	-	-	-	-	-	-	139.471376
16		Value										
17	Down Moves	0	1	2	3	4	5	6	7	8	9	10
18	0	2.41E+07	2.70E+07	3.12E+07	3.42E+07	3.65E+07	3.77E+07	3.71E+07	3.41E+07	2.78E+07	1.69E+07	0.00E+00
19	1	-	1.79E+07	2.07E+07	2.33E+07	2.52E+07	2.64E+07	2.62E+07	2.43E+07	2.00E+07	1.23E+07	0.00E+00
20	2	-	-	1.29E+07	1.50E+07	1.67E+07	1.79E+07	1.81E+07	1.70E+07	1.41E+07	8.74E+06	0.00E+00
21	3	-	-	-	8.82E+06	1.04E+07	1.15E+07	1.20E+07	1.15E+07	9.72E+06	6.10E+06	0.00E+00
22	4	-	-	-	-	5.61E+06	6.73E+06	7.40E+06	7.39E+06	6.42E+06	4.12E+06	0.00E+00
23	5	-	-	-	-	-	3.17E+06	3.97E+06	4.30E+06	3.95E+06	2.63E+06	0.00E+00
24	6	-	-	-	-	-	-	1.45E+06	1.98E+06	2.09E+06	1.52E+06	0.00E+00
25	7	-	-	-	-	-	-	-	4.37E+05	7.03E+05	6.86E+05	0.00E+00
26	8	-	-	-	-	-	-	-	-	3.65E+04	6.02E+04	0.00E+00
27	9	-	-	-	-	-	-	-	-	-	0.00E+00	0.00E+00
28	10	-	-	-	-	-	-	-	-	-	-	0.00E+00

To find p note that p(1.2) + (1-p).9 = 1.1. This ensures that gold yields, on average, the risk-free rate of return each period. Therefore we find

$$p = \frac{1.1 - .9}{1.2 - .9} = \frac{2}{3}$$

We now proceed as follows:

Generating Gold Prices

Step by Step

Step 1: We compute p in cell F1 with the formula

> =(1+D1-D3)/(D2-D3).

Step 2: In rows 4 through 15 we generate the tree of gold prices for Years 1-10. We assume that our revenue is received at times 0, 1, 9. Then in rows 18-28 we will generate the discounted expected value of cash flows from **wherever we are to end of problem.** For example, cell J18 gives the expected discounted value of cash flows (at beginning of year 8) received during the last two years of the lease (given price of gold is $1719..93). To begin we enter the current price of gold, $400, in cell A5.

Step 3: To compute the price for each year when there have been no down moves copy from C5 to D5:L5 the formula

> =u*B5

Note that as we move down one row in a given column, the price of gold is multiplied by d/u. Therefore in cell C6 we can compute the Year 1 price following a down move with the formula

> =IF($A6<=C$4,(d/u)*C5,"-").

Copying this formula to C6:L15 generates all other gold prices and enters a "_" in cells where no price is defined.

Finding Value of Lease

We begin in Column K by finding value of lease at beginning of last year. Then we work backwards to find value of lease at earlier times. Remember at each node we will not mine any gold if the current price of gold is under $200.

Step by Step

Step 1: In K18 we compute the value of the lease at the beginning of year 9 if current gold price is $2063.91. Since we assume payments are received at end of year (based on beginning of year price) the value of the lease at Time 9 if gold price is at its highest level is

$$max(0, \frac{10000(2063.9 - 200)}{1.1}) = 16.94 \, million$$

To implement this idea enter in K18 the formula

$$=MAX(0,(K5-\$G\$2)*10000/(1+\$E\$1)).$$

Copying from K18 to K19:K27 generates the value of the lease for all possible gold prices at the beginning of the last year.

Step 2: To work backwards to Time 8 we compute in J18 the expected discounted value of the lease if gold is at its highest price. Note that this value is given by

$$\frac{1}{1+r} max(0, 10000(current \, gold \, price - 200))$$

$$+ \frac{1}{1+r} (p(Time \, 9 \, value \, after \, up) + (1 - p)(Time \, 9 \, value \, after \, down))$$

To operationalize this idea enter into J18 the formula

$$=IF(\$A18<=J\$17,(1/(1+\$E\$1)*MAX((J5-\$G\$2)*10000,0)+(\$G\$1*K18+(1-\$G\$1)*K19)*(1/(1+\$E\$1))),"-")$$

Copying this formula to B18:J26 computes the value of the lease for all other possible combinations of Year and gold prices. Note that a "-" is placed in any cell for which a value of the lease is undefined. We find the value of the lease to be $24.1 million.

Remark

The key value of the real option approach is that it lets us value flexibility. In our problem the flexibility is due to the fact that if gold prices go down, we do not have to mine the gold.

References

Luenberger, D., *Investment Science*, Oxford Press, 1997.

Chapter 41: Valuing an Option to Purchase a Company

The binomial tree approach to valuing an option is very flexible. It can be used to value many "real investment options" such as an option to purchase, and option to contract operations and an option to expand. Here is an example of how to use the binomial tree approach to value the option to purchase a company.

Example 41.1

Corpco is currently worth $50 million. The value of Corpco has an annual volatility of 40% and the risk-free rate is 10%. During each of the next five years we will have the option to buy Corpco at the following prices (in millions):

Year	Purchase Price
Now	$40
1 year later	$41
2 years later	$42
3 years later	$43
4 years later	$50
5 years later	$70

Assume that Corpco earns roughly 12% of its value during each year. Now, value the option to purchase Corpco. How sensitive is the value of this option to changes in volatility and interest rates? Determine a range of values for Corpco during each year for which you would purchase Corpco.

Solution

Our work is in file **Purchase.xls**. See Figure 41.1.

Figure 41.1

	A	B	C	D	E	F	G
1	American Option						
2	to purchase						
3	Current price	$ 50.00					
4	r	0.1	payout rate	0.12			
5	drift	-0.02	df	$ 0.91			
6	sigma	0.4					
7	t						
8	deltat	1					
9	u	1.491825					
10	d	0.67032					
11	a	0.980199					
12	p	0.377209					
13	q	0.622791					
14		Time					
15	Stock Prices	0	1	2	3	4	5
16	0	$ 50.00	$ 74.59	$ 111.28	$ 166.01	$ 53.22	$ 79.40
17	1		$ 33.52	$ 50.00	$ 74.59	$ 23.91	$ 35.68
18	2		-	$ 22.47	$ 33.52	$ 10.75	$ 16.03
19	3		-	-	$ 15.06	$ 4.83	$ 7.20
20	4		-	-	-	$ 2.17	$ 3.24
21	5		-	-	-	-	$ 1.45
22	Purchase Price	$ 40.00	$ 41.00	$ 42.00	$ 43.00	$ 50.00	$ 70.00
23		Purchase Value				$ 3.22	
24	Down Moves	0	1	2	3	4	5
25	0	$ 13.62	$ 33.59	$ 69.28	$ 123.01	$ 3.22	$ 9.40
26	1	-	$ 3.71	$ 10.83	$ 31.59	$ -	$ -
27	2	-	-	$ -	$ -	$ -	$ -
28	3	-	-	-	$ -	$ -	$ -
29	4	-	-	-	-	$ -	$ -
30	5	-	-	-	-	-	$ -

We note that the drift that keys our computation of u, d, and p will not equal r in this example. The reason is the firm pays out 12% of its value each year. Therefore, in a risk neutral world the firm would grow at r -.12 = -2% per year.

We use the same formulas to generate the possible values of Corpco that we used to generate stock prices in our American put example. All we need to do is change Δt to 1, because we are looking at the value of Corpco at yearly time intervals. We also use a drift rate of -2% for the stock price, due to 12% value payout. A smaller value of Δt would make our calculations more accurate. If, for example, we let Δt = .125 we would only allow purchase during periods 8, 16, 24, 32, and 40 but we would use the other periods to generate our possible prices during these periods.

Step 1: We enter the yearly purchase prices in B22:G22.

Step 2: In Year 5 we will purchase if and only if Corpco's value is at least as large as the purchase price ($70 million). We therefore determine in cell G25 the value of the purchase option if each price move for 5 years has been up with the formula

=MAX(G16-$G$22,0).

Copying this formula to G26:G30 computes the value of the purchase option for all other possible Year 5 prices.

Step 3: Suppose it is Year t and there have been I down moves. Then the value at Year t of the option to purchase is given by

(1) Maximum (Current value - Current Purchase Price), $\left(\dfrac{1}{1+r}\right)$ **(p*(Year t+1,I+1 up move value)+ q*(Year t+1, I up move value).*

If this Maximum is attained by Current value - Current Purchase Price, then we buy Corpco this year, otherwise we continue. To implement (1) we enter in cell F25 the formula

=IF($A25<=F$24,MAX(F16-F$22,df(*p*G25+q*G26)),"-").

We have defined our discount factor in cell D5 with the formula

=1/(1+B4).

Copying this formula to B25:F30 computes the value of the purchase option for all possible Corpco values during Years 0-4.

From cell B25 we find the option has a value of $13.62 million.

Step 4: To show in bold face the cells where purchasing Corpco is optimal use Conditional Formatting to enter the following format in cell G25

and select a bold-faced font. Using Edit>Copy> Paste Special>Formats we copy this format to the cell range B25:G30. Now any cell in which it is optimal to exercise our purchase option will be noted in bold face. This is because it is optimal to exercise the purchase option if and only if (Corpco value - Purchase price) = (Current value of option).

Sensitivity Analysis

Running a one-way data table on the volatility and risk-free rate (using column input cells sigma and r_, respectively) yields the results in Figure 41.2.

Figure 41.2

	H	I	J	K
5	Sensitivity Analysis			
6				
7	Volatility	13.62227	r	13.62227
8	0.1	10	0.01	15.00917
9	0.2	10	0.02	15.4777
10	0.3	11.19175	0.03	16.12656
11	0.4	13.62227	0.04	16.94568
12	0.5	15.94915	0.05	17.78608
13	0.6	18.17529	0.06	18.64767
14	0.7	20.29652	0.07	19.55564
15			0.08	20.68822
16			0.09	21.86826
17			0.1	23.09725
18			0.11	24.37675
19			0.12	25.70836

Note that an increase in either the volatility or the risk-free rate increases the value of the purchase option. The risk-free rate, however, has little impact on the value of the option to purchase.

When Do We Buy?

For each year t we determine a "cutoff point" p(t) defined as follows. If Year t value of Corpco is at least as large as the cutoff point, we will purchase (if we have not already done so) Corpco during Year t; if Year t value of Corpco is less than p(t) we will not purchase Corpco during Year t. The value p(t) is simply **the smallest value during Year t for which the value obtained by purchasing during Year t is at least as large as the value of continuing onward.** We illustrate the determination of p(3). See Figure 41.3.

Figure 41.3

	A	B	C	D	E	F	G
1	American Option						
2	to purchase						
3	Current price	$ 50.00					
4	r	0.1	payout rate	0.12			
5	drift	-0.02	df	$ 0.91			
6	sigma	0.4					
7	t						
8	deltat	1					
9	u	1.491825		Purchase in Year 3			
10	d	0.67032		if value>=$52.93.			
11	a	0.980199					
12	p	0.377209					
13	q	0.622791					
14		Time					
15	Stock Prices	0	1	2	3	4	5
16	0	$ 50.00	$ 74.59	$ 111.28	$ 52.93	$ 78.97	$ 117.81
17	1		$ 33.52	$ 50.00	$ 23.78	$ 35.48	$ 52.93
18	2		-	$ 22.47	$ 10.69	$ 15.94	$ 23.78
19	3		-	-	$ 4.80	$ 7.16	$ 10.69
20	4		-	-	-	$ 3.22	$ 4.80
21	5		-	-	-	-	$ 2.16
22	Purchase Price	$ 40.00	$ 41.00	$ 42.00	$ 43.00	$ 50.00	$ 70.00
23		Purchase Value			$ 9.93		
24	Down Moves	0	1	2	3	4	5
25	0	$ 13.07	$ 33.59	$ 69.28	$ 9.93	$ 28.97	$ 47.81
26	1	-	$ 2.74	$ 8.00	$ -	$ -	$ -
27	2	-	-	$ -	$ -	$ -	$ -
28	3	-	-	-	$ -	$ -	$ -
29	4	-	-	-	-	$ -	$ -
30	5	-	-	-	-	-	$ -

Step by Step

Step 1: Enter a trial Year 3 value for Corpco in cell E16.

Step 2: In cell E23 compute the value of purchasing in Year 3 with the formula

=E16-E22.

Step 3: The following Solver Window will determine p(3):

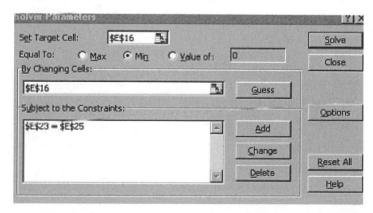

We seek the smallest Year 3 Corpco value (E16) for which it is optimal to purchase Corpco during Year 3 (it will be optimal to purchase Corpco if E23 = E25). We find p(3) = $52.93. Thus if we have not yet purchased Corpco, we should do so during Year 3 if its value is at least $52.93 million. In a similar fashion we find that the following "cutoff points" for firm value during each period. During a period we purchase if the firm value exceeds the cutoff point.

Year	Purchase Cutoff
1	Buy if value $\geq$ $79.16
2	Buy if value $\geq$ $59.63
3	Buy if value $\geq$ $52.93
4	Buy if value $\geq$ $53.22

Chapter 42: Valuing an Option to Abandon the Internet Startup

Let's recall our first real options example.

Example 42.1

We are thinking (see file **Startupabandon.xls**) of investing in a potential Internet start-up. We are quite sure that today and every three months for the next 21 months we will have to invest $0.5 million to keep the project going. Our present estimate of the NPV of revenues (less future operating costs) to be received from this project (revenues begin two years from now) is $22 million. We will have to spend $12 million two years from now to complete the start-up. Assume a risk-free rate of 5%. Should we go ahead with this project? Recall that today we believe the NPV of project revenues is $14.54 million. We also assume a 40% annual volatility.

By looking at this situation as a European call option we found its value to be $1.19 million. Now let's suppose that during each of the next seven quarters we may, if things look bad, abandon the project. For example, if during quarter 3 our estimate of the value of revenues is $3 million it hardly seems worthwhile to pump in $0.5 million during each quarter. By how much does the abandonment option increase the project's value?

Solution

Our work is in sheet abandon of file **Startupabandon.xls**. See Figure 42.1. In A1:B7 we compute the relevant parameters for our binomial tree. We use $\Delta t = .25$ years. In cell B8 we compute our discount factor per period as $\dfrac{1}{1+.25(.05)} = .99$.

We now proceed as follows:

Step by Step

Step 1: We begin by generating the set of possible revenue values for each quarter. We enter the current estimate of revenue value ($14.54 million) in cell B19. Then we generate the possible prices for each quarter by copying from J11 to C11:J19 the formula

$$=IF(\$A11>J\$9,"",IF(\$A11=J\$9,u*I12,(d/u)*J10)).$$

If a price is not possible, a blank is entered in the cell. For example we cannot have 7 up moves in 6 periods so cell H12 is blank. The highest possible price during each period is computed as u times time highest possible price during the previous period. In any other cell the price is computed as d/u times the price in the cell directly above.

Step 2: We now value the situation without the abandonment option. This will of course approximate the Black-Scholes answer of $1.19 million. We begin by finding the value of each period 8 node. This is simply Max (Revenue Value – 12,0). By copying from J22 to J23:J30 the formula

$$=MAX(J11\text{-}12,0)$$

we compute the value of the situation at Time 2 (Period 8) for each possible stock price.

Step 3: We now compute that value of each node in Periods 0-7. Let node (t,j) be period t node with j up moves of the stock. Let the value of the situation from the node (t,j) onward equal V(t,j). Then

$$V(t,j) = -.5 + \frac{1}{df}(pV(t+1, j+1) + (1-p)V(t+1, j)).$$

Here df = discount factor and p =risk neutral probability of an up move. This result follows because at any node we obtain with probability p a value V(t+1, j+1) and with probability 1-p obtain a value V(t + 1, j). Of course we must also pay $0.5 million during the current period. Copying from I23 to B30:I23 the following formula computes all node values

$$=IF(\$A23>I\$20, "", -0.5 + df^*(p^*J22 + (1-p)^*J23)).$$

This formula also puts a blank space in any cells for which there is no defined value.

We find that the value of the situation is $1.27 million. Choosing a smaller value of Δt would have resulted in a value closer to our Black-Scholes value of $1.19 million.

Step 4: We can now determine the amount by which our abandonment option increases the value of the situation. In J33:J42 we compute the period 8 value by copying from J33 to J34:J42 the formula

$$=MAX(J19\text{-}12,0).$$

If we define V(t,j) as before then we see that

$$V(t,j) = \max(0, -.5 + \frac{1}{df}(pV(t+1, j+1) + (1-p)V(t+1, j)).$$

This follows because at any node we can abandon (and earn 0 from that point onward) or pay $0.5 million and continue as before. By copying from I34 to B41:I34 the formula

=IF($A34>I$31,"",MAX(0,-0.5+df*(p*J33+(1-p)*J34)))

we compute the value of each time, stock price combination.

We find the value today (with the abandonment option) is $1.79 million. Thus the abandonment option is worth around $520,000.

When Should We Abandon?

To obtain the value of the abandonment option we must know at each time the range of revenue values for which abandonment is optimal. For example, during quarter 4 what ranges of revenue values lead to abandonment? To answer this question (see sheet Value) we go to the quarter 4 stock price with the highest value (cell F15) and put any number in that cell. The largest number in F15 (call it r*) that will make the project value (found in F37) equal to 0 represents the "boundary" between abandoning and not abandoning the project. If the quarter 4 revenue value exceeds r* we should keep going while if the quarter 4 revenue estimate is less than r* we should abandon the project. To find r* we simply solve the following Solver model.

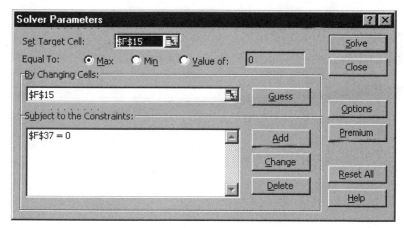

We find the largest Quarter 4 revenue value that makes the project value from Quarter 4 onward equal to 0. We find that if our Quarter 4 revenue estimate is less than $10.37 million we should abandon the project. Otherwise we should continue.

Figure 42.1

	A	B	C	D	E	F	G	H	I	J
1	r	0.05		Abandonment						
2	sigma	0.40								
3	deltat	0.25								
4	a	1.01								
5	u	1.22								
6	d	0.82								
7	p	0.48		1.01						
8	df	0.99								
9	**Firm Value**	0.00	1.00	2.00	3.00	4.00	5.00	6.00	7.00	8.00
10	up moves	0.00	0.25	0.50	0.75	1.00	1.25	1.50	1.75	2.00
11	8.00									72.02
12	7.00								58.96	48.27
13	6.00							48.27	39.52	32.36
14	5.00						39.52	32.36	26.49	21.69
15	4.00					32.36	26.49	21.69	17.76	14.54
16	3.00				26.49	21.69	17.76	14.54	11.90	9.75
17	2.00			21.69	17.76	14.54	11.90	9.75	7.98	6.53
18	1.00		17.76	14.54	11.90	9.75	7.98	6.53	5.35	4.38
19	0.00	14.54	11.90	9.75	7.98	6.53	5.35	4.38	3.59	2.94
20	**No abandonment**	0.00	1.00	2.00	3.00	4.00	5.00	6.00	7.00	8.00
21	Value from now on	0.00	0.25	0.50	0.75	1.00	1.25	1.50	1.75	2.00
22	8.00									60.02
23	7.00								46.62	36.27
24	6.00							35.58	27.18	20.36
25	5.00						26.49	19.67	14.14	9.69
26	4.00					18.99	13.46	9.00	5.41	2.54
27	3.00				12.87	8.47	5.02	2.43	0.71	0.00
28	2.00			7.98	4.61	2.12	0.44	-0.42	-0.50	0.00
29	1.00		4.17	1.71	0.04	-0.91	-1.21	-0.99	-0.50	0.00
30	0.00	1.27	-0.42	-1.44	-1.87	-1.83	-1.48	-0.99	-0.50	0.00
31	**Abandonment**	0.00	1.00	2.00	3.00	4.00	5.00	6.00	7.00	8.00
32		0.00	0.25	0.50	0.75	1.00	1.25	1.50	1.75	2.00
33	8.00									60.02
34	7.00								46.62	36.27
35	6.00							35.58	27.18	20.36
36	5.00						26.49	19.67	14.14	9.69
37	4.00					18.99	13.46	9.00	5.41	2.54
38	3.00				12.87	8.47	5.02	2.43	0.71	0.00
39	2.00			8.01	4.67	2.23	0.66	0.00	0.00	0.00
40	1.00		4.33	2.01	0.56	0.00	0.00	0.00	0.00	0.00
41	0.00	1.79	0.45	0.00	0.00	0.00	0.00	0.00	0.00	0.00

Chapter 43: Valuing an Option to Purchase with an Abandonment Option

When considering purchase of a company, it is important to add the option value of available opportunities to the straight DCF value in order to fairly value the purchase opportunity. Here is an example.

Example 43.1

You are thinking of buying Walco. You believe the current value of this business to be $100 million with a 45% annual volatility. The risk free rate is 5% and Walco pays out 20% of its value annually in cash flow. If you purchase Walco and things go sour at any time during the next five years in the US you can move Walco's assets to Europe where they are worth $75 million. Walco is willing to sell for $115 million. Should you take their offer?

Solution

We need to value a five-year American abandonment option with exercise price of $75 million. Our work is in file **Teleabd.xls**. Recall that in a risk-neutral world we grow the underlying asset (value of Walco) at risk-free rate less cash outflow rate (5%-20% = -15%). In Figure 43.1 we use our binomial approximation to compute p, u, d, and our discount factor. We will use $\Delta t = .1$, so 10 periods represents a year.

Figure 43.1

	A	B	C	D	E
1	drift	-0.15			**Telecom P**
2	sigma	0.45		r	0.05
3	deltat	0.1			
4	a	0.985112			
5	u	1.152925			
6	d	0.867359			
7	p	0.412349		0.985112	
8	df	0.995025			

Generating the Asset Values

In rows 9-61 we generate 50 periods of Walco asset values. See Figure 43.2

Figure 43.2

	A	B	C	D	E	AV	AW	AX	AY	AZ
9	Firm Value	Time	1	2	3	46	47	48	49	50
10	up moves	0	0.1	0.2	0.3	4.6	4.7	4.8	4.9	5
11	50									123043.7
12	49								106723	92567.18
13	48							92567.18	80288.96	69639.34
14	47						80288.96	69639.34	60402.3	52390.47
15	46					69639.34	60402.3	52390.47	45441.34	39413.94
16	45					52390.47	45441.34	39413.94	34186.03	29651.56
17	44					39413.94	34186.03	29651.56	25718.54	22307.2
18	43					29651.56	25718.54	22307.2	19348.35	16781.96
19	42					22307.2	19348.35	16781.96	14555.98	12625.26
52	9					1.86023	1.613487	1.399472	1.213845	1.052839
53	8					1.399472	1.213845	1.052839	0.913189	0.792063
54	7					1.052839	0.913189	0.792063	0.687003	0.595878
55	6					0.792063	0.687003	0.595878	0.51684	0.448286
56	5					0.595878	0.51684	0.448286	0.388825	0.33725
57	4					0.448286	0.388825	0.33725	0.292517	0.253717
58	3				153.2511	0.33725	0.292517	0.253717	0.220064	0.190874
59	2			132.9237	115.2925	0.253717	0.220064	0.190874	0.165557	0.143597
60	1		115.2925	100	86.73588	0.190874	0.165557	0.143597	0.12455	0.10803
61	0	100	86.73588	75.23114	65.25239	0.143597	0.12455	0.10803	0.0937	0.081272

To do this enter Walco's current asset value ($100 million) in cell B61. Then copy from AZ11 to AZ11:C61 the formula

$$=IF(\$A11>AZ\$9,"",IF(\$A11=AZ\$9,u*AY12,(d/u)*AZ10)).$$

The first part of the formula places a blank in any cell that corresponds to a number of up moves exceeding the period number. The second part of the formula makes sure that during period t the firm value for t up moves is u times the previous period's value for t – 1 up moves. The final part of the formula computes all other firm values as d/u times the firm value computed in the cell directly above.

Working Backwards to Determine the Option Value

In Rows 62-113 (see Figure 43.3) we compute the value of the option from the current time onward at any stage for any given number of up moves. More formally, let V(t, k) = Value of abandonment option if we are in stage t and have seen k up moves.

Figure 43.3

	A	B	C	D	E	AV	AW	AX	AY	AZ
62	Abandonment	0	1	2	3	46	47	48	49	50
63	50									0
64	49								0	0
65	48							0	0	0
66	47						0	0	0	0
67	46					0	0	0	0	0
68	45					0	0	0	0	0
69	44					0	0	0	0	0
102	11					72.14918	72.52731	72.85529	73.13977	73.13977
103	10					72.85529	73.13977	73.38651	73.60053	73.60053
104	9					73.38651	73.60053	73.78616	73.94716	73.94716
105	8					73.78616	73.94716	74.08681	74.20794	74.20794
106	7					74.08681	74.20794	74.313	74.40412	74.40412
107	6					74.313	74.40412	74.48316	74.55171	74.55171
108	5					74.48316	74.55171	74.61118	74.66275	74.66275
109	4					74.61118	74.66275	74.70748	74.74628	74.74628
110	3				24.30056	74.70748	74.74628	74.77994	74.80913	74.80913
111	2			27.48174	29.94776	74.77994	74.80913	74.83444	74.8564	74.8564
112	1		30.59861	33.04605	35.50125	74.83444	74.8564	74.87545	74.89197	74.89197
113	0	33.60957	36.00829	38.39324	40.74918	74.87545	74.89197	74.9063	74.91873	74.91873

During stage 50 we will exercise the option if and only if firm value is less than $75 million. Then the option will yield $75 million – Stage 50 firm value. More formally,

$$V(50,k) = \max(0, 75 - Stage\,50\,asset\,value).$$

We implement this formula by copying from AZ60 to AZ61:AZ113 the formula

= IF(AZ11<75,75-AZ11,0).

During any stage before stage 50 our option is worth the maximum of what we can get by exercising the option during the current period and the expected discounted value of what we can get by keeping the option "live." Of course, our expected discounted value is computed in a risk neutral world. In short for t<50 we have that

$$V(t,k) = \max(75 - Asset\,value\,at\,time\,t\,after\,k\,up\,moves, df*(pV(t+1,k+1) + (1-p)V(t+1,k)).$$

We implement this formula by copying from AY64:B113 the formula

= IF($A64>AY$62," ",MAX(75-AZ12,df*(p*AZ63+(1-p)*AZ64))).

Note the first part of the formula enters a space during stage t in any cell that corresponds to more than t up moves.

From cell B113 we find the abandonment option to be worth $33.6 million. Therefore the total worth of Walco to us is nearly $134 million. Buying Walco for $115 million would be a bargain, **but only if we recognize the worth of the abandonment option**.

Chapter 44: Using Simulation to Value European Real Options

The risk-neutral approach discussed in Chapter 35 is very powerful. It enables us to value many quantities that **derive** their value from an underlying asset. In most books, you do this by finding a combination of puts and calls which replicates the payoffs of what you are trying to value. We do not need to do this. Just use the lognormal to simulate the future value of the underlying asset (growing at risk-free rate) and then make your output cell be the discounted value of the payoffs you receive. The mean of your output cell is the value you seek. **This approach only works for European options, because for American options the timing of the cash flows is unknown.** Here are six examples:

Example 44.1

The current price of IBM is 145 and 1/8. In 64 days Gerstner will be paid as follows: For every $1 increase in stock price up to $10 he receives $1 million; for every $1 increase in stock price over $10 Gerstner receives $500,000. What is a fair market value for Lou's option?

Solution

We need the volatility of the price of IBM stock. By looking at traded options we can estimate the implied volatility (see file **IBMvols.xls** and Figure 44.1).

Figure 44.1

		A	B	C	D
1	IBM OPTIONS	April	April	April
2	Current Price	145.125	145.125	145.125
3	Duration	0.175342	0.175342	0.175342
4	Volatility	0.327147	0.327147	0.327147
5	Exercise Price	140	150	160
6	Risk-free Rate	0.0636	0.0636	0.0636
7	d1	0.412352	-0.09128	-0.5624
8	d2	0.275362	-0.22827	-0.69939
9	N(d1)	0.659959	0.463633	0.28692
10	N(d2)	0.608481	0.409717	0.242153
11	Option Price(theory)	11.53395	6.50882	3.324504
12				
13	Option Price(actual)	12	6.25	3.125
14	Squared Error	0.217206	0.066988	0.039802
15				
16	SSE	0.323996		

In row 13 we have listed the price of three call options which expire in 64 days (exercise prices $140, $150, and $160. We have created a Black-Scholes template that, upon entering volatility in row 4 computes a Black-Scholes price in Row 11. We want to find a single volatility which best predicts these prices. We choose B4 to be our changing cell for volatility and minimize sum of squared errors (actual-predicted price)^2 for the three options (cell B16). Our Solver Window is as follows:

Figure 44.2

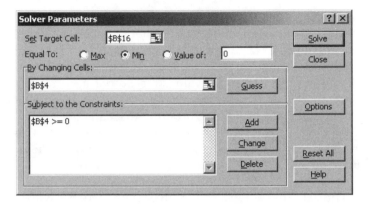

We find an implied volatility of 32.7%. We can now value our option. (See Figure 44.3 and file **Gerstner.xls**).

Figure 44.3

	A	B	C	D	E	F
4	Current Price	145.125				
5	Volatility	0.327				
6	Riskfree rate	0.0636				
7	Duration	0.175342			Name	Discounted payoff
8	Normal	0			Description	Output
9	Later Stock Price	145.3831			Cell	B11
10	Payoff(millions)	0.258143			Minimum =	0
11	Discounted payoff	0.25528			Maximum =	47.52227
12					Mean =	6.374745
13					Std Deviation =	8.484468
14					Variance =	71.98619
15					Skewness =	1.281692
16					Kurtosis =	4.098358

Step 1:In B4-B7 we enter relevant parameters, including the implied volatility.

Step 2: In B8 we enter a Normal (0,1) variable with formula

   =RiskNormal(0,1).

Step 3: In B9 we compute the stock price in 64 days using lognormal growth at the risk-free rate and known volatility:

   =B4*EXP((B6-0.5*B5^2)*B7+B8*SQRT(B7)*B5)

Step 4: In B10 we compute Gerstner's payoff with the statement

   =IF(AND((B9-B4)>=0,(B9-B4)<10),(B9-B4),IF(B9-B4)>=10,10+0.5*(B9-
   (B4+10)),0)).

This pays Lou $1 million per dollar increase up to $10 and $0.5 million per dollar increase beyond that point.

Step 5: In B11 we discount this payoff back to the current time with the formula

   =EXP(-B6*B7)*B10.

Step 6: After making B11 our output cell we find our best estimate is that the fair market value is $6.37 million.

Example
44.2

An asset is currently worth $553,000 and has an annual volatility of 28%. The risk-free rate is 5%. A year from now I may sell the asset for a salvage value of $500,000. How much is this abandonment option worth?

Let V = value of asset one year from now. Then a year from now option returns

   Max(0, $500,000 - V) (1)

If we let the asset grow for one year at the risk-free rate and with the given volatility and take a discounted value of (1) as our output cell, then the mean of our output cell is the value of the abandonment option. Our work is in Figure 44.4 and file **Abandonment.xls**.

Figure 44.4

	A	B	C	D	E	F	G
1	Abandonment						
2	Abandonment value		$ 500,000.00				
3	r	Volatility	Current Price	Normal(0,1	Price 1 year from now	Value of Option	Discounted value
4	0.05	0.28	$ 553,000.00	0.387636	$ 623,093.16	0	0

We proceed as follows:

Step 1: In D4 enter a standard normal (mean 0, sigma of 1) random variable with the formula

 =RiskNormal(0,1)

Step 2: In E4 generate the value of the asset a year from now using the lognormal random variable. The formula is

 =C4*EXP((A4-0.5*B4^2)+B4*D4).

Step 3: In F4 we exploit (1) to generate the value of the option's cash flows one year from now with the formula

 =IF(E4<C2,C2-E4,0).

Step 4: In cell G4 compute the discounted value of the option's cash flows with the formula

 =EXP(-A4)*F4.

Step 5: After choosing G4 as our output cell we find the option is worth $34,093.

	D	E
7	Name	Discounted value
8	Description	Output
9	Cell	G4
10	Minimum =	0
11	Maximum =	280536.9
12	Mean =	34,092.91
13	Std Deviation =	54,870.25
14	Variance =	3.01E+09

Example 44.3

This example describes an option to postpone (based on Trigeorgis (1995)). The current risk-free rate is 8%. We can build a plant now costing $104 million and gain revenues worth (risk adjusted) $100 million. Revenues begin one year from now. Therefore current value of project is -$4 million and project does not appear worthwhile. Suppose, however, project's value has a 60% annual volatility and we can wait one year before investing in this project. What is the worth of this option? Assume that construction costs grow at the risk-free rate.

Solution   Our work is in Figure 44.5 and the file **Postpone.xls**. Let V = value of project one year from now. Then value of option to postpone is

$$=max(0, V - e^{.08}(104)) \quad (2)$$

This is because we will invest one year from now only if the value of the project exceeds the cost (which one year from now will be $e^{.08}(104)$).

Figure 44.5

	A	B	C	D	E	F	G	H	I
1	Postpone Investment								
2									
3									
4	r	Current value	Investment cost	Value with no option	Volatility	Normal (0,1)	Value One year from now	Cash flows in one year from waiting	Discounted value of cash flows
5	0.08	100	104	-4	0.6	1.6431	242.5075	129.8456	119.86261
6									

We now proceed as follows:

Step by Step   **Step 1: Enter the needed parameters in A5-E5.**

Step 2: In F5 enter a Normal(0,1) with the formula

$$=RiskNormal(0,1)$$

Step 3: In G5 use the lognormal to compute the value of the asset one year from now with the formula

$$=B5*EXP((A5-0.5*E5^2)+F5*E5).$$

Step 4: In H5 we use (2) to determine the cash flows obtained in one year with the formula

$$=MAX(0,G5-C5*EXP(A5)).$$

Step 5: Discount the value of the cash flows back to time 0 in cell I5 with the formula

$$=EXP(-A5)*H5.$$

Step 6: Make I5 an output cell and find that with the option our situation is worth \$22.14 million.

	D	E
8		
9	Name	Discounted value of cash flows
10	Description	Output
11	Cell	I5
12	Minimum =	0
13	Maximum =	664.8685
14	Mean =	22.14528
15	Std Deviation =	50.32
16	Variance =	2532.108
17	Skewness =	4.171664
18	Kurtosis =	31.00052

Thus the option to postpone improves our position by 22.14 - (-4) = $26.14 million relative to our position if we did the project without having the option to postpone the project.

Valuing the Option to Expand

We now modify Example 44.3 to show how we evaluate an option to expand a project.

Example 44.4

Assume you have the option to spend $40 million one year from now on a plant expansion that will increase the project's value by 50%. Value this expansion option.

Solution

Our work is in the file **Expand.xls**. See Figure 44.6

Figure 44.6

	A	B	C	D	E	F
1	Expand for 40 million by 50%?					
2						
3						
4	r	Current value	Investment cost	Value with no option	Volatility	Normal (0,1)
5	0.08	100	104	-4	0.6	-0.16196

	G	H	I	J	K
3					
4	Value One year from now	Cash Flows in One Year	Discounted value of cash flows	Expansion cost	Expansion factor
5	82.10484	83.15726	-27.236177	40	0.5

We proceed as follows:

Step by Step

Step 1 : In A5:E5 and J5:K5 we enter relevant parameters for the problem.

Step 2: In cell F5 we enter

  =RiskNormal(0,1).

This will help us generate the value of the project one year from now.

Step 3: In cell G5 we generate the (random) value of the project one year from now with the formula

  =B5*EXP((A5-0.5*E5^2)+F5*E5).

Step 4: Note that if we choose to expand, our cash flows in one year will equal

1.5*(value in one year) - 40.

If we do not expand, our cash flows in one year will simply equal the value of the project. Therefore in H5 we compute our cash flows in one year with the formula

  =MAX((1+K5)*G5-J5,G5).

Step 5: In cell I5 we compute the discounted value of our cash flows with the formula

  =EXP(-A5)*H5-C5.

Step 6: We now select cell I5 as our output cell. We find after 4000 iterations that with the option to expand our situation is worth an average of $14.08 million. Thus the option to expand improves our position over doing the project right away by $18.08 million.

	D	E
11	Cell	I5
12	Minimum =	-91.8832
13	Maximum :	987.4983
14	Mean =	14.08345
15	Std Deviati	95.02
16	Variance =	9029.213
17	Skewness	2.609704

Valuing the Option to Contract

Now we modify Example 44.3 to value the option to contract a project.

Example 44.5

Instead of paying the entire $104 million plant cost now you must only pay $50 million now. A year from now you may pay the remaining $54 million cost (with interest) and obtain the full project value or you may contract the scale of the project by paying only $25 million. If you contract the scale of the project the project will be worth only 50% of what it would have actually been worth. Value this contraction option.

Solution

Our work is in the file **Contract.xls**. See Figure 44.7.

Figure 44.7

	A	B	C	D	E	F	G	H
1	Contract Project?							
2	Pay 50 million now							
3	One year from now pay 25 million and get .5 of value or pay 54*exp(.08) and get whole project							
4	r	Current value	Investment cost now	Volatility	Normal (0,1)	Value One year from now	Cash Flows in One Year	Discounted value of cash flows
5	0.08	100	50	0.6	0	90.48374	31.98624	-20.472979

	I	J	K
3			
4	Cost if Contracted	Cost in one year to keep going(today's $s)	Contraction Factor
5	25	54	0.5

We proceed as follows:

Step by Step

Step 1: Enter the relevant parameters in cells A5:D5 and I5:K5.

Step 2: In cell E5 enter

  =RiskNormal(0,1).

This random variable will be used in F5 to generate the value of the project in one year.

Step 3: In cell F5 we generate the value of the project in one year with the formula

=B5*EXP((A5-0.5*D5^2)+E5*D5).

Step 4: In G5 we compute the cash flows from the project in one year. Note that if we contract the project our cash flows in one year are given by

.5*(Value of project) - $25 million.

If we do not contract the project our cash flows in one year are given by

(Value of Project) - e$^{.08}$*($54 million)

Since we can choose the better of these options in G5 we compute the cash flows from the project in one year with the formula

=MAX(F5-EXP(A5)*J5,K5*F5-I5).

Step 5: In cell H5 we compute the total discounted value of the cash flows from the project with the formula

=EXP(-A5)*G5-C5.

Step 6: Choosing cell H5 as an output cell yields a mean of -$1.28 million. This improves our situation over immediately doing project by $2.72 million.

	D	E
10	Name	Discounted value of cash flows
11	Description	Output
12	Cell	H5
13	Minimum =	-68.05699
14	Maximum =	515.879
15	Mean =	-1.28
16	Std Deviation	62.90
17	Variance =	3956.415
18	Skewness =	2.348511
19	Kurtosis =	11.81437

A "Pioneer" Option

Often companies enter into small projects that have a negative NPV. The reason for this is that participation in the smaller project gives the company the option to later participate in a larger project that may have a large positive NPV. Merck Pharmaceuticals, led by their CFO Judy Lewent (see Nichols (1994)) has "pioneered" the use of real option theory. Here is an example of this idea, again based on Trigeorgis (1996).

Example 44.6

Merck is debating whether to invest in a pioneer biotech project. They estimate the worth of this project to be -$56 million. Investing in the pioneer project gives Merck the option to own, if they desire, a much bigger technology that will be available in 4 years. If Merck does not participate in the Pioneer project **they cannot own the bigger project**. The big project will require $1.5 billion in cash 4 years from now. Currently Merck estimates the NPV of the cash flows from the bigger project to be $597 million. What should Merck do? Risk free rate is 10% and annual volatility of big project is 35%.

Solution

Our solution is in the file **Pioneer.xls**. See Figure 44.8.

Figure 44.8

	A	B
1	**Buying a Pioneer Project**	
2		
3	NPV of pioneer project	-5.6E+07
4	Current NPV of new technology	5.97E+08
5	Year 4 cost of New Technology	1.5E+09
6	r	0.1
7	Annual volatility	0.35
8	Normal (0,1)	0.513126
9	Value of project in 4 years	9.98E+08
10	NPV in year 4 of doing new Project	0
11	Discounted NPV of doing new project	0

We proceed as follows:

Step 1: Enter relevant parameter values in B3:B7

Step 2: In B8 generate a standard normal that will be used to generate the value of the project in four years with the formula

=*RiskNormal(0,1).*

Step 3: In cell B9 generate the value of the project in four years with the formula

=*B4*EXP((B6-0.5*B7^2)*4+B8*SQRT(4)*B7).*

Step 4: In cell B10 we compute the NPV (in Year 4 \$s) of doing the new Project

=*MAX(B9-B5,0).*

This assumes, of course, that we only do the new project if it is worthwhile.

Step 5: In cell B11 we compute the value (in today's dollars) of doing the new project.

=*EXP(-4*B6)*B10.*

Step 6: We choose B11 as our Output cell. We obtain a mean of \$69 million. This more than outweighs the negative NPV of the Pioneer project, so we should go ahead with the Pioneer project.

A natural question is what is the smallest volatility that would make the option value at least \$56 million? This question can easily be answered using RISKOptimizer. See Winston (1999) for an introduction to the use of RISKOptimizer. Simply find the smallest volatility that makes the mean of cell B11 at least \$56 million. See file **Pioneer2.xls** and Figure 44.9. The RISKOptimizer settings are given below.

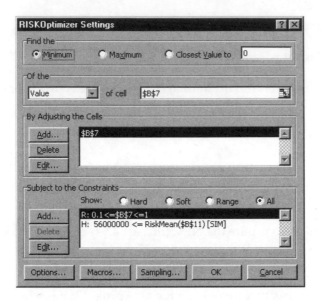

Figure 44.9

	A	B	C
1	**Buying a Pioneer Project**		
2			
3	NPV of pioneer project	-56000000	
4	Current NPV of new technology	597000000	
5	Year 4 cost of New Technology	1.5E+09	
6	r	0.1	
7	Annual volatility	0.3198152	
8	Normal (0,1)	0	
9	Value of project in 4 years	725857434	
10	NPV in year 4 of doing new Project	0	
11	Discounted NPV of doing new project	0	.319
12	Mean of B11	56166698	
13			

We find that a 32% volatility is the smallest volatility for which the value of the option is enough to compensate for the negative NPV of the project.

Remarks

Chapter 21 of Brealey and Myers (1996) contains an excellent introduction to real options. The two books by Trigeorgis contain a comprehensive (though advanced) discussion of real options. We refer the reader to Luenberger (1997) for an excellent discussion of real options.

Of course, it is difficult to come up with volatility for a project. Looking at implied volatilities for companies in a similar industry may be helpful. Probably the best strategy is to use a data table to value the option for a wide range of volatilities.

References

Brealey, S. and Myers, R., *Principles of Corporate Finance,* Prentice Hall, 1996

Luenberger, D., *Investment Science*, Oxford Press, 1997

Nichols, N., "Scientific Management at Merck," *Harvard Business Review,* Vol. 72, No. 1, pages 89-99, 1994.

Trigeorgis, L., *Real Options,* MIT Press, 1996

Trigeorgis, L., *Real Options and Capital Investment*, Praeger, 1995

Winston, W., *Decision Making Under Uncertainty Using RISKOptimizer*, Palisade, 1999.

Chapter 45: Using Simulation to Value an Option to Develop Vacant Land

A classic example in the real options literature is the option to develop vacant land. The idea is that if we wait a while before building on the land, the land may substantially increase in value. Our simulation approach makes this an easy problem to solve. Here is an example (based on Titman).

Example 45.1

Georgia Woodward is trying to determine whether or not you should develop vacant land into a 6 or 9 unit apartment complex. It will cost $480,000 to build a six-unit complex and $810,000 to build a 9-unit complex (cost will remain unchanged if you build next year). Current market value of an apartment unit is $100,000. The risk free rate is 10% and the annual volatility of the value of an apartment unit is 30%. Also the apartment pays 8% of its value in profits each year. Georgia has the option to build now or wait a year. What value would you place on the option to wait a year?

Solution

We first determine the value of the current situation and then the value of the situation with the option. The difference represents the value of waiting. If we build a 9 unit complex now we earn 9*(100,000) – 810,000 = $90,000. If we build a six unit complex now we earn 6*(100,000) – 480,000 = $120,000. Therefore the current situation indicates that we will earn $120,000 by building a 6-unit complex. If we wait, then the current value of a unit ($100,000) will grow according to a lognormal random variable. In risk neutral valuation the drift will not equal the risk-free rate. **It will equal the risk-free rate less the "dividend or payout rate" of 8%.** Thus value of a unit will grow at average rate of 2% per year. Now we can generate a random value of a unit a year from now and choose (based on that unit value) the optimal decision between our three options: build nothing, build a 6-unit complex, or build a 9 unit complex. Our work is in file **Landsim.xls**.

Figure 45.1

	A	B	C	D	E	F	G	H
1	Developing Vacant land							
2								
3	Build 6 units	480000						
4	Build 9 units	810000						
5	Current unit value	100000						
6	Volatility	0.3						
7	r	0.1						
8	payout rate	0.08						
9	Profit for 6 now	120000						
10	Profit for 9 now	90000						
11	Build 6 now	120000						
12	Normal (0,1)	-0.797526809						
13	Unit value in one year	76777.53952						
14	Build 6 next year	-19334.76285						
15	Build 9 next year	-119002.1443						
16	Do Nothing next year	0						
17	Profit next year	0						
18	PV of next year's profit	0						
19						If we have option to wait a year before building situation is worth		
20						$165,000, which is $45,000 better than building now.		
21								
22	Mean value	165017.7845						
23								
24		0						
25	1	30037.78067						
26	2	91136.8592						
27	3	205330.438						
28	4	423243.2302						

Step by Step

Step 1: In cell B12 we generate a normal random variable that is used in B12 to generate next year's value of a unit.

$$= RiskNormal(0,1)$$

Step 2: In cell B13 we use our lognormal simulation formula (with μ = .10 - .08 and σ = .30) to generate a random value of a unit in one year's time.

$$=B5*EXP((B7-0.5*B6\wedge2-B8)+B12*B6).$$

Step 3: In cells B14:B16 we compute the value of each option (Build 6 units next year, Build 9 units next year, and Build nothing next year) with the following formulas:

$$=6*B13-B3 \ (Build \ 6 \ units)$$

$$=9*B13-B4 \ (Build \ 9 \ units)$$

$$=0 \ (Build \ nothing).$$

Step 4: In B17 we compute our Year 1 profit by choosing the best of our three possible profits:

=MAX(B14,B15,B16).

Step 5: In cell B18 we compute our discounted profit with the formula

=EXP(-B7)*B17.

Step 6: After running 1600 iterations of @RISK we found an average discounted profit of $165,000. This indicates that the option to wait one year before developing the land is worth around $165,000 - $120,000 = $45,000.

Reference

Titman, S., "Urban Prices Under Uncertainty," *American Economic Review*, Vol. 75 No. 3, June, 1985, pages 505-514.

Chapter 46: Using Simulation to Value a Compound Option

The development of many high-tech projects (such as a new drug or a software product) proceeds as follows:

At time 0 we spend an amount of money (D) to get the project going. We also have some idea of the eventual revenues the project will earn.

At time $t_1 < T$ we need to spend some more money (D') in order to keep the project going. We also have the option to stop the project at time t_1. Clearly if our current estimate of future project revenues is favorable we will keep going. Otherwise we will stop.

If we have kept the project going at time t_1, then at time T we can, if we desire, spend D'' to complete the project. Clearly if our current estimate of future project revenues exceeds D'' we will keep going. Otherwise we will stop.

This type of situation is known as a **compound option**. Essentially at time t_1 we have an option to pay D'. If we pay D' we gain the right or option to pay D'' at time T and complete the project. Essentially a compound option is an "option on an option." We now show how to value a compound option. Our example (but not solution method) is based on Perlitz et. al.

Example 46.1

A drug company is undertaking development of a new drug. Today they will make a $25 million investment that is used to screen many potential compounds. After three years, the screening process will be complete and they can conduct clinical trials, if desired, at a cost of $90 million. Finally, 10 years from now we can, if desired, invest $500 million and bring the drug to market. Our current estimate of the cash inflows from the drug is $800 million (in Time 10 dollars). This estimate would, of course, have some adjustment for risk contained in its computation. Annual volatility of revenues is estimated to be 60%. The company's cost of capital is 14% and the risk-free rate for a ten-year bond is 4%. How would you value this opportunity?

Solution

We begin with the traditional DCF approach. Our work is in sheet **Compopt.xls**. See Figure 46.1.

Figure 46.1

	A	B	C	D	E	F
1	**Compound Option**	vol	0.6			
2		r	0.04	0.039221		
3		wacc	0.14			
4	Time	Payment	Revenue	DF		
5	0	25		1		
6	3	90		0.674972		
7	10	500	800	0.269744		
8	NPV	220.6193	215.795			
9						
10	Project value DCF	-4.824294				
11	Option Approach		Normal RV			
12	Revenue value now	215.795				
13	Revenue value in 3 yrs	141.4564	0			
14	Cutoff	390				
15	Go ahead?	no				
16	Revenue value in 10 years	52.80132	0			
17						
18	Cash Flows	Time	Amount	DF		
19		0	-25	1		
20		3	0	0.888996		
21		10	0	0.675564		
22						
23		DCF	-25			
24						
25						
26					Mean = 47.4001	
27						

In cells E4:E6 we compute the NPV (at 14%) of all the project's cash flows. For example NPV of Time 10 cash flow is $\dfrac{300}{1.14^{10}} = \$80.92$. Note from cell E7 the traditional DCF approach yields an NPV of -$4.82 million, indicating that we should not undertake the project.

We now value this opportunity using the risk-neutral approach. We assume our revenue estimate will change according to a lognormal random variable having

μ = Ln(1 +.04) and σ = .25. We use this lognormal random variable to generate revenue values at Time 3 and Time 10. Based on our revenue value at Time 3, we must decide to continue. For some cutoff point c* we will continue (and pay $90 million at Time 3) if Time 3 revenue estimate is at least c*. Otherwise we will stop development. If we have continued at Time 3 we look at our Time 10 revenue estimate. If it exceeds $500 million, then we complete the project. For many possible values of c* we simulate the project's DCF in a risk neutral world many times. The mean DCF for the value of c* yielding the largest mean DCF gives our estimate of the project's value! Here is how things go:

Step by Step

Step 1: In cell B12 compute the value in today's dollars of our current revenue estimate with the formula

$$=C7/((1+C3)^{\wedge}10)$$

Step 2: After entering a standard normal random variable in cell C13 use the lognormal random variable to generate in cell B13 a Year 3 revenue estimate with the formula

$$=B12*EXP((D2-0.5*vol^{\wedge}2)*A6+C13*SQRT(A6)*vol)$$

Step 3: After entering a standard normal random variable in cell C16 use the lognormal random variable to generate in cell B16, conditioned on our Year 3 revenue estimate, a Year 10 revenue estimate with the formula

$$=B13*EXP((D2-0.5*vol^{\wedge}2)*(A7-A6)+C16*SQRT(A7-A6)*vol).$$

Step 4: In cell B14 we entered a trial value c* for our Year 3 revenue estimate. If during Year 3 our revenue estimate is greater than c* we pay $90 million and have an option to complete the project at Time 10. If our Year 3 revenue estimate is less than c*, then we terminate the project and do not pay the $90 million.

Note we only have a Year 10 cash flow if our Year 10 revenue estimate is at least $500 million.

Step 5: In C19 we compute our cash flow at Time 0 (-$25 million). In cell C20 compute our Year 3 cash flow with the formula

$$=IF(B13>B14,-B6,0).$$

This incurs the cost of continuing at Year 3 if and only if Year 3 revenue exceeds our cutoff for continuing. In cell C21 we compute the Year 10 cash flow with the formula

$$=IF(AND(B15="yes",B16>B7),B16-B7,0)$$

If we went ahead at Year 3 and Year 10 Revenue Value is at least $500 million, then at Year 10 we get Year 10 Revenue Value -$500 million. Otherwise we get $0.

Step 6: In cells D20:D22 we compute the discount factor for each cash flow by copying from D20 to D21:D22 the formula

$$=EXP(-\$D\$2*B19).$$

Step 7: In cell C23 we compute the total NPV of all cash flows with the formula

=SUMPRODUCT(C19:C21,D19:D21).

Step 8: We now use RISKOptimizer (see Winston (1999) for a discussion of RISKOptimizer) to determine the cutoff point maximizes mean NPV. Our settings are as follows.

We choose a cutoff point that is an integer between 1 and 1000 that maximizes our mean NPV. RISKOptimizer yields a cutoff point of $390 million. This gives us a mean NPV of $47.4 million. Thus if we continue with project at Year 3 if revenue estimate is at least $390 million and finish project at Year 10 if the Year 10 revenue estimate is at least $500 million, we will earn an average NPV of $47.4 million.

Remark

Note that the option value for the situation is much higher than the traditional DCF value. This is because the traditional DCF valuation does not allow for the possibility of bailing out at Year 3 when things look bad or bailing out at Year 10 when things look bad.

Reference

Perlitz, M., Peske, T., Schrank, R., "Real Options Valuation: the New Frontier in R&D Project Evaluation?", *R&D Management*, Vol. 29. , No. 3, July 1999, pages 255-269.

Winston, W., *Decision-Making with RISKOptimizer*, Palisade, 1999.

Chapter 47: Using Simulation to Value a Licensing Agreement

Often a company likes to purchase a new product with the fee being tied to the profitability of the product. Simulation and the risk neutral valuation approach can be used to value such an agreement.

Example 47.1

We are thinking of purchasing the rights to sell a software package. Our current estimate of the value (to us) of future sales is $400 million. We are offering to compensate the developer by paying him (beginning in one year and through the end of year 20) each year 40% of all profits in excess of $50 million. What is this payment worth? Assume a risk-free rate of 6%, annual volatility of 50%, and that the project earns an average of 12% of its value each year.

Solution

We simply use the lognormal random variable (with μ = .06 -.12 and σ = 50%) to generate the project value for each year. Then we generate each year's profits. Whenever a year has profits in excess of $50 million, we credit 40% of the excess profit. Then we sum up the discounted cash flows. Finally we use @RISK to simulate the DCF cell. The average value of the DCF is a fair value for the licensing agreement. See file **licensesim.xls** and Figure 47.1.

Figure 47.1

	A	B	C	D	E	F	G	H	I	J	K
1											
2	Licensing										
3	Software	values in millions									
4											
5	Current value	400									
6	r	0.06									
7	q	0.12									
8	sigma	0.5									
9	Payout	0.4									
10											
11											
12											
13				DCF		0					
14											
15		Time	Curent value	Payout	Discounted payout	Rand #			Name	Workbook	Mean
16		0	400						Output 1	DCF	licensesim.xls	77.89199
17		1	408.4805272	0	0	0.411959					
18		2	194.8543262	0	0	-1.110384					
19		3	144.3301778	0	0	-0.230297					
20		4	99.11914317	0	0	-0.381562					
21		5	56.62270223	0	0	-0.749825					
22		6	42.588448	0	0	-0.199654					
23		7	40.26940647	0	0	0.269018					
24		8	36.57169053	0	0	0.177365					
25		9	41.98405132	0	0	0.646031					
26		10	40.55740968	0	0	0.300857					
27		11	69.42953052	0	0	1.445188					
28		12	66.82143568	0	0	0.293423					
29		13	73.39619059	0	0	0.557696					
30		14	155.8790516	0	0	1.876417					
31		15	72.80869924	0	0	-1.15249					
32		16	44.22675141	0	0	-0.627011					
33		17	44.39863203	0	0	0.377758					
34		18	13.1112139	0	0	-2.069482					
35		19	10.78595349	0	0	-0.020446					
36		20	12.97020514	0	0	0.73882					

Step 1: In C17:C36 we use the lognormal random variable (keying off standard normal random variables entered in F17:F36) to compute the project value each year by copying from C17 to C18:C36 the following formula:

$=C16*EXP((r\_-q-0.5*sigma^2)*1+SQRT(1)*sigma*F17).$

Note we reduce the risk-free rate by the payout rate of 12%.

Step 2: In D17:D36 we compute the payout to the licensee by copying from D17: to D18:D36 the formula

$=IF(q*C17>50,0.4*(q*C17-50),0).$

Again, during each year we pay the licensee 40% of any profits exceeding $50 million.

Step 3: In E17:E36 we compute the discounted cash flow of the licensee's payout for each year by copying from E17 to E18:E36 the formula

$=EXP(-r\_*B17)*D17.$

Step 4: In cell E13 we compute our total DCF in the risk neutral world with the formula

$=SUM(E17:E36).$

Step 5: After selecting cell E13 as an output cell we found the mean DCF to be $78 million.

Therefore a fair value for the licensing agreement is $78 million.

Chapter 48: Using the Jump Diffusion Model to Value Real Options

The lognormal model of stock prices and project values has been criticized as not accurately reflecting the movement of stock prices and asset values. For example, when looking at the value of a new product, the entrance of a major competitor may almost instantly reduce the project value by say, 30%. The lognormal random variable does not allow for sudden jumps in stock or project value. **The jump diffusion model** does allow for sudden jumps. The jump diffusion model assumes that at each point in time there is a small chance of a jump. At times when a jump does not occur, the change in stock or asset value follows a traditional lognormal random variable. In the file **Jumpdiffusion.xls** we have included templates that let you value puts or calls under a jump diffusion process. See Figure 48.1. Cell N15 of sheet call yields the call price.

Figure 48.1

	A	B	C	D	E	F	G	H	I	J	K	L	M	N
1														
2	Jump Diffusion													
3	Call Price													
4	Input data													
5														
6	Stock price	$100												
7	Exercise price	$80												
8	Duration	0.25	T		sigma	0.25								
9	Interest rate	8.00%			delta	0.068465								
10	dividend rate	0			z	0.125								
11	Sigma(I)	25.00%												
12	%age vol in jumps	0.75	gamma											
13	jumps per year	10	lambda											
14				Predicted										
15	Call price		=	$21.69									Call price	21.73865
16	put			$0.11						Call				
17													c(I)	C(I)*Mult
18									I		Multiply	Sigma(I)	$21.69	
19	Other quantities for option price									0	0.082085	0.125	21.58417	1.771737
20	d1	2.007648			N(d1)	0.97766				1	0.205212	0.185405	21.59527	4.431618
21	d2	1.882648			N(d2)	0.970126				2	0.256516	0.230489	21.64826	5.553118
22										3	0.213763	0.268095	21.74746	4.648803
23										4	0.133602	0.30104	21.88223	2.923507
24										5	0.066801	0.330719	22.04193	1.472422
25										6	0.027834	0.357940	22.21859	0.618426
26										7	0.009941	0.383243	22.40661	0.222736
27										8	0.003106	0.406971	22.6021	0.070212
28										9	0.000863	0.429389	22.80234	0.019676
29										10	0.000216	0.450694	23.00542	0.004963
30										11	4.9E-05	0.471036	23.20995	0.001138
31										12	1.02E-05	0.490535	23.41495	0.000239
32										13	1.96E-06	0.509289	23.61971	4.64E-05
33										14	3.51E-07	0.527376	23.82371	8.36E-06
34										15	5.85E-08	0.544862	24.02657	1.4E-06
35										16	9.13E-09	0.561805	24.22802	2.21E-07
36										17	1.34E-09	0.578252	24.42786	3.28E-08
37										18	1.87E-10	0.594243	24.62596	4.59E-09
38										19	2.45E-11	0.609816	24.82222	6.09E-10
39										20	3.07E-12	0.625	25.01657	7.68E-11
40														

In addition to our traditional Black-Scholes template, we need to input two additional quantities in cells B12 and B13. Note that value of sigma is now entered in cell F8 as well as B11.

In cell B13 we enter the average number of jumps per year. For instance, 1 indicates we believe that, on average, the stock or asset value will experience 1 "sudden jumps" per year.

In cell B12 we enter the percentage of all variance that is due to the jumps. By entering 75%, we are saying that 75% of all variation in stock prices is due to sudden jumps and only 25% is due to everyday drift or variability.

Suppose we want to value a 3-month call with current stock price of $100, risk free rate of 8%, annual volatility of 25%, no dividends and exercise price of $80. We find that with the jumps the call is worth $21.74. Note the ordinary Black-Scholes price of this option is $21.69.

Applying the Jump Diffusion Model to our Web TV Example

Let's recall our Web TV example.

In April 1997 Microsoft purchased Web TV for $425 million. Let's assume that Microsoft felt that the true value of Web TV at this point in time was $300 million. Could the purchase of Web TV still be worthwhile? If the purchase of Web TV gives Microsoft the "option" to enter another business in the future, then the value of this option might outweigh the -$125 million NPV of the Web TV deal. More concretely let's suppose that buying Web TV gives us the opportunity (for $2 billion) to enter (in three years) another Internet related business that has a current value of $ billion. Assume a risk-free rate of 5%. Assume an annual volatility of 50% for the value of the Internet related business. Does the "pioneer" option created by Web TV exceed our Web TV NPV of -$125 million?

Using the traditional Black-Scholes model we found the value of the pioneer option to be $170 million. Let's now model the value of the Internet related business as jump diffusion process with an average of 5 jumps per year and assume these jumps represent 50% of all volatility. From Figure 48.2 we find the value of the pioneer option is now $156 million. This still makes the purchase of Web TV worthwhile venture.

Figure 48.2

	A	B	C	D	E	F	G	H	I	J	K	L	M	N
1														
2	Jump Diffusion													
3	Call Price													
4	Input data													
5														
6	Stock price	$1												
7	Exercise price	$2												
8	Duration	3	T		sigma	0.50								
9	Interest rate	5.00%			delta	0.158114								
10	dividend rate	0			z	0.353553								
11	Sigma(I)	50.00%												
12	%age vol in jumps	0.5	gamma											
13	jumps per year	5	lambda											
14				Predicted										
15	Call price		=	$0.17									Call price	0.155848
16	put			$0.90						Call				
17													c(I)	C(I)*Mult
18	Other quantities for option price									I	Multiply	Sigma(I)	$0.17	
19										0	3.06E-07	0.353553	0.080313	2.46E-08
20	d1	-0.19416			N(d1)	0.423025				1	4.59E-06	0.365148	0.087156	4E-07
21	d2	-1.060185			N(d2)	0.14453				2	3.44E-05	0.376386	0.093923	3.23E-06
22										3	0.000172	0.387298	0.100607	1.73E-05
23										4	0.000645	0.397911	0.107208	6.92E-05
24										5	0.001936	0.408248	0.113723	0.00022
25										6	0.004839	0.41833	0.120151	0.000581
26										7	0.01037	0.428174	0.126493	0.001312
27										8	0.019444	0.437798	0.132749	0.002581
28										9	0.032407	0.447214	0.13892	0.004502
29										10	0.048611	0.456435	0.145006	0.007049
30										11	0.066287	0.465475	0.15101	0.01001
31										12	0.082859	0.474342	0.156933	0.013003
32										13	0.095607	0.483046	0.162776	0.015562
33										14	0.102436	0.491596	0.16854	0.017265
34										15	0.102436	0.5	0.174229	0.017847
35										16	0.096034	0.508265	0.179842	0.017271
36										17	0.084736	0.516398	0.185383	0.015709
37										18	0.070613	0.524404	0.190852	0.013477
38										19	0.055747	0.532291	0.196251	0.01094
39										20	0.04181	0.540062	0.201582	0.008428

Remark

By using the put sheet we may value a European abandonment option where the project has sudden jumps in value.

Applying the Jump Diffusion Model to our Web TV Example

Chapter 49: Pricing Options When Stock Price is Not Lognormal

On June 29, 2001 MSFT sold for $69.79. We assume a risk free rate of 5% a year. August call options (duration 52/365 of a year) sold for the following prices:

Exercise Price	Option Price
$65	$7.20
$70	$4.20
$75	$2.00

What is a fair price for these options? One approach is to assume underlying stock price of MSFT follows a lognormal random variable. Then there is probably a sigma that 'best fits' these option prices. As we know this is called the **implied volatility** for MSFT stock.

Our goal is to find a single volatility that fits Black Scholes predicted option prices as closely as possible to the actual option prices. Our spreadsheet has the Black-Scholes formula for pricing calls embedded in Row 11 of workbook **Volkappa.xls**.

Figure 49.1

	A	B	C	D	E
1	**MSFT Options**				
2	Current Price	69.79	69.79	69.79	
3	Duration	0.142466	0.142466	0.142466	
4	Volatility	0.381918	0.381918	0.381918	
5	Exercise Price	65	70	75	
6	Risk-free Rate	0.04879	0.04879	0.04879	
7	d1	0.613544	0.099453	-0.379153	
8	d2	0.46939	-0.0447	-0.523307	
9	N(d1)	0.730242	0.539611	0.352287	
10	N(d2)	0.680605	0.482173	0.30038	
11	Option Price(theory)	7.030703	4.141126	2.213641	
12					
13	Option Price(actual)	7.2	4.2	2	
14	Squared Error	0.028662	0.003466	0.045643	
15					
16	SSE	0.07777			

Our criteria for "best fit" will be to minimize the sum of the squared differences between the actual option price and the Black Scholes price.

Step 1: In cell B4 enter a trial value for volatility. Copy this value across by copying the formula

    =$B$4

from C4 to D4.

Step 2: In cells B14:D14 we compute our squared error for pricing each option by copying from B14 to C14:D14 the formula

    =(B11-B13)^2.

Step 3: In cell B16 compute the sum of the squared errors with the formula

    =SUM(B14:D14).

Step 4: We now invoke the following settings in Solver.

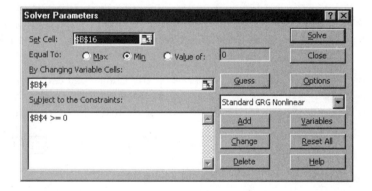

We choose a non-negative volatility value (cell B4) to minimize the sum of square errors (cell B16). The model is nonlinear because the Black Scholes formula is nonlinear function of volatility. We find the best estimate of MSFT's annual volatility to be 38%. Now we could go ahead and price other options of this duration assuming 38% volatility. The relatively close fit of the BS prices to the actual prices indicates the market is probably using BS as a base model to price MSFT options. If MSFT prices follow a lognormal random variable, then daily percentage changes should look like a normal random variable. We used Palisade's BestFit capability to see if that is the case. We pasted the last six month's of daily MSFT returns into BestFit and autofit the data. The resulting best fitting normal random variable is shown in Figure 49.2. The fit is not bad, but 11 random variable fit this data better than the Normal random variable!

For more volatile stocks and volatile FX currencies it seems unlikely that the assumption of a lognormal random variable will give proper option prices. We now detail an approach to price options that uses the actual past returns on the stock to generate option prices.

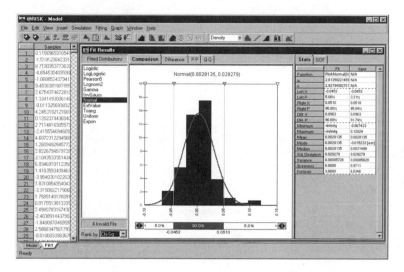

To begin we assume the underlying distribution for daily percentage changes in MSFT price during the duration of the option is equally likely to be one of the daily returns actually realized during the last six months (1/2/01 through 6/26/01). The question becomes how to risk neutralize this distribution. There are an infinite number of ways to adjust the probabilities of each possible daily return that yield a risk neutral probability measure. Since the risk-free rate is .05/252 = .00019 per day any set of probabilities that makes expected daily return .00019 would be a risk neutral measure. A more intuitive approach to creating a risk neutral measure is to not change the probabilities but change the underlying values of the random variable. All we do is simply subtract a constant c from each possible daily percentage stock return. Of course c must be chosen to ensure that the average daily percentage return equals the risk-free rate. Note that this choice of a risk neutral measure preserves all moments and the shape of the original distribution. Here's how things go (see workbook **msftriskneutral.xls**).

Figure 49.2

	A	B	C	D	E	F	G	H
1			historical sigma	0.464796197	implied sigma	0.39		
2			Mean return	0.002813502	0.000198413			Risk free rate annual
3	Obs #	Date	Close	Return	Risk neutralized return	Deviation	Adjusted deviation	Adjusted risk neutral
4		2-Jan-01	84.6136					
5	1	3-Jan-01	94.4031	0.115696531	0.113081442	0.11288303	0.094717602	0.094916015
6	2	4-Jan-01	92.969	-0.01519124	-0.01780633	-0.0180047	-0.01510737	-0.01490896
7	3	5-Jan-01	93.7796	0.008719035	0.006103946	0.00590553	0.0049552	0.005153612
8	4	8-Jan-01	93.3431	-0.00465453	-0.00726962	-0.007468	-0.00626626	-0.00606784
9	5	9-Jan-01	92.3454	-0.01068852	-0.01330361	-0.013502	-0.01132925	-0.01113083
10	6	10-Jan-01	93.2184	0.009453638	0.006838549	0.00664014	0.005571588	0.005770001
11	7	11-Jan-01	93.4678	0.002675437	6.0348E-05	-0.0001381	-0.00011585	8.25657E-05
12	8	12-Jan-01	93.5925	0.001334149	-0.00128094	-0.0014794	-0.00124129	-0.00104288
13	9	16-Jan-01	92.5325	-0.01132569	-0.01394078	-0.0141392	-0.01186388	-0.01166547
14	10	17-Jan-01	96.4608	0.042453192	0.039838103	0.03963969	0.033260769	0.033459182
15	11	18-Jan-01	108.059	0.120237444	0.117622354	0.11742394	0.098527779	0.098726192
16	12	19-Jan-01	110.989	0.027114817	0.024499727	0.02430131	0.020390685	0.020589097
17	13	22-Jan-01	108.308	-0.02415555	-0.02677064	-0.026969	-0.02262912	-0.02243071
18	14	23-Jan-01	108.807	0.004607231	0.001992142	0.00179373	0.001505078	0.00170349
19	15	24-Jan-01	110.179	0.012609483	0.009994393	0.00979598	0.008219586	0.008417999
20	16	25-Jan-01	110.49	0.002822679	0.00020759	9.1772E-06	7.70042E-06	0.000206113
21	17	26-Jan-01	113.92	0.031043533	0.028428444	0.02823003	0.023687182	0.023885595
22	18	29-Jan-01	114.71	0.006934691	0.004319601	0.00412119	0.003457997	0.003656409
23	19	30-Jan-01	116.337	0.014183593	0.011568504	0.01137009	0.009540387	0.0097388
24	20	31-Jan-01	111.737	-0.0395403	-0.04215539	-0.0423538	-0.03553812	-0.03553971
25	21	1-Feb-01	113.783	0.018310855	0.015695765	0.01549735	0.013003479	0.013201892
26	22	2-Feb-01	110.011	-0.03315082	-0.03576591	-0.0359643	-0.03017685	-0.02997844
27	23	5-Feb-01	111.957	0.01768914	0.015074051	0.01487564	0.012481812	0.012680225
28	24	6-Feb-01	113.922	0.017551381	0.014936292	0.01473788	0.012366222	0.012564634
29	25	7-Feb-01	116.769	0.024990783	0.022375694	0.02217728	0.018608456	0.018806869
30	26	8-Feb-01	113.962	-0.02403891	-0.026654	-0.0268524	-0.02253126	-0.02233284
31	27	9-Feb-01	111.865	-0.01840087	-0.02101596	-0.0212144	-0.0178005	-0.01760209
32	28	12-Feb-01	114.761	0.025888348	0.023273258	0.02307485	0.019361582	0.019559995
33	29	13-Feb-01	113.613	-0.0100034	-0.01261849	-0.0128169	-0.01075437	-0.01055596
34	30	14-Feb-01	114.961	0.011864839	0.00924975	0.00905134	0.007594773	0.007793185
35	31	15-Feb-01	116.639	0.014596254	0.011981165	0.01178275	0.009886641	0.010085054
36	32	16-Feb-01	114.861	-0.01524361	-0.0178587	-0.0180571	-0.01515132	-0.01495291
37	33	20-Feb-01	111.365	-0.03043679	-0.03305188	-0.0332503	-0.02789957	-0.02770116
38	34	21-Feb-01	107.38	-0.03578324	-0.03839832	-0.0385967	-0.03238565	-0.03218724
39	35	22-Feb-01	108.768	0.012926057	0.010310967	0.01011255	0.008485217	0.008683629
40	36	23-Feb-01	103.874	-0.04499485	-0.04760994	-0.0478084	-0.04011491	-0.0399165
41	37	26-Feb-01	105.173	0.012505536	0.009890446	0.00969203	0.008132366	0.008330779
42	38	27-Feb-01	102.466	-0.02573855	-0.02835363	-0.028952	-0.02375738	-0.02375897
43	39	28-Feb-01	99.7793	-0.0262204	-0.02883549	-0.0290339	-0.0243617	-0.02416328
44	40	1-Mar-01	105.922	0.061562869	0.05894778	0.05874937	0.049295268	0.049493681
45	41	2-Mar-01	102.176	-0.03536565	-0.03798074	-0.0381791	-0.03203526	-0.03183685
46	42	5-Mar-01	104.783	0.025514798	0.022899708	0.0227013	0.019048145	0.019246558
47	43	6-Mar-01	105.872	0.010392907	0.007777818	0.00757941	0.006359708	0.00655812
48	44	7-Mar-01	107.42	0.01462143	0.0120634	0.01180793	0.009907765	0.010106178
49	45	8-Mar-01	106.341	-0.01004468	-0.01265977	-0.0128582	-0.01078901	-0.0105906
50	46	9-Mar-01	99.1701	-0.06743307	-0.07004816	-0.0702466	-0.05894231	-0.0587439
51	47	12-Mar-01	95.3747	-0.03827162	-0.04088671	-0.0410851	-0.0344736	-0.03427518
52	48	13-Mar-01	98.2712	0.030369689	0.0277546	0.02755619	0.023121775	0.023320187
53	49	14-Mar-01	94.8453	-0.03486169	-0.03747678	-0.0376752	-0.0316124	-0.03141399
54	50	15-Mar-01	95.4446	0.006318711	0.003703621	0.00350521	0.002941141	0.003139554
55	51	16-Mar-01	89.9912	-0.05713681	-0.0597519	-0.0599503	-0.05030295	-0.05010454
56	52	19-Mar-01	92.4881	0.027746046	0.025130957	0.02493254	0.020920335	0.021118748
57	53	20-Mar-01	88.1933	-0.04643624	-0.04905133	-0.0492497	-0.04132435	-0.04112594
58	54	21-Mar-01	88.9724	0.008834004	0.006218915	0.0060205	0.005051668	0.00525008
59	55	22-Mar-01	88.9924	0.000224789	-0.0023903	-0.0025887	-0.00217213	-0.00197372
60	56	23-Mar-01	93.397	0.049494114	0.046879025	0.04668061	0.039168648	0.039367061
123	119	22-Jun-01	112.87	0.002397869	-0.00021722	-0.0004156	-0.00034875	-0.00015034
124	120	25-Jun-01	112.65	-0.00194915	-0.00456423	-0.0047626	-0.00399623	-0.00379782
125	121	26-Jun-01	113.04	0.003462051	0.000846961	0.00064855	0.000544182	0.000742595

Figure 49.3

	I	J	K	L	M
1					
2	0.05	Risk free rate daily	0.000198413	Shift to make return risk free	0.00261509
3			Call Ex Price	65	
4			Option Value	0.532356197	
5	Day	Price	Return		
6	0	$ 69.79	0.022425205		
7	1	$ 71.36	-0.007451854		
8	2	$ 70.82	-0.014929968		
9	3	$ 69.77	-0.006067845		
10	4	$ 69.34	-0.022430708		
11	5	$ 67.79	-0.001042879		
12	6	$ 67.72	0.024496603		
13	7	$ 69.38	-0.032187239		
14	8	$ 67.14	-0.010392091		
15	9	$ 66.44	-0.01026703		
16	10	$ 65.76	0.005441247		
17	11	$ 66.12	0.008417999		
18	12	$ 66.68	-0.023758966		
19	13	$ 65.09	0.0097388		
20	14	$ 65.73	-0.009818572		
21	15	$ 65.08	0.006943933		
22	16	$ 65.53	0.008330779		
23	17	$ 66.08	-0.004383817		
24	18	$ 65.79	0.019246558		
25	19	$ 67.06	0.006018296		
26	20	$ 67.46	0.015985191		
27	21	$ 68.54	0.007902155		
28	22	$ 69.08	0.005770001		
29	23	$ 69.48	-0.001973718		
30	24	$ 69.34	-0.005797915		
31	25	$ 68.94	-0.034275183		
32	26	$ 66.58	0.005441247		
33	27	$ 66.94	0.060635755		
34	28	$ 71.00	0.049493681		
35	29	$ 74.51	0.005441247		
36	30	$ 74.92	0.013201892		
37	31	$ 75.91	0.000472351		
38	32	$ 75.94	-0.050104542		
39	33	$ 72.14	-0.020183267		
40	34	$ 70.68	-0.0587439		
41	35	$ 66.53	-0.014908959		
42	36	$ 65.54	-0.020183267		
43					

Columns A-D (we have hidden some rows) give the actual daily prices and returns on MSFT during the January-June 2001 period.

Step 2: In cell K2 we determined the daily risk free rate (.05/252 = .0001984).

Step 3: In cell M2 we compute the amount we must reduce each daily percentage return by to risk neutralize our distribution

=D2-K2.

We find that a reduction in each day's percentage return of .00261 will risk neutralize our distribution.

Step 4: By copying from E5 to E125 the formula

=D5-$M$2

we create in column E our risk neutralized daily percentage returns.

Step 5: In a straightforward fashion we now generate the evolution of MSFT's price during the duration of the option (36 trading days) and value the option as the mean value of the discounted cash flows from the option. In cells K5:K58 we generate daily percentage returns by copying the formula

=RiskDuniform(AdjRNreturns)

from K5 to K6:K42. Note the range AdjRNreturns is E5:E125.

Step 6: By copying from J7 to J8:J42 the formula

=(1+K6)*J6

we generate MSFT prices during the next 36 days.

Step 7: In cell L3 we list the exercise prices for our three options

=RiskSimtable({65,70,75}).

Step 8: In cell L4 we compute the discounted cash flow from the option with the formula

(1/(1+K2)^ 36)*IF(J42>$L$3,J42-$L$3,0).

Cell L4 is our output cell.

Step 9: After running 3 simulations (because the RiskSimtable contains three possible exercise prices) and selecting cell L4 as our output cell we obtain the following estimated prices for the three call options:

Figure 49.4

	N	O	P	Q
11				
12	EX Price	Sim#	Mean	Actual Price
13	$ 65.00	1	$ 7.06	$ 7.50
14	$ 70.00	2	$ 4.22	$ 4.20
15	$ 75.00	3	$ 3.23	$ 2.00

Calibrating Risk Neutralization to Market Prices

In the workbook **MSFTcalibrate.xls** we calibrate our risk neutral distribution to actual market prices

Step by Step

Step 1: In cells F5:F125 we compute the deviation of our risk neutralized probability from the mean by copying from F5 to F6:F125 the formula

=E5-$E$2.

Step 2: In cell F1 we enter a trial "squeeze factor". A squeeze factor of k means that we will make MSFT's percentage change for that scenario equal to

(Daily risk-free rate)+ k*(Column F deviation) (1).

A choice k<1 squeezes in deviations and reduces variability. A choice of k<1 would occur when implied volatility< historical volatility. A choice of k>1 would occur when implied volatility>historical volatility.

Step 3: In cells G5:G125 we compute the squeezed deviation by copying from G5 to G6:G125 the formula

=F5*$F$1.

Step 4: In cells H5:H125 we compute the squeezed percentage return for the day by copying from H5 to H6:H125 the formula

=$E$2+G5.

Step 5: In Column K we compute the daily percentage returns by changing the formula to

$=RiskDuniform(AdjRNreturns).$

The range AdjRNreturns is H5:H125.

Step 6: In L4:N4 we compute the discounted cash flow from each call option by copying from L4 to M4:N4 the formula

$=(1/(1+\$K\$2)^\wedge 36)*IF(\$J42>M\$3,\$J42-M\$3,0).$

Step 7: In cells L5:N5 we compute the mean discounted cash flow for each option by copying from L5 to M5:N5 the formula

$=RiskMean(L4).$

Step 8: In L6:N6 we enter the actual price of the three options. Then in L7:N7 we compute the squared percentage error based on our estimated option price and the actual option price. To do this we copy from L7 to M7:N7 the formula

$=(100*(L5-L6)/L6)^\wedge 2.$

Step 9: In P7 we compute the sum of our squared estimation errors with the formula

$=SUM(L7:N7).$

Step 10: We now use RISKOptimizer to determine the value of k that minimizes the sum of our squared percentage estimation errors. Our dialog box follows:

Calibrating Risk Neutralization to Market Prices

We choose the squeeze factor (cell F1) to be between 0 and 2 and minimize the sum of our squared estimation errors. We find the appropriate squeeze factor to be .83 and we obtain the following option prices:

Figure 49.5

	N	O	P	Q
12	EX Price	Sim#	Mean	Actual Price
13	$ 65.00	1	$ 6.92	$ 7.50
14	$ 70.00	2	$ 4.06	$ 4.20
15	$ 75.00	3	$ 2.17	$ 2.00

Note we underestimate the $65 and $70 call prices but overestimate the $75 call price.

Remark

Of course, the big question is whether or not trading based on the option prices estimated by this method would yield significant excess (after adjusting for risk) returns. For example, if we buy options for which our price exceeds the market price by say 20% and short options for which our price is less than actual market price by more than 20%, would we make significant profits?

Figure 49.6

	A	B	C	D	E	F	G	H
1			historical sigma	0.464796197	squeeze factor	0.826898924		
2			Mean return	0.002813502	0.000198413			Risk free rate annual
3	Obs #	Date	Close	Return	Risk neutralized return	Deviation	Adjusted deviation	Adjusted risk neutral
4		2-Jan-01	84.6136					
5	1	3-Jan-01	94.4031	0.115696531	0.113081442	0.112883029	0.093342855	0.093541268
6	2	4-Jan-01	92.969	-0.01519124	-0.01780633	-0.01800474	-0.0148881	-0.01468969
7	3	5-Jan-01	93.7796	0.008719035	0.006103946	0.005905533	0.004883279	0.005081692
8	4	8-Jan-01	93.3431	-0.00465453	-0.00726962	-0.00746803	-0.00617531	-0.0059769
9	5	9-Jan-01	92.3454	-0.01068852	-0.01330361	-0.01350203	-0.01116481	-0.0109664
10	6	10-Jan-01	93.2184	0.009453638	0.006838549	0.006640136	0.005490721	0.005689134
11	7	11-Jan-01	93.4678	0.002675437	6.0348E-05	-0.00013806	-0.00011417	8.42471E-05
12	8	12-Jan-01	93.5925	0.001334149	-0.00128094	-0.00147935	-0.00122328	-0.00102486
13	9	16-Jan-01	92.5325	-0.01132569	-0.01394078	-0.0141392	-0.01169169	-0.01149327
14	10	17-Jan-01	96.4608	0.042453192	0.039838103	0.03963969	0.032778017	0.03297643
15	11	18-Jan-01	108.059	0.120237444	0.117622354	0.117423941	0.097097731	0.097296143
16	12	19-Jan-01	110.989	0.027114817	0.024499727	0.024301315	0.020094731	0.020293144
17	13	22-Jan-01	108.308	-0.02415555	-0.02677064	-0.02696905	-0.02230068	-0.02210227
18	14	23-Jan-01	108.807	0.004607231	0.001992142	0.001793729	0.001483233	0.001681645
19	15	24-Jan-01	110.179	0.012609483	0.009994393	0.009795981	0.008100286	0.008298699
20	16	25-Jan-01	110.49	0.002822679	0.00020759	9.17724E-06	7.58865E-06	0.000206001
21	17	26-Jan-01	113.92	0.031043533	0.028428444	0.028230031	0.023343382	0.023541795
22	18	29-Jan-01	114.71	0.006934691	0.004319601	0.004121189	0.003407807	0.003606219
23	19	30-Jan-01	116.337	0.014183593	0.011568504	0.011370091	0.009401916	0.009600329
24	20	31-Jan-01	111.737	-0.0395403	-0.04215539	-0.0423538	-0.03502231	-0.0348239
25	21	1-Feb-01	113.783	0.018310855	0.015695765	0.015497353	0.012814744	0.013013157
26	22	2-Feb-01	110.011	-0.03315082	-0.03576591	-0.03596432	-0.02973886	-0.02954045
27	23	5-Feb-01	111.957	0.01768914	0.015074051	0.014875638	0.012300649	0.012499062
28	24	6-Feb-01	113.922	0.017551381	0.014936292	0.014737879	0.012186736	0.012385149
29	25	7-Feb-01	116.769	0.024990783	0.022375694	0.022177281	0.01833837	0.018536782
30	26	8-Feb-01	113.962	-0.02403891	-0.026654	-0.02685242	-0.02220423	-0.02200582
31	27	9-Feb-01	111.865	-0.01840087	-0.02101596	-0.02121437	-0.01754214	-0.01734373
32	28	12-Feb-01	114.761	0.025888348	0.023273258	0.023074845	0.019080565	0.019278977
33	29	13-Feb-01	113.613	-0.0100034	-0.01261849	-0.0128169	-0.01059828	-0.01039987
34	30	14-Feb-01	114.961	0.011864839	0.00924975	0.009051337	0.007484541	0.007682954
35	31	15-Feb-01	116.639	0.014596254	0.011981165	0.011782752	0.009743145	0.009941558
36	32	16-Feb-01	114.861	-0.01524361	-0.0178587	-0.01805712	-0.01493141	-0.014733

	H	I	J	K	L	M	N	O	P	Q
2	Risk free rate annual	0.05	Risk free rate daily	0.000198413	Shift to make return risk free	0.00261509				
3	Adjusted risk neutral				Call Ex Price	65	70	75		
4					Option Value	16.01813115	11.0537147	6.089298193		
5	0.093541268	Day	Price	Return	16.01813115	11.0537147	6.089298193	Mean		
6	-0.01468969	0	$ 69.79	0.005176759	7.5	4.2	2	actual		
7	0.005081692	1	$ 70.15	0.008298699	12899.29926	26628.9143	41805.89928	sq %age err	81334.11283	
8	-0.0059769	2	$ 70.73	-0.003887429					SSE	
9	-0.0109664	3	$ 70.46	-0.027296217						
10	0.005689134	4	$ 68.54	0.009941558						
11	8.42471E-05	5	$ 69.22	-0.017487315						
12	-0.00102486	6	$ 68.01	0.001681645			EX Price	Sim#	Mean	Actual Price
13	-0.01149327	7	$ 68.12	-0.027296217			$ 65.00	1	$ 6.92	$ 7.50
14	0.03297643	8	$ 66.26	0.013577935			$ 70.00	2	$ 4.06	$ 4.20
15	0.097296143	9	$ 67.16	-0.010115132			$ 75.00	3	$ 2.17	$ 2.00
16	0.020293144	10	$ 66.48	0.003389501						
17	-0.02210227	11	$ 66.71	0.093541268						
18	0.001681645	12	$ 72.95	-0.017487315						
19	0.008298699	13	$ 71.67	-0.022502958						
20	0.000206001	14	$ 70.06	0.009137584						
21	0.023541795	15	$ 70.70	0.03340909						
22	0.003606219	16	$ 73.06	0.03340909						
23	0.009600329	17	$ 75.50	-0.007340817						
24	-0.0348239	18	$ 74.95	0.022984594						
25	0.013013157	19	$ 76.67	0.002817136						
26	-0.02954045	20	$ 76.89	-0.001024863						
27	0.012499062	21	$ 76.81	0.003096866						
28	0.012385149	22	$ 77.04	0.009941558						
29	0.018536782	23	$ 77.81	0.01897009						
30	-0.02200582	24	$ 79.29	0.006465815						
31	-0.01734373	25	$ 79.80	0.015756059						
32	0.019278977	26	$ 81.06	0.001681645						
33	-0.01039987	27	$ 81.19	0.053687601						
34	0.007682954	28	$ 85.55	-0.001942192						
35	0.009941558	29	$ 85.39	0.008560473						
36	-0.014733	30	$ 86.12	-0.011493273						
37	-0.02729622	31	$ 85.13	-0.039428985						
38	-0.03171719	32	$ 81.77	0.002817136						
39	0.008560473	33	$ 82.00	-0.031717188						
40	-0.03933426	34	$ 79.40	0.014034245						
41	0.008212745	35	$ 80.51	0.007682954						
42	-0.02341124	36	$ 81.13	-0.049374436						

Chapter 50: An Option to Start Up and Shut Down a Gold Mine

Let's add to the complexity of the gold mine situation by assuming that during each year the mine is open there is a fixed cost of operating the mine (this cost is incurred even if no gold is extracted). If the mine is open at the beginning of a year we may shut the mine down (shutting the mine down incurs a shutdown cost). If the mine is closed at the beginning of a year we may open the mine (opening the mine incurs an opening cost). How do we value the worth of this type of situation? The key is to realize we now need **three lattices**: a price lattice, a lattice to track the value of each price time combination when the mine is shut down at the beginning of the year, and a lattice to track the value of each price time combination when the mine is open at the beginning of the year. Here are the specifics of our example.

Example 50.1

The current price of gold is $400. The risk-free rate is 10% and the annual volatility for changes in gold prices is 30%. Gold prices are assumed to follow a lognormal random variable. Each year the mine is open a fixed cost of $1 million is incurred. **This cost is incurred even if no gold is mined during the year.** If we open the mine a cost of $2 million is incurred. If we shut the mine a cost of $1.5 million is incurred. During the current year and each of the next ten years we can, if the mine is open, mine up to 10,000 ounces of gold at a variable cost of $250 per ounce. What is the worth of this situation?

Solution

Our work is in file **Goldstartshut.xls**. We begin by generating the possible prices of gold in the usual way. See Figure 50.1.

Figure 50.1

	A	B	C	D	E	J	K	L
1	Option to							
2	**Startup and Shutdown**							
3	Current price	$ 400.00		fc	1.00E+06			
4	Exercise price	$ 50.00		shutc	$ 1,500,000.00			
5	r	0.1		startc	$ 2,000,000.00			
6	sigma	0.3		extc	$ 250.00			
7	t	20		df	0.909090909			
8	deltat	1		rate	10000			
9	u	1.349858808						
10	d	0.740818221						
11	a	1.105170918						
12	p	0.598240421						
13	q	0.401759579						
14			Time					
15	**Gold Prices**		0	1	2	3	8	9	10
16	0	$ 400.00	$ 539.94	$ 728.85	$ 983.84	$ 4,409.27	$ 5,951.89	$ 8,034.21
17	1		$ 296.33	$ 400.00	$ 539.94	$ 2,419.86	$ 3,266.47	$ 4,409.27
18	2		-	$ 219.52	$ 296.33	$ 1,328.05	$ 1,792.68	$ 2,419.86
19	3		-	-	$ 162.63	$ 728.85	$ 983.84	$ 1,328.05
20	4		-	-	-	$ 400.00	$ 539.94	$ 728.85
21	5		-	-	-	$ 219.52	$ 296.33	$ 400.00
22	6					$ 120.48	$ 162.63	$ 219.52
23	7					$ 66.12	$ 89.25	$ 120.48
24	8					$ 36.29	$ 48.98	$ 66.12
25	9					-	$ 26.88	$ 36.29
26	10					-		$ 19.91

Next we compute the expected discounted value of being in each price-time situation when the mine is shutdown at the beginning of Year 10. If the mine is shutdown at the beginning of Year 10 we have 2 choices: do nothing and earn $0 or start the mine up, incur the fixed cost and mine 10,000 ounces of gold. Thus the value of each price-time combination when the mine is shutdown at the beginning of Year 10 may be computed by copying from L28 to L29:L38 the formula

$$=MAX((L26\text{-}extc)*rate\text{-}startc\text{-}fc,0).$$

See Figure 50.2 Also note we have used the range names for cells E3:E8 that are specified in cells D3:D8.

Figure 50.2

	A	B	C	D	E	J	K	L
27	Down move	value if shut						
28	0	$19,292,843.18	$ 29,741,423.50	$ 42,736,676.13	$ 57,486,486.13	$ 121,326,528.31	$ 110,635,824.25	$ 74,842,147.6
29	1		$ 8,536,462.97	$ 13,604,936.67	$ 21,535,967.77	$ 61,363,184.85	$ 56,801,092.38	$ 38,592,705.5
30	2			$ 3,114,017.16	$ 5,181,566.33	$ 28,454,604.22	$ 27,255,965.10	$ 18,698,589.8
31	3				$ 810,426.11	$ 10,393,992.25	$ 11,041,255.46	$ 7,780,467.6
32	4					$ 1,165,173.36	$ 2,142,434.13	$ 1,788,475.2
33	5					$ -	$ -	$ -
34	6					$ -	$ -	$ -
35	7					$ -	$ -	$ -
36	8					$ -	$ -	$ -
37	9						$ -	$ -
38	10							$ -
39								

Next we compute the expected discounted value of being in each price-time situation when the mine is open at the beginning of Year 10. If the mine is open at the beginning of Year 10 we have 2 choices: do not mine and simply incur the fixed cost of operation or mine 10,000 ounces. Note shutting down would cost more than leaving mine open and not mining so it does not make sense to shut mine down in this situation. By copying from L41 to L42:L51 the formula

$$= MAX((L16\text{-}extc)*rate\text{-}fc,\text{-}fc)$$

we compute the expected discounted value of being in each price with an open mine at the beginning of Year 10. See Figure 50.3.

Figure 50.3

	A	B	C	D	E	J	K	L
40	Down move	value if open						
41	0	$20,779,582.72	$ 31,741,423.50	$ 44,736,676.13	$ 59,486,486.13	$ 123,326,528.31	$ 112,635,824.25	$ 76,842,147.69
42	1		$ 8,260,010.72	$ 15,090,863.87	$ 23,535,967.77	$ 63,363,184.85	$ 58,801,092.38	$ 40,592,705.52
43	2			$ 1,614,017.16	$ 4,902,889.90	$ 30,454,604.22	$ 29,255,965.10	$ 20,698,589.86
44	3				$ (689,573.89)	$ 12,393,992.25	$ 13,041,255.46	$ 9,780,467.69
45	4					$ 2,522,771.54	$ 4,142,434.13	$ 3,788,475.20
46	5					$ (1,500,000.00)	$ (630,035.63)	$ 500,000.00
47	6					$ (1,500,000.00)	$ (1,500,000.00)	$ (1,000,000.00)
48	7					$ (1,500,000.00)	$ (1,500,000.00)	$ (1,000,000.00)
49	8					$ (1,500,000.00)	$ (1,500,000.00)	$ (1,000,000.00)
50	9						$ (1,500,000.00)	$ (1,000,000.00)
51	10							$ (1,000,000.00)

Next we compute the value of each price-time situation for years before the final year given that mine is shutdown at the beginning of the year. Note we have two choices. First, we can open the mine and extract 10,000 ounces of ore. During the current year this action incurs a startup cost and fixed cost as well as earning profit from extraction.

If we are at beginning of Year t and there have been j down moves then with probability p we earn profit from beginning of Year t+1 with j down moves and an open mine and with probability q we earn profit from beginning of Year t+1 with j+1 down moves and an open mine. Second, we can leave the mine shut and earn no profit during current year. If we are at beginning of Year t and there have been j down moves then with probability p we earn profit from beginning of Year t+1 with j down moves and a shut mine and with probability q we earn profit from beginning of Year t+1 with j+1 down moves and a shut mine. Copying from cell K28 to the range B28:K38 the following formula

=IF($A28>K$15,"_",MAX((K16-extc)*rate-startc+df*(p*L41+q*L42)-fc,df*(p*L28+q*L29)))

computes the expected discounted value of each price-time situation when the mine is shutdown at the beginning of a year.

Next we compute the value of each price-time situation for years before the final year given the mine is open at the beginning of the year. Note we have three choices. First, we may keep the mine open during the current year and extract 10,000 ounces. During the current year this action incurs a fixed cost and earns a profit from extraction. If we are at the beginning of Year t and there have been j down moves then with probability p we earn profit from beginning of Year t+1 with j down moves and an open mine and with probability q we earn profit from beginning of Year t+1 with j+1 down moves and an open mine. Second, we may keep the mine open during the current year and perform no extraction. This incurs the fixed cost during the current year and if we are at beginning of Year t and there have been j down moves then with probability p we earn profit from the beginning of Year t+1 with j down moves and an open mine and with probability q we earn profit from beginning of Year t+1 with j+1 down moves and an open mine. Third, we may shut the mine down during the current year. This incurs the shutdown cost during the current year and if we are at the beginning of Year t and there have been j down moves then with probability p we earn profit from the beginning of Year t+1 with j down moves and a shut mine and with probability q we earn profit from beginning of Year t+1 with j+1 down moves and a shut mine. Thus copying the formula

=IF($A41>K$15,"_",MAX((K16-extc)*rate-fc+df*(p*L41+q*L42),-fc+df*(p*L41+q*L42),-shutc+df*(p*L28+q*L29))

from K41 to B41:K51 computes the expected discounted value of each price-time situation when the mine is open at the beginning of the year.

We find that if the mine is shutdown at Time 0 the worth of the situation is $19,292,843. If the mine is open at Time 0 the worth of the situation is $20,792,843.

Chapter 51: Using Trend Curve to Estimate Product Demand

How can we use Solver to determine a profit maximizing-price? One way is to derive a demand curve by breaking the market into segments and identify a low price, medium price and high price. For each of these prices and market segments, ask company experts to estimate product demand. Then we can use Excel's trend curve fitting capabilities to fit a quadratic function that can be used to estimate each segment's demand for different prices. Finally, we can add the segment demand curves to derive an aggregate demand curve and use the Solver to determine the profit-maximizing price. The procedure is illustrated in the following example (based on Dolan and Simon (1996):

Example 51.1

A candy bar costs 55 cents to produce. We are considering charging a price of between $1.10 and $1.50 for this candy bar. For a price of $1.10, $1.30, and $1.50, the marketing department estimates the following demand (in thousands) for the candy bar in the three regions where the candy bar will be sold.

What price will maximize profit? See file **Expdem.xls**

Figure 51.1

	C	D	E	F	G
			Region 1 demand	Region 2 demand	Region 3 demand
3	Price				
4	Low	$ 1.10	35	32	24
5	Medium	$ 1.30	32	27	17
6	High	$ 1.50	22	16	9
7	Unit cost	0.55			

Step by Step

Step 1: We begin by "fitting" a quadratic curve to the three demands specified in Figure 51.1 for each region. For example, for Region 1 we use the X-Y Chart Wizard option to plot D4:E6. Click the points on the graph until they turn yellow and choose Insert>Trendline>Polynomial (2) and check the equation option to make sure the quadratic equation that exactly fits the three points is listed.

Figure 51.2

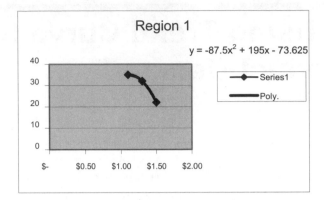

Thus we estimate Region 1 Demand = -87.5*(price)^2 + 195*(price) - 73.625.

Similarly, in Regions 2 and 3 we find the following demand equations for Regions 2 and 3.

Figure 51.3

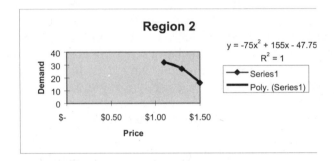

Region 2 Demand = -75*(price)^2 + 155*(price) - 47.75.

Figure 51.4

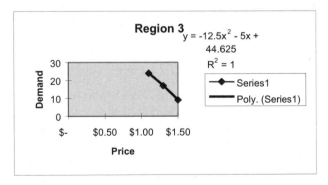

Region 3 Demand = -12.5*(price)^2 - 5*(price) + 44.625.

Step 2: We now enter a trial price in cell H4 and determine in cells I4:K4 the demand (in thousands of units) for that price in each region:

Region 1 Demand (cell I4) =-87.5*H4^2+195*H4-73.625

Region 2 Demand (cell J4) = -75*(H4)^2 + 155*H4 - 47.7

Region 3 Demand (cell K4) = -12.5*(H4)^2 - 5*H4 + 44.625

Step 3: In cell L4 compute the total demand (in thousands of units) with the formula

= SUM(I4:K4).

Step 4: In cell I6 compute our profit (in thousands of $s).

= (H4-I2)*L4.

Step 5: We are now ready to invoke the Solver to find the profit-maximizing price. We simply maximize profit (cell I6) with price (H4) being a changing cell. Since our demand curves are, in theory, only valid for prices between $1.10 and $1.50 we add the constraints H4>=1.10 and H4<=1.50 (see Figure 51.5 for the Solver window).

Figure 51.5

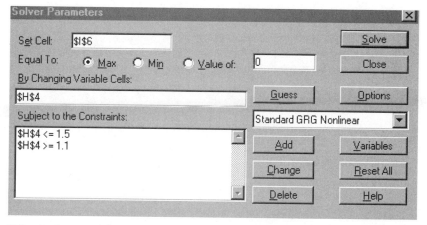

Why is the model nonlinear? As shown in Figure 51.6, we find the profit-maximizing price to be $1.29.

Figure 51.6

	H	I	J	K	L
2	Variable cost	0.55			
3	Price	Region 1 demand	Region 2 demand	Region 3 demand	Total demand
4	1.286324543	32.42809	27.53299	17.51049	77.47157
5					
6	Profit	57.04422			
7	(000's)				

Reference

Dolan, R. and Simon, J., *Power Pricing*, Free Press, 1996.

Chapter 52: Pricing for a Subscription-Based Service

In today's hi-tech age there are many products which require the consumer to initially buy a piece of hardware and then purchase a monthly subscription to continue obtaining value from the hardware. Examples include Web TV and Direct TV.

There are at least two important pricing decisions to be made when marketing a product such as Web TV (all numbers in this example are entirely fictitious)

- The price of the hardware (the Web TV Unit).

- The price of the monthly subscription fee.

These prices should not be determined separately, but should be determined together in order to maximize the long-term profitability of the company. Here is a first pass at a pricing model. The key determinants of the pricing strategy will be the following:

- Sensitivity of demand for the hardware to the hardware price.

- Sensitivity of the "churn rate" to the monthly subscription rate.

We will use the Excel Trend Curve feature to estimate both of these demand curves. Our inputs are as follows:

- Annual percentage of market that will purchase hardware for lowest, highest, and an intermediate price.

- Annual churn rate for lowest, highest, and intermediate monthly subscription price.

Given this information we will use the Trend Curve feature to determine the dependence of hardware demand and churn rate on price. Then we can determine the long-term discounted profit of the company (generated by hardware sales and subscription fees). Finally we use Solver to determine the pricing strategy that maximizes NPV of the company's profit.

**Example
52.1**

Our work is in the file **webtv.xls.** It costs us $300 to provide a Web TV hardware unit and one year of service. The current market size for our product is assumed to be 10 million. Our price for the hardware unit and one year of service will be between $250 and $500. The percentage of the market that will purchase the hardware and one year of service during a year is given in Figure 52.1.

For example, if we charge $250 we estimate 4% of the market will buy while if we charge $500 we estimate only 1% of the market will buy.

It costs $100 to provide one year of Web TV service. The fraction of subscribers who will terminate their Web TV service during a year is, of course, price-dependent. We estimate, for example, that if we charge $100 per year only 5% of subscribers will terminate our service during a year and if we charge $400 per year 30% of our subscribers will terminate our service during a year. Given these assumptions what prices for hardware + one year of service and annual subscription rate will maximize our long-term profit?

**Example
52.1**

	C	D	E
1			
2	**Web TV Purchase + 1 Year**		
3	Market Size	1.00E+07	
4	Our Cost	$ 300.00	%age buying
5		Price(100's)	
6	Low Price	$ 2.50	4
7	Medium Price	$ 3.50	3
8	High Price	$ 5.00	1
9			
10	**Annual Fee**		
11	Our Cost	$ 100.00	Churn rate
12		Price 100's	Percent churn
13	Low Price	$ 1.00	5
14	Medium Price	$ 3.00	12
15	High Price	$ 4.00	30

Solution

We begin by estimating the demand curve for hardware and churn rate.

Step 1: Use the Chart Wizard to plot Percentage Buying Hardware as a function of price (in hundreds of dollars). With the chart selected click on the points until they turn gold and choose Chart>Add Trendline. Select the Polynomial (2) Option and choose Show Equation from Options. You will obtain the following graph:

Figure 52.2

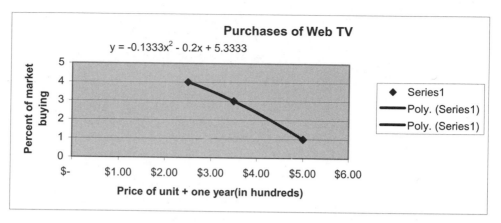

This graph allows us to determine (for any price between $250 and $500) the percentage of the market that will purchase Web TV during a year.

Purchase Percentage = -.1333*(Price)² -.2*(Price) + 5.3333.

Note we should not extrapolate this relationship beyond the ranges of $150 and $500.

In a similar fashion (see Figure 52.3) we obtain the sensitivity of the churn rate to the annual subscription fee.

Figure 52.3

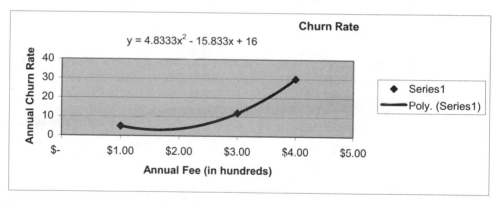

We are now ready to model the long-term NPV of Web TV's profit.

Step by Step

Step 1: In C36 and E36 we enter trial prices for Web TV hardware + one year subscription and annual subscription rate.

Step 2: In cell D36 we compute the percentage of the non-purchasers of Web TV that will purchase the product during a year with the formula

=-0.1333*(C36/100)^2-0.2*(C36/100)+5.333

Figure 52.4

	B	C	D	E	F	G	H	I	J	K
35		Initial Price		% buying	Subs Rate	Churn Rate		NPV			799,622,083
36			264.2485503	3.87370504	294.3909791	11.2747776					
37	Year	Non Purchasers		New Buyers	Total Owners	New Subscribers	Hold over Subscribers	Total Subscribers	Revenue	Cost	Profit
38	1	1.00E+07		3.87E+05	3.87E+05	3.87E+05	0.00E+00	3.87E+05	1.02E+08	1.16E+08	-1.38E
39	2	9.61E+06		3.72E+05	7.60E+05	3.72E+05	3.44E+05	7.16E+05	2.00E+08	1.46E+08	5.35E
40	3	9.24E+06		3.58E+05	1.12E+06	3.58E+05	6.35E+05	9.93E+05	2.82E+08	1.71E+08	1.11E
41	4	8.88E+06		3.44E+05	1.46E+06	3.44E+05	8.81E+05	1.23E+06	3.50E+08	1.91E+08	1.59E
42	5	8.54E+06		3.31E+05	1.79E+06	3.31E+05	1.09E+06	1.42E+06	4.07E+08	2.08E+08	2.00E
43	6	8.21E+06		3.18E+05	2.11E+06	3.18E+05	1.26E+06	1.58E+06	4.54E+08	2.21E+08	2.33E
44	7	7.89E+06		3.06E+05	2.42E+06	3.06E+05	1.40E+06	1.70E+06	4.92E+08	2.32E+08	2.61E
45	8	7.58E+06		2.94E+05	2.71E+06	2.94E+05	1.51E+06	1.81E+06	5.23E+08	2.39E+08	2.83E
46	9	7.29E+06		2.82E+05	2.99E+06	2.82E+05	1.60E+06	1.88E+06	5.46E+08	2.45E+08	3.01E
47	10	7.01E+06		2.71E+05	3.26E+06	2.71E+05	1.67E+06	1.94E+06	5.64E+08	2.49E+08	3.15E
48	11	6.74E+06		2.61E+05	3.52E+06	2.61E+05	1.72E+06	1.99E+06	5.77E+08	2.51E+08	3.26E
49	12	6.48E+06		2.51E+05	3.78E+06	2.51E+05	1.76E+06	2.01E+06	5.85E+08	2.51E+08	3.33E
50	13	6.22E+06		2.41E+05	4.02E+06	2.41E+05	1.79E+06	2.03E+06	5.89E+08	2.51E+08	3.38E
51	14	5.98E+06		2.32E+05	4.25E+06	2.32E+05	1.80E+06	2.03E+06	5.91E+08	2.49E+08	3.41E
52	15	5.75E+06		2.23E+05	4.47E+06	2.23E+05	1.80E+06	2.02E+06	5.89E+08	2.47E+08	3.42E
53	16	5.53E+06		2.14E+05	4.69E+06	2.14E+05	1.80E+06	2.01E+06	5.85E+08	2.44E+08	3.41E
54	17	5.31E+06		2.06E+05	4.89E+06	2.06E+05	1.78E+06	1.99E+06	5.79E+08	2.40E+08	3.39E
55	18	5.11E+06		1.98E+05	5.09E+06	1.98E+05	1.76E+06	1.96E+06	5.72E+08	2.36E+08	3.36E
56	19	4.91E+06		1.90E+05	5.28E+06	1.90E+05	1.74E+06	1.93E+06	5.63E+08	2.31E+08	3.32E
57	20	4.72E+06		1.83E+05	5.46E+06	1.83E+05	1.71E+06	1.90E+06	5.53E+08	2.26E+08	3.27E

Step 3: In cell F36 we compute the annual churn rate with the formula

$=4.833*(E36/100)^2-15.833*(E36/100)+16.$

Step 4: In C38 we enter the initial market size.

Step 5: In cell D38 we compute the number of new purchasers of Web TV during the first year as a fraction of the number of current non-purchasers

$=(\$D\$36/100)*C38:$

Step 6: In cell E38 and F38 we recopy the number of new purchasers as the number of New Subscribers and Holdover Subscribers.

Step 7: In cell G38 we enter 0 (the number of holdover subscribers) and in H38 we enter the number of total subscribers at the end of the year with the formula

$=F38 + G38.$

Step 8: In I38 we compute the first year revenue with the formula

$=G38*\$E\$36+D38*\$C\$36.$

Step 9: In J38 we compute the total first year cost with the formula

$=\$D\$4*D38+\$D\$11*G38.$

Step 10: In cell K38 we compute the first year profit with the formula

$=I38-J38.$

Step 11: In cell C39 we compute the number of people who have yet to purchase the product at beginning of Year 2. We simply subtract Year 1 purchasers from non-purchasers at the beginning of Year 1 with the formula.

=C38-D38.

Step 12: In cell D39 we compute the number of purchasers during Year 2 by copying the formula in D38 to D39.

Step 13: In cell E39 we compute total owners of hardware at end of Year 2 by adding Year 2 purchasers to Year 1 owners with the formula

=D39+E38.

Step 14: In cell F39 we compute the number of new subscribers during Year 2 (same as new buyers) with the formula

=D39.

Step 15: In cell G39 we compute the number of holdover subscribers from Year 1 still with us at end of Year 2 by subtracting from Year 1 subscribers those who churn. The appropriate formula is

=(1-$F$36/100)*H38.

Step 16: In cell H39 we compute the total number of subscribers at the end of Year 2 with the formula

=F39+G39.

Step 17: Copying from I38:K38 to I39:K39 computes costs, revenues, and profits for Year 2.

Step 18: Copying all our formulas from C39:K39 to C40:K57 computes all relevant quantities for Years 2-20.

Step 19: Assuming a 20% annual discount rate and profits received at the end of the year we compute our total NPV of 20 years of profits in cell K36 with the formula

=NPV(0.2,K38:K57)

Step 20: We now use Solver to determine the price for the hardware and one-year subscription and annual subscription charge that maximizes profit.

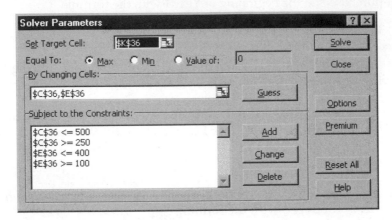

We maximize our 20-year NPV (K36) by changing the hardware + one year price and the annual subscription charge (C36 and E36). We restrict each price to be between the limits used to construct the Trend Curves. This is because extrapolating beyond the ranges used to create the charts could lead to demands that are increasing functions of price!

We find that initial hardware and one year subscription should be sold for $264 (below cost) while subsequent subscriptions should be sold for $294 per year.

Chapter 53: Optimal Product Bundling

In many situations companies bundle products in an attempt to get customers to purchase more products than they would have without bundling. Here are some examples:

- Phone companies may bundle call-waiting, voice mail and caller-ID features.

- Automobile companies often bundle popular options such as air conditioning, cassette players, and power windows.

- Computer mail order companies often bundle computers with printers, scanners, and monitors.

- The most successful bundle in history is Microsoft Office!

The following example shows how to use the INDEX and MATCH function to model the profitability associated with a set of product prices.

Example 53.1

In the file **Phone1.xls** we are given the amount of money 77 randomly chosen customers are willing to pay for Call Waiting, Voice Mail and Caller ID. For example, the first customer was willing to pay up to $0.50 for Call Waiting, up to $1.00 for Voice Mail, and up to $0.50 for Caller ID. Phoneco is thinking of offering the following product combinations for sale:

- Call Waiting by itself.

- Voice Mail by Itself

- Caller ID by itself

- Call Waiting and Voice Mail

- Call Waiting and Caller ID

- Voice Mail and Caller ID

- All three products

Figure 53.1

	A	B	C
5	Call Waiting	Voice Mail	Caller ID
6	0.5	1	0.5
7	2.5	5	0.5
8	4	4	7
9	10	10	0
10	0	1	2
11	0	10	0
12	3	5	1.5
13	1	3	0
14	0.75	1	0.3
15	3	4	4
77	0	8	5
78	0	1	0
79	5	5	8
80	3	4	4
81	0	6	1
82	5	5	0.25

Since we are offering individual products as well as bundles of products this situation is called **mixed bundling**.

Set up a spreadsheet to show how to determine the revenue associated with any set of product prices.

Solution

We assume that each customer represents an equal share of the market, so it suffices to determine a set of prices that maximizes revenue received from all 77 customers. Each consumer has seven purchase options (plus the option of purchasing nothing). **We assume a consumer will always purchase the option that gives her the maximum non-negative surplus; if no product combination yields a non-negative surplus the consumer will purchase nothing**. Here is how to proceed: See Figure 53.2 and file **Phone1.xls**.

Figure 53.2

	C	D	E	F	G	H	I	J
3								
4	Price	2	4	6	8	10	12	14
5	Caller ID	CW	VM	CID	CW,VM	CW,CID	VM,CID	CW,VM,CID
6	0.5	-1.5	-3	-5.5	-6.5	-9	-10.5	-12
7	0.5	0.5	1	-5.5	-0.5	-7	-6.5	-6
8	7	2	0	1	0	1	-1	1
9	0	8	6	-6	12	0	-2	6
10	2	-2	-3	-4	-7	-8	-9	-11
11	0	-2	6	-6	2	-10	-2	-4
12	1.5	1	1	-4.5	0	-5.5	-5.5	-4.5
13	0	-1	-1	-6	-4	-9	-9	-10
14	0.3	-1.25	-3	-5.7	-6.25	-8.95	-10.7	-11.95
15	4	1	0	-2	-1	-3	-4	-3
16	3	3	3	-3	4	-2	-2	1
67	0.5	-1	-2	-5.5	-5	-8.5	-9.5	-10.5
68	10	23	46	4	67	25	48	71
69	2	-2	-2	-4	-6	-8	-8	-10
70	0	-0.25	1	-6	-1.25	-8.25	-7	-7.25
71	6	3	2	0	3	1	0	3
72	0	3	4	-6	5	-5	-4	-1
73	0	3	2	-6	3	-5	-6	-3
74	1	4	3.5	-5	5.5	-3	-3.5	0.5
75	1	1	-1	-5	-2	-6	-8	-7
76	3.95	1.95	2.95	-2.05	2.9	-2.1	-1.1	0.85
77	5	-2	4	-1	0	-5	1	-1
78	0	-2	-3	-6	-7	-10	-11	-13
79	8	3	1	2	2	3	1	4
80	4	1	0	-2	-1	-3	-4	-3
81	1	-2	2	-5	-2	-9	-5	-7
82	0.25	3	1	-5.75	2	-4.75	-6.75	-3.75

	K	L	M
3		total	278
4			
5	max surp	bought?	revenue
6	-1.5	0	0
7	1	2	4
8	2	1	2
9	12	4	8
10	-2	0	0
11	6	2	4
12	1	1	2
13	-1	0	0
14	-1.25	0	0
15	1	1	2
16	4	4	8
67	-1	0	0
68	71	7	14
69	-2	0	0
70	1	2	4
71	3	1	2
72	5	4	8
73	3	1	2
74	5.5	4	8
75	1	i	2
76	2.95	2	4
77	4	2	4
78	-2	0	0
79	4	7	14
80	1	1	2
81	2	2	4
82	3	1	2

Step 1: Enter trial prices for each product combination in D4:J4.

Step 2: In D6:F82 we compute the surplus for each customer for a purchase of Call Waiting, Voice Mail and Caller ID. Customer 1's surplus for purchasing Call Waiting is computed in D6 with the formula

$=A6-D\$4.$

Copying this formula to D6:F82 computes the product surplus of each customer for Call Waiting, Voice Mail and Caller ID.

Step 3: In G6:G82 we compute each customer's surplus for the Call Waiting and Voice Mail combination by copying the formula

$=A6+B6-G\$4$

from G6 to G7:G82. This computes the amount each customer is willing to pay for Call Waiting and Voice and subtracts off the price.

Step 4: By mimicking Step 3, we compute in H6:J82 the surplus each customer associates with the other product bundle combinations.

Step 5: In K6:K82 we compute each customer's maximum product surplus by copying from K6 to K7:K82 the formula

$= MAX(D6:J6).$

Step 6: In L6:L82 we compute the number of the product combination (if any) purchased by each customer by copying from L6:L82 the formula

$=IF(K6<0,0,MATCH(K6,D6:J6,0)).$

Discussion of the MATCH Function

The MATCH function's first argument is the lookup cell and the second is the lookup array. The MATCH function will return the relative position of the first element in the lookup array that matches the lookup cell. The 0 is required because the elements in the lookup array are not ordered from smallest to largest. A "1" requires lookup array to be in ascending order and returns the relative position of the largest value that is less than or equal to the lookup value. A "-1" requires lookup array to be in descending order and returns the relative position of the smallest value greater than or equal to the lookup value.

This formula will return a 0 if all surpluses are negative, a "1" if CW is most preferred, ... a "7" if the bundle of CW, VM and Caller ID is most preferred.

Step 7: In M6:M82 we compute the revenue received from each customer by copying from M6 to M7:M82 the formula

> =IF(L6=0,0,INDEX($D$4:$J$4,1,L6)).

If the consumer purchases nothing, column L will contain a 0 and the customer generates no revenue. Otherwise the index function returns the price of the product purchased by the consumer. Basically, the INDEX function is a two-way Lookup Table. We lookup in the range D4:J4 the number in row "1" and column "L6". This is exactly the price of the option purchased by the customer.

Step 8: In cell M3 we compute our total revenue with the formula

> =SUM(M6:M82).

How to Find Revenue Maximizing Prices?

This is tricky. An ordinary Solver model will not work because a small change in a price can drastically change the profit. Simply changing the price a penny could cause you to lose a customer and perhaps $10 of revenue. Fortunately, Evolver can come to the rescue.

Evolver uses **genetic algorithms** to obtain good solutions. We begin with a population containing, say, 100 sets of values for changing cells. For example if we have changing cells x and y a population would consist of 100 points such as (1,2) (2,3) etc. where first number is x value and second number is y value. Those members of the populations that yield good target cell values have more chance of surviving to the next "generation" or population. Those members of the population that yield poor target cell values have little chance of surviving to the next generation.

Using Evolver to Find Optimal Bundle Prices

We are now ready to use Evolver to find the set of bundle prices that maximize revenue. Our dialog box is as follows

We want to maximize total revenue (M3) by changing our prices (D4:J4). We will constrain each price to be between $0 and $25.

	C	D	E	F	G	H	I	J	K	L	M	N	O	P	Q
3										total	480.1347				
4	Price	15.875	4.92	2.989	18.9551	7.968072	25	9.90747432							
5	Caller ID	CW	VM	CID	CW,VM	CW,CID	VM,CID	CW,VM,CID	max surp	bought?	revenue				
6	0.5	-15.38	-3.9	-2.489	-17.455	-6.96807	-23.5	-7.9074743	-2.488558	0	0				
7	0.5	-13.38	0.08	-2.489	-11.455	-4.96807	-19.5	-1.9074743	0.082759	2	4.917241				
8	7	-11.88	-0.9	4.011	-10.955	3.031928	-14	5.09252568	5.092526	7	9.907474		Product	Frequency	
9	0	-5.875	5.08	-2.989	1.0449	2.031928	-15	10.0925257	10.09253	7	9.907474		0	19	
10	2	-15.88	-3.9	-0.989	-17.955	-5.96807	-22	-6.9074743	-0.988558	0	0		1	0	
11	0	-15.88	5.08	-2.989	-8.9551	-7.96807	-15	0.09252568	5.082759	2	4.917241		2	14	
12	1.5	-12.88	0.08	-1.489	-10.955	-3.46807	-18.5	-0.4074743	0.082759	2	4.917241		3	3	
13	0	-14.88	-1.9	-2.989	-14.955	-6.96807	-22	-5.9074743	-1.917241	0	0		4	0	
14	0.3	-15.13	-3.9	-2.689	-17.205	-6.91807	-23.7	-7.8574743	-2.688558	0	0		5	2	
15	4	-12.88	-0.9	1.011	-11.955	-0.96807	-17	1.09252568	1.092526	7	9.907474		6	0	
16	3	-10.88	2.08	0.011	-6.9551	0.031928	-15	5.09252568	5.092526	7	9.907474		7	39	
67	0.5	-14.88	-2.9	-2.489	-15.955	-6.46807	-22.5	-6.4074743	-2.488558	0	0				
68	10	9.1248	45.1	7.011	56.0449	27.03193	35	75.0925257	75.09253	7	9.907474				

Maximum revenue of $480.14 was obtained. To determine the products purchased by each customer we copied from P9:P16 the formula

=COUNTIF($L$6:$L$82,O9).

We find that for most consumers CW and the entire bundle are purchased. Almost 25% of our potential customers buy nothing. The prices do not look satisfying, however. In the real world we cannot charge more for CW than for the entire bundle. How can we ensure that the insertion of products never leads to a lower price? We could add constraints to do this, but a better way is to keep track of each time adding a product leads to a lower price and penalize our target cell for each occurrence. This is done in file **Phonefinal.xls**. We begin by copying our set of optimal prices to the sheet Phonefinal.xls.

Step by Step

Step 1: In O69:Q79 we determine the total amount by which adding a product raises price. For example, in P70 we compute the amount by which VM price exceeds VM-CW price with the formula

$=E4-G4.$

Then in cell Q70 we compute the amount by which VM-CW price exceeds VM price with the formula

$=IF(P70>0,P70,0).$

In cell Q79 we compute our Total "price reversals" with the formula

$=SUM(Q70:Q78).$

	O	P	Q
69	Penalty	dev	penalty
70	VM-CWVM	-5	0
71	CW-CWVM	-3.23988	0
72	CID-CWCID	-4.99997	0
73	CW-CWCID	-2.23984	0
74	VM-VMCID	-4.99999	0
75	CID-VMCID	-6	0
76	CWVM-all	-1.89999	0
77	CWCID-all	-2.90003	0
78	VMCID-all	-1.9	0
79		total	0

Step 2: We now change our Total formula in M3 to

$=SUM(M6:M82)-50*Q79.$

This penalizes us severely for any price reversal. We now set our Evolver dialog box as follows:

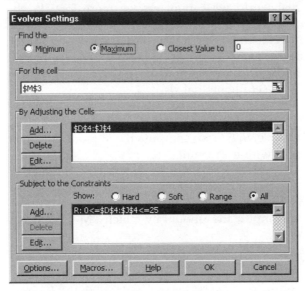

We obtain the following solution:

	C	D	E	F	G	H	I	J	K	L	M	N	O	P
3										total	492.4994			
4	Price	6.7601	5	4	10	8.999952	10	11.8999846						
5	Caller ID	CW	VM	CID	CW,VM	CW,CID	VM,CID	CW,VM,CID	max surp	bought?	revenue			
6	0.5	-6.26	-4	-3.5	-8.5	-7.99995	-8.5	-9.8999846	-3.49998	0	0			
7	0.5	-4.26	0	-3.5	-2.5	-5.99995	-4.5	-3.8999846	5.07E-07	2	4.999999			
8	7	-2.76	-1	3	-2	2.000048	1	3.10001539	3.100015	7	11.89998		Product	Frequenc
9	0	3.2399	5	-4	10	1.000048	1E-05	8.10001539	10	4	9.999998		0	2
10	2	-6.76	-4	-2	-9	-6.99995	-7	-8.8999846	-1.99998	0	0		1	
11	0	-6.76	5	-4	1.7E-06	-8.99995	1E-05	-1.8999846	5.000001	2	4.999999		2	1
12	1.5	-3.76	0	-2.5	-2	-4.49995	-3.5	-2.3999846	5.07E-07	2	4.999999		3	
13	0	-5.76	-2	-4	-6	-7.99995	-7	-7.8999846	-2	0	0		4	
14	0.3	-6.01	-4	-3.7	-8.25	-7.94995	-8.7	-9.8499846	-3.69998	0	0		5	
15	4	-3.76	-1	2E-05	-3	-1.99995	-2	-0.8999846	1.5E-05	3	3.999985		6	
16	3	-1.76	2	-1	2	-0.99995	1E-05	3.10001539	3.100015	7	11.89998		7	2

Note there are no price reversals and revenue is actually up $12 to $492! Also note that somebody purchases every combination except Call Waiting.

Using Evolver to Find Optimal Bundle Prices

Chapter 54: Optimal Quantity Discounts with Evolver

Evolver can easily be used to determine a revenue or profit maximizing strategy for quantity discounts. Here is an example of how to find a quantity discount strategy with a single price break.

Example 54.1

Three customer segments are thinking of ordering up to 5000 copies of Office. The value each segment associates with each 500 copies ordered are given in Figure 54.1. For example, Segment 1 values the first 500 purchased at $200 each, the next 500 purchased at $190 each, etc. We are thinking of adapting the following price strategy. Charge a price (High Price) for each of the first N units ordered and another price (Low Price) for remaining units. What strategy will maximize our revenue from the three segments?

Figure 54.1

	C	D	E	F
1	Size	500	400	300
2	Cuts	C1 Value	C2 Value	C3 Value
3	500	$ 200	$ 220	$ 190
4	1000	$ 190	$ 160	$ 180
5	1500	$ 160	$ 130	$ 170
6	2000	$ 130	$ 110	$ 160
7	2500	$ 100	$ 80	$ 150
8	3000	$ 90	$ 75	$ 140
9	3500	$ 60	$ 55	$ 130
10	4000	$ 40	$ 36	$ 90
11	4500	$ 25	$ 20	$ 70
12	5000	$ 15	$ 5	$ 60

Solution

We define a customer's consumer surplus as the value they attach to a given number of units - the cost of those units. To solve problems of this type we assume that **each customer will purchase the number of units that maximizes their consumer surplus. If each possible order quantity** has a negative surplus, the segment will purchase nothing.

Our spreadsheet computes the following quantities:

- Cost of buying each quantity.
- Value each segment associates with each order quantity.
- Each segment's surplus for each order quantity.
- The quantity purchased by each segment.
- The revenue we earn from each segment and the total revenue.

Our work is in file **Qd.xls** (sheet qd). Also see Figure 54.2. We have named the range C16:E16 with the names in C15:E15 (Cut, HP, and LP),

Step 1: In cell G3 we compute the value associated by Segment 1 to the first 500 items purchased with the formula

$=500*D3.$

Step 2: In cell G4 we compute the total value associated by Segment 1 with the first 1000 items with the formula

$=G3+500*D4.$

Thus value for first 1000 = value for first 500 + value for next 500. Copying this formula from G4 to G5:G13 yields value Segment 1 associates with 1000, 1500, ... 5000 items.

Step 3: Copying the formulas from G3:G12 to H3:I12 computes the value Segments 2 and 3 associate with each possible order quantity.

Step 4: In J3:J12 we compute the cost of ordering 500, 1000, ... 5000 units. Simply copy from J3 to J3:J12 the formula

$=IF(C3<=Cut,HP*C3,Cut*HP+(C3-Cut)*LP).$

These formula charges the High Price for all units purchased up to the cutoff, and charges the Low Price for all remaining units purchased.

Step 5: In cells K3:M12 compute the surplus obtained by each customer segment for each possible purchase quantity by copying from K3 to K3:M12 the formula

$=G3-\$J3.$

Figure 54.2

	C	D	E	F
1	Size	500	400	300
2	Cuts	C1 Value	C2 Value	C3 Value
3	500	$ 200	$ 220	$ 190
4	1000	$ 190	$ 160	$ 180
5	1500	$ 160	$ 130	$ 170
6	2000	$ 130	$ 110	$ 160
7	2500	$ 100	$ 80	$ 150
8	3000	$ 90	$ 75	$ 140
9	3500	$ 60	$ 55	$ 130
10	4000	$ 40	$ 36	$ 90
11	4500	$ 25	$ 20	$ 70
12	5000	$ 15	$ 5	$ 60
13				
14				
15	Cut	HP	LP	
16	1211	325.0747	14.99984	

Figure 54.3

	G	H	I	J	K	L	M
2	C1 Cum	C2 Cum	C3 Cum	Cost	C1 Sur	C2 Sur	C3 Sur
3	$ 100,000	$ 110,000	$ 95,000	$ 162,537	$ (62,537)	$ (52,537)	$ (67,537)
4	$ 195,000	$ 190,000	$ 185,000	$ 325,075	$ (130,075)	$ (135,075)	$ (140,075)
5	$ 275,000	$ 255,000	$ 270,000	$ 398,000	$ (123,000)	$ (143,000)	$ (128,000)
6	$ 340,000	$ 310,000	$ 350,000	$ 405,500	$ (65,500)	$ (95,500)	$ (55,500)
7	$ 390,000	$ 350,000	$ 425,000	$ 413,000	$ (23,000)	$ (63,000)	$ 12,000
8	$ 435,000	$ 387,500	$ 495,000	$ 420,500	$ 14,500	$ (33,000)	$ 74,500
9	$ 465,000	$ 415,000	$ 560,000	$ 428,000	$ 37,000	$ (13,000)	$ 132,000
10	$ 485,000	$ 433,000	$ 605,000	$ 435,500	$ 49,500	$ (2,500)	$ 169,500
11	$ 497,500	$ 443,000	$ 640,000	$ 443,000	$ 54,500	$ 0	$ 197,000
12	$ 505,000	$ 445,500	$ 670,000	$ 450,500	$ 54,500	$ (5,000)	$ 219,500
13				max surplus	$ 54,500	$ 0	$ 219,500
14				bought	5000	4500	5000
15				revenue	$ 225,249,956	$177,199,997	$ 135,149,974
16				total	$ 537,599,926		

Step 6: In K13:M13 we compute the maximum surplus for each segment. This will be used to determine the number of units purchased by each segment. Simply copy from K13 to L13:M13 the formula

=MAX(K3:K12).

Step 7: In K14:M14 we compute the number of units purchased by each segment by copying from K14 to K14:M14 the formula

=IF(K13<0,0,500*MATCH(K13,K3:K12,0)).

If the maximum surplus is negative, then no units are purchased. Otherwise, the MATCH function finds the ranking in rows 3-12 (max surplus in row 3 yields a 1, max surplus in row 4 yields a 2, etc.) of the maximum surplus and multiplies it by 500 to obtain number of units purchased. For example, Segment 1's maximum surplus of 50.002 was obtained by the seventh order quantity. Multiplying 7 by 500 yields the number of units purchased.

Step 8: In K15:M15 we compute the revenue earned from each segment by copying from K15 to L15:M15 the formula

$$D1*IF(K14=0,0,VLOOKUP(K14,\$C\$3:\$J\$12,8)).$$

If no items are purchased, then we earn no revenue. Otherwise we look up in Column J of spreadsheet the cost corresponding to the number of items purchased (obtained from Row 14!) and multiply this cost by the size of the segment.

Step 9: In K16 we obtain our total revenue by adding the revenues for the different segments.

$$=SUM(K15:M15).$$

Step 10: We are now ready to invoke Evolver. The settings are as follows.

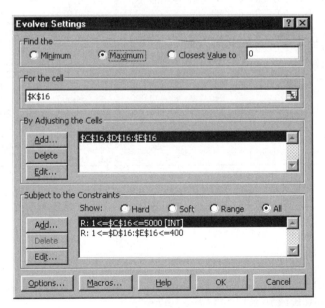

We maximize revenue (K16) by changing the Cutoff and the High and Low prices (C16:E16). We constrain each price to be between $0 and $400. The cutoff for the discount is constrained to be an integer between 0 and 5000 units. We find maximum revenue of nearly $538,000,000 can be obtained. We charge $325.07 for the first 1211 units and $14.99 for remaining units.

Remark

If we just charged a single price for each unit the revenue-maximizing price would be $129 and our profit would equal $342,000,000. Note how much more money we make with the quantity discount strategy. See sheet Single Price for this analysis.

Chapter 55: Price Response to Currency Fluctuation

Suppose Eli Lilly is selling a drug in Germany. Their goal is to maximize their profit in dollars, but when the drug is sold in Germany they receive marks. In order to maximize their dollar profit, how should the price in marks vary with the exchange rate? To illustrate the ideas involved consider the following example (based on Dolan and Simon (1997)):

Example 55.1

The drug Taxoprol costs $60 to produce. Currently the exchange rate is .667 $/mark and we are charging 150 marks for Taxoprol. Current demand for Taxoprol is 100 units, and it is estimated that the elasticity for Taxoprol is 2.5. Assuming a linear demand curve, determine how the price (in marks) for Taxoprol should vary with the exchange rate.

Solution

See sheet Linear Elastic Demand in file **intrprice.xls**. We begin by determining the linear demand curve that relates demand to the price in marks. Currently demand is 100 and the price is 150 marks. Since the elasticity is 2.5, a 1% increase in price (to 151.5) will result in a 2.5% decrease in demand (to 100 - 2.5 = 97.5). In the file Intprice.xls (sheet Linear Demand) we entered these two points in B12:C13. We now find the slope and intercept of the demand curve.

$$Slope = \frac{97.5 - 100}{151.5 - 150} = -1.6667 \quad \text{(thus demand is elastic)}$$

(Computed in D13 with formula =*(B13 - B12)/(A13-A12)*).

Intercept = 100 + (-150)(-1.6667) = 350

(Computed in D14 with the formula =*B12 + (-A12)*(D13)*).

Thus *Demand* = 350 – 1.6667(Price in Marks).

Figure 55.1

	A	B	C	D	E
1	**Price dependence**				
2	**on exchange rate**				
3					
4	Current $/DM	0.66667			
5	Unit Cost US $	60			
6	Current price DM	149.9998			
7	Current demand	100.0004			
8	Current profit US$	4000.05			
9	Elasticity	2.5			
10					
11	Price DM	demand			
12	150	100			
13	151.5	97.5	slope	-1.66667	
14	Demand = 350-(5/3)*price		intercept	350	
15					
16					

We now can compute (for a trial price) our profit for a given exchange rate. Then we use Solver to find the price maximizing profit. Finally we will use the SolverTable to find the profit maximizing price for different exchange rates.

Step by Step

Step 1: Enter a trial value for the exchange rate ($/mark) (say .66667) in cell range B4

Step 2: In B5 we enter the unit cost in dollars ($60).

Step 3: In B6 we enter trial prices (in marks) for Taxoprol.

Step 4: Observe that demand for any exchange rate is given by

350 - 1.66667(price in marks)*

In cell B7 we determine the demand for each exchange rate. In B7 we find the demand for the exchange rate of .6667 $/mark with the formula

*= $D$14 + $D$13*B6.*

Step 5: Observe that profit in dollars is given by

*(($/mark)*price in marks - cost in dollars)*(demand).*

In cell B8 we compute the dollar profit (for the trial prices) for each exchange rate. In B8 we find the profit for our current exchange rate (.66667 $/mark) and current price (150 marks) with the formula

*= (B4*B6 - B5)*B7.*

Step 6: We now use Solver to determine the profit-maximizing price for each exchange rate. By changing the price (B6) in marks we can maximize the profit (B8) in dollars. Our Solver window follows:

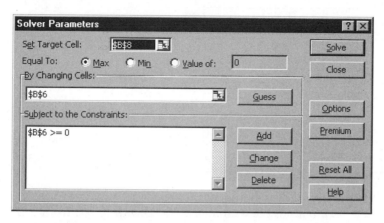

We find for an exchange rate of $.66667 per mark that we should charge 150 marks.

Step 7: We now use SolverTable to tell us how our profit and price will change with changes in the exchange rate. We select Data>SolverTable and select One Way Table. Fill in the dialog box as follows:

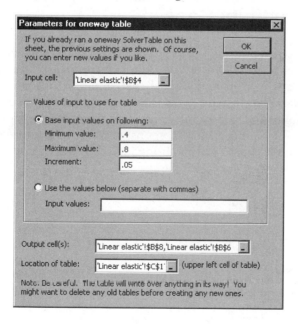

This dialog box will have Solver solve for optimal price in marks for exchange rates of .4, .45, ..., .75 and .80 dollars/mark. For each exchange rate, the SolverTable records the profit-maximizing price in marks and the profit. The results follow:

	C	D	E
17	$/DM	Profit$s	Price DM
18	0.4	600.0001	180
19	0.45	1102.084	171.6667
20	0.5	1687.5	165
21	0.55	2333.523	159.5455
22	0.6	3025	155
23	0.65	3751.443	151.1538
24	0.7	4505.357	147.8571
25	0.75	5281.25	145
26	0.8	6075	142.5

Note, for example, we should not force the Germans to bear the entire brunt of currency devaluation. For example, if the DM dropped from $0.75 to $0.50 (a 33% decrease) then we would only increase the price from 145 DM to 165 DM (14%). The reason we cannot force the Germans to bear the entire brunt of the price increase is the elastic nature of demand.

Constant Elasticity Case

If Demand $=a(Price)^{-b}$, then for any price, demand will have an elasticity of b. That is, a 1% increase in price will decrease demand by b%. In the sheet Constant Elasticity in Intprice.xls we have analyzed this situation. We used Goal Seek to choose the parameter a so demand equals 100 when exchange rate is $0.66667 per mark. From the following SolverTable we find that for demand of constant elasticity, price should be much more responsive to changes in exchange rates. It turns out that we should always price to bring in $100 per unit of the drug.

$/DM	Profit $	Price dm
0.4	1115.419	250
0.45	1497.337	222.2222
0.5	1948.557	200
0.55	2472.834	181.8182
0.6	3073.734	166.6667
0.65	3754.668	153.8461
0.7	4518.905	142.8571
0.75	5369.592	133.3333
0.8	6309.764	125

Reference

Dolan, R. and Simon, J. , *Power Pricing*, Free Press, 1997

Chapter 56: Pricing in the Presence of Gray Imports and Piracy

Suppose Eli Lilly must set a price for Taxoprol in the US, Germany, and United Kingdom. They know that the profit-maximizing price in Germany and the UK is much higher than the profit-maximizing price in the US. Unfortunately for Lilly, if the US price is much lower than the UK or German price, unscrupulous entrepreneurs can make money by purchasing Taxoprol in the US and "pirating" it illegally to Germany or the UK. Such imports are often called **"gray imports."** In this section we discuss how international prices need to be modified to account for gray imports.

Example 56.1

Lilly produces Taxoprol in the US and sells it in Germany and UK (as well as US). The demand for the product in each country depends on the price in the following fashion. Assume \$1.50 = 1 British pound and \$0.50 = 1 dm

Country	Demand
US	10,000-4000(\$ price)
UK	6000 - 1300(pound price)
Germany	6500- 600(dm price)

It costs Lilly 50 cents to produce the drug in the US, and 15 cents/unit to ship to the UK and 25 cents per unit to ship to Germany. If the US price is much lower than the UK or German price, a certain percentage of the UK and German demand will be satisfied by illegal imports purchased in the US. Specifically, Lilly believes that if the US price is more than 10% lower than the UK price, then for every percentage point difference between UK and US prices exceeding 10% of UK price(in \$), .9% of all UK demand will be satisfied from the US. For example, if the US price = \$2.10 and the UK Price = \$3.00, the US price is 30% lower than the UK price and .9(30 - 10) = 18% of UK demand will be satisfied from the US. Similarly, if the US price is more than 10% lower than the German price, then for every percentage point difference between the German and US prices (in \$s) exceeding 10%, .9% of all German demand will be satisfied from the US. How should Lilly price Taxoprol?

Our solution is in **Grayimports.xls**.

*Figure 56.1
Solution
with Gray
Imports*

	A	B	C	D	E	F	G	H	I
1	Gray Imports		$/mark	0.5					
2			$/pound	1.5					
3		Demand			Unit Cost	Price(native currency	Price $s	Sold	Profit
4	US Demand	2458.066	>=	0	$ 0.50	1.885484	$ 1.89	3910.57	$ 5,418.0:
5	UK Demand	3344.409	>=	0	$ 0.65	2.042762	$ 3.06	2487.585	$ 6,005.3!
6	German Demand	3251.122	>=	0	$ 0.75	5.414797	$ 2.71	2655.442	$ 5,197.7(
7			%age Gray Imports					Total	16621.174!
8	US/UK price	0.384662	0.256195912						
9	US/Germany price	0.303581	0.183222964						

Figure 56.1 shows what we need to keep track of:

- Price in each country(in native currency and in $s).

- Demand in each country

- Gray imports to UK and Germany

- Amount Sold in each country

- Profit Earned in each country(in $s)

- Total Profit(in $s)

We proceed as follows:

Step 1: Enter trial prices for each country (in native currency)in F4:F6.

Step 2: Compute the overall demand for each country in B4:B6. For example, the demand in US is computed in B4 with the formula

$= 10000 - 4000*F4.$

Similarly, we compute the UK demand in B5 with formula

$=6000-1300*F5.$

and German demand in B6 with the formula

$=6500-600*F6.$

Step 3: In G4:G6 compute the price of the drug in each country (in $s). In G4 compute price in US in $s with formula

   $= F4$.

In G5 compute UK price in $s with formula

   $= F5*D2$.

In G6 compute German price in $s with formula

   $=F6*D1$.

Step 4: We enter unit costs (in $s) for selling in each country in E4:E6.

Step 5: In B8:C9 we compute the percentage of UK and German demand that will be met with gray imports. In B8 we compute the percentage amount by which US price is lower than UK price with formula

   $=(G5-\$G\$4)/G5$.

Copying this formula to B9 computes the percentage amount by which US price is lower than German price. Then in C8:C9 we can compute the percentage of Gray imports to each country. In C8 we compute the percentage of gray imports to UK with the formula

   $= IF(B8>.1,.9*(B8-.1),0)$.

This ensures that we lose .9% of UK imports to US for each percentage increase in price differential over 10%.

Similarly, in C9 we compute the percentage of gray imports to Germany with the formula

   $= IF(B9>.1, .9*(B9-.1),0)$.

Step 6: We now compute the total sold in each country in H4:H6. For the US amount sold = (original US demand) + (gray imports to UK) + (gray imports to Germany).

Thus in H4 we compute US sales with the formula

   $= B4+B5*C8+B6*C9$.

For UK

amount sold = (original UK demand) - (Gray Imports), so we compute UK sales in H5 with the formula

   $= B5-B5*C8$.

Copying this formula to H6 computes German sales.

Step 7: In I4:I6 we compute Lilly's profit in each country by the formula

(profit) = (units sold in country)*(country price in \$s - country unit cost in \$s).

Thus in I4 US profit is computed with the formula

= H4*(G4-E4).

Copying this formula to I5:I6 computes the profit in UK and Germany. Then total profit is computed in I7 with the formula

=SUM(I4:I6).

Step 7: We are now ready to use Evolver to find the profit-maximizing set of prices. We do not use the ordinary Solver because the problem is highly nonlinear. The two causes of the Nonlinearities are the IF statements in C8:C9 and the quotients involving changing cells in B8:B9. Evolver may not find exactly the profit-maximizing solution, but it usually comes within 1%-2% of the maximum profit. In using Evolver just remember that it requires each changing cell to have a lower bound (usually 0) and an upper bound.

Figure 56.2

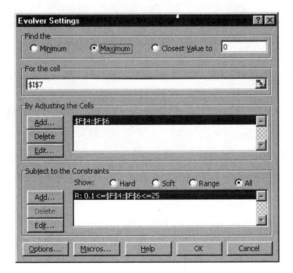

To specify our problem for Evolver (see Figure 56.2) we choose our Evolver Target Cell to be I7 (total profit). Our Changing cells are just the price in each country (F4:F6). Since a price exceeding 25 units will induce negative demand everywhere, we constrain prices to be at most 25 (F4:F6<=25). The lower bound on the prices is tricky. If we use 0, then the formulas in B8 and B9 may involve dividing by 0, which will cause an error. Therefore we force each price to exceed .10 units. (F4:F6>=.1) After hitting start Evolver finds the solution in Figure 56.1; a \$1.89 US price, 2.04 pounds UK price, and a 5.41 dm Germany price. Total profit is \$16,621

Remarks

If we assumed that gray imports did not exist we could have run Evolver (see Figure 56.3 and file **grayimports2.xls**) to maximize profit and found that a maximum profit of $19,059 could be earned by charging $1.50 in US, 2.52 pounds in UK and 6.18 DM in Germany. To use Evolver here just put 0 in the Gray import cells (C8:C9). Note how gray import threat drives up US price and down UK price.

Figure 56.3 Solution if there are No Gray Imports

	A	B	C	D	E	F	G	H	I
1	No Gray Imports		$/mark	0.5					
2			$/pound	1.5					
3		Demand			Unit Cost	Price(native currency	Price $s	Sold	Profit
4	US Demand	4000	>=	0	$ 0.50	1.5	$ 1.50	4000	$ 4,000.00
5	UK Demand	2718.333	>=	0	$ 0.65	2.524359	$ 3.79	2718.333	$ 8,526.16
6	German Demand	2800.456	>=	0	$ 0.75	6.165907	$ 3.08	2800.456	$ 6,533.33
7			%age Gray Imports					Total	19059.49021
8	US/UK price	0.60386	0						
9	US/Germany price	0.513454	0						

In reality, several countries may send gray imports to a given country. This would make the setup of our model more difficult. We might model, say gray imports to, say, China to depend on the price differentials between China and Japan and China and India.

Chapter 57: Conjoint Analysis

It is important for marketers to understand which attributes of a product are most important to customers. Knowledge of the relative importance of product attributes can be used to design a product or predict the market share for a product. Conjoint analysis provides a way of assessing attribute importance and is particularly valuable when the set of key attributes is relatively limited. Conjoint analysis has been used to design many products such as soap, shampoo, gasoline, panty hose, auto insurance, branch banks, copying machines, hotels, PCs, airline service, automobiles, car rental services, and cameras. The well-known hotel chain Courtyard by Marriott was designed after an extensive conjoint study. Here are some examples of product attributes.

Product	Attributes
PC	brand name, price, computer speed, RAM, hard drive space, service policy
Hotel Room	location, room size and setup, services, leisure facilities, security and price
New Drug	Efficacy, side effects, taste, cost, convenience, medical endorsements

To set up a conjoint analysis the researcher must define a number of levels (usually 2-7) for each attribute. For example, the attribute Entertainment in the Courtyard by Marriott study had the following levels:

- Color TV with local stations

- Color TV with local stations and pay movies

- Color TV with 30 cable stations

- Color TV with local stations HBO and ESPN

- Color TV with 30 cable stations and free movies.

In this case the Entertainment attribute has five levels.

We now discuss a classic conjoint study conducted by Green and Wind (see Lehmann et. al (1998)).

Example 57.1

A new carpet cleaning fluid is under design. A consumer's purchase decision may depend on

- Package design (either A, B, or C)
- Which brand (1,2, or 3)
- Price (either $1.19, $1.39, or $1.59)
- Did Good Housekeeping approve product?
- Is product guaranteed?

Thus the product has 5 attributes. Package Design, Brand, and Price each have three levels while Good Housekeeping approval and Guarantee each have two levels. This means that there are 3x3x3x2x2 = 108 different product combinations under consideration. Usually, consumers are asked to rank different product combinations. It is impractical, however, to ask a consumer to rank 108 product combinations. For this reason Green and Wind chose to use 18 combinations. The combinations they chose (and the rank assigned by a particular consumer) are given in Figure 57.1.

Figure 57.1

	A	B	C	D	E	F
1	design	Brand	PRICE	Approved?	Guarantee?	Rank
2	A	1	1.19	No	No	13
3	A	2	1.39	No	Yes	11
4	A	3	1.59	Yes	No	17
5	B	1	1.39	Yes	Yes	2
6	B	2	1.59	No	No	14
7	B	3	1.19	No	No	3
8	C	1	1.59	No	Yes	12
9	C	2	1.19	Yes	No	7
10	C	3	1.39	No	No	9
11	A	1	1.59	Yes	No	18
12	A	2	1.19	No	Yes	8
13	A	3	1.39	No	No	15
14	B	1	1.19	No	No	4
15	B	2	1.39	Yes	No	6
16	B	3	1.59	No	Yes	5
17	C	1	1.39	No	No	10
18	C	2	1.59	No	No	16
19	C	3	1.19	Yes	Yes	1

For example, the consumer felt the most preferred product was Package C, Brand 3, $1.19 price, with a Guarantee and Good Housekeeping seal of approval.

Choice of Combinations

How were these 18 combinations chosen? Most conjoint researchers choose the combination of attribute levels to be an **orthogonal design**. Basically this means that the levels for any attribute are uncorrelated with the levels of any other attribute. In most cases this means that a given level of an attribute appears an equal number of times with each level of the other attributes. For example, a $1.19 price appears twice with each brand and 3 times with a guarantee and three times without a guarantee. This ensures that when we determine the effect of a $1.19 price the effects of the other attributes should "balance out." If, for example, we always had a Guarantee when we charged $1.19 we could not determine if a consumer preferred the product because of the low price or the Guarantee. Addelman (1962) contains tables of orthogonal designs. The seven basic plans are used in the following situations

Plan	Number of trials	Combinations of Attribute levels that can be handled
1	8	$4,3,2^7$
2	9	$3^4, 2^4$
3	16	$4^5,3^5,2^{15}$
4	18	$3^7, 2^7$
5	25	$5^6,4^6,3^6,2^6$
6	27	$9,8,7,6,5,4,3^{13},2^{13}$
7	32	$4^9,3^9,2^{31}$

For example, Plan 6 uses 27 trials or combinations. Plan 6 allows you to handle one attribute with 9, 8, 7, 6, 5, or 4 levels, up to 13 attributes with three levels, and up to 13 attributes with two levels.

We illustrate the use of these tables for the carpet-cleaning example. For each of our attributes with 3 levels we label the levels as 0, 1, 2. For each of our two level attributes we label the levels as 0 and 1. Our correspondence of 0, 1, and 2 to actual attribute levels will be as follows:

Table 57.1

Attribute #	Level Code	Meaning of Level
1	0	Design A
1	1	Design B
1	2	Design C
2	0	Brand 1
2	1	Brand 2
2	2	Brand 3
3	0	$1.19 price
3	1	$1.39 price
3	2	$1.59 price
4	0	No Good Housekeeping Approval
4	1	Good Housekeeping Approval
5	0	No Guarantee
5	1	Guarantee

Green and Wind used Basic Plan 4 reproduced below. Note the first set of seven columns is for three level factors (it contains 0, 1, and 2) while the second set of seven columns is for two level factors (it contains only 0 and 1). Green and Wind chose Columns 1-3 for the three level factors and columns 4 and 5 for the two level factors.

Basic Plan 4

Plan 4:$3^7,2^7$
18 trials

Row	1	2	3	4	5	6	7	1	2	3	4	5	6	7
1	0	0	0	0	0	0	0	0	0	0	0	0	0	0
2	0	1	1	2	1	1	1	0	1	1	0	1	1	1
3	0	2	2	1	2	2	2	0	0	0	1	0	0	0
4	1	0	1	1	1	2	0	1	0	1	1	1	0	0
5	1	1	2	0	2	0	1	1	1	0	0	0	0	1
6	1	2	0	2	0	1	2	1	0	0	0	0	1	0
7	2	0	2	2	1	0	2	0	0	0	0	1	0	0
8	2	1	0	1	2	1	0	0	1	0	1	0	1	0
9	2	2	1	0	0	2	1	0	0	1	0	0	0	1
10	0	0	2	1	0	1	1	0	0	0	1	0	1	1
11	0	1	0	0	1	2	2	0	1	0	0	1	0	0
12	0	2	1	2	2	0	0	0	0	1	0	0	0	0
13	1	0	0	2	2	2	1	1	0	0	0	0	0	1
14	1	1	1	1	0	0	2	1	1	1	1	0	0	0
15	1	2	2	0	1	1	0	1	0	0	0	1	1	0
16	2	0	1	0	2	1	2	0	0	1	0	0	1	0
17	2	1	2	2	0	2	0	0	1	0	0	0	0	0
18	2	2	0	1	1	0	1	0	0	0	1	1	0	1

This yields the following design:

Figure 57.2

Plan 4   18 trials
3x3x3x2x2

1	2	3	4	5
0	0	0	0	0
0	1	1	0	1
0	2	2	1	0
1	0	1	1	1
1	1	2	0	0
1	2	0	0	0
2	0	2	0	1
2	1	0	1	0
2	2	1	0	0
0	0	2	1	0
0	1	0	0	1
0	2	1	0	0
1	0	0	0	0
1	1	1	1	0
1	2	2	0	1
2	0	1	0	0
2	1	2	0	0
2	2	0	1	1

With the Excel CORREL function you can check any pair of columns in Figure 57.2 has a 0 correlation. Essentially this says that knowing the level of one attribute will give you no information about the level of another attribute. Now by referring to Table 57.1 we can see where attribute combinations in Figure 57.1 came from. For example, first trial in Figure 57.2 has all codes of 0. This represents Design A, Brand 1, $1.19 price with no Good Housekeeping seal or Guarantee. Combination 18 has codes 2, 2, 0, 1, and 1. This corresponds to Design C, Brand 3, $1.19, Good Housekeeping seal and Guarantee.

Using Dummy Variables to Evaluate Importance of Attribute Levels

By using regression with dummy variables we can determine the relative importance of the product attributes. We rescale the consumer's rankings so that the highest ranked product combination receives a score of 18 and the lowest ranked product combination receives a score of 1. To do this just subtract 19 from the product combination's actual ranking. We call this the **Inverse Ranking**. Then we run regression using dummy variables to determine the effect of each product attribute on the Inverse rankings. This requires us to leave out one level of each attribute. We left out Design C, Brand 3, a $1.59 price, no Good Housekeeping approval, and no Guarantee. After rescaling the rankings, a positive coefficient for a dummy variable will indicate that the given level of the attribute makes the product more preferred than the left-out level of the attribute and a negative coefficient for a dummy variable will indicate that the given level of the attribute makes the product less preferred than the left-out level of the attribute. Figure 57.3 gives (see file **Conjoint.xls** and the **data** tab) the coding of the data.

Figure 57.3

	A	B	C	D	E	F	G	H	I	J
20	A?	B?	Brand 1?	Brand 2?	1.19?	1.39?	Approved?	Guarantee	Rank(1=Best)	Rank(1=worst)
21	1	0	1	0	1	0	0	0	13	6
22	1	0	0	1	0	1	0	1	11	8
23	1	0	0	0	0	0	1	0	17	2
24	0	1	1	0	0	1	1	1	2	17
25	0	1	0	1	0	0	0	0	14	5
26	0	1	0	0	1	0	0	0	3	16
27	0	0	1	0	0	0	0	1	12	7
28	0	0	0	1	1	0	1	0	7	12
29	0	0	0	0	0	1	0	0	9	10
30	1	0	1	0	0	0	1	0	18	1
31	1	0	0	1	1	0	0	1	8	11
32	1	0	0	0	0	1	0	0	15	4
33	0	1	1	0	1	0	0	0	4	15
34	0	1	0	1	0	1	1	0	6	13
35	0	1	0	0	0	0	0	1	5	14
36	0	0	1	0	0	1	0	0	10	9
37	0	0	0	1	0	0	0	0	16	3
38	0	0	0	0	1	0	1	1	1	18

For example, the first row of data indicates that if we charge $1.19 for Brand 1 and Package Design A with no Guarantee or Good Housekeeping approval, the combination is rated 6th from worst (or 13th overall). After running a regression with Y-Range J20:J38 and X-Range A20:H38 (and checking Labels included box) we obtain the equation given in Figure 57.4.(see Regression sheet).

Figure 57.4

	A	B	C	D	E	F	G	H	I
1	SUMMARY OUTPUT								
2									
3	Regression Statistics								
4	Multiple R	0.991536							
5	R Square	0.983144							
6	Adjusted R Sq	0.968161							
7	Standard Error	0.952579							
8	Observations	18							
9									
10	ANOVA								
11		df	SS	MS	F	ignificance F			
12	Regression	8	476.3333	59.54167	65.61735	4.49E-07			
13	Residual	9	8.166667	0.907407					
14	Total	17	484.5						
15									
16		Coefficients	andard Err	t Stat	P-value	Lower 95%	Upper 95%	ower 95.0%	Jpper 95.0%
17	Intercept	4.833333	0.635053	7.610915	3.29E-05	3.396743	6.269924	3.396743	6.269924
18	A?	-4.5	0.549972	-8.182236	1.85E-05	-5.744124	-3.255876	-5.744124	-3.255876
19	B?	3.5	0.549972	6.363961	0.000131	2.255876	4.744124	2.255876	4.744124
20	Brand 1?	-1.5	0.549972	-2.727412	0.023323	-2.744124	-0.255876	-2.744124	-0.255876
21	Brand 2?	-2	0.549972	-3.636549	0.00543	-3.244124	-0.755876	-3.244124	-0.755876
22	1.19?	7.666667	0.549972	13.94011	2.13E-07	6.422543	8.910791	6.422543	8.910791
23	1.39?	4.833333	0.549972	8.788327	1.04E-05	3.589209	6.077457	3.589209	6.077457
24	Approved?	1.5	0.47629	3.149344	0.01175	0.422557	2.577443	0.422557	2.577443
25	Guarantee?	4.5	0.47629	9.448032	5.73E-06	3.422557	5.577443	3.422557	5.577443

All independent variables are significant at the .05 level (all p-values are smaller than .05). Our best prediction for the inverse rank of a product is as follows:

Predicted Inverse Rank = 4.833 -4.5A + 3.5B –1.5(Brand 1) –2(Brand 2)

+7.667($1.19 Price) + 4.83($1.39 Price) +1.5(Approved?) + 4.5(Guarantee).

The meaning of this equation follows:

- Design C leads to a rank 4.5 higher than Design A and 3.5 lower than Design B.

- Brand 3 leads to a rank 1.5 higher than Brand 1 and 2 higher than Brand 2.

- A $1.19 price leads to a rank 7.67 higher than $1.59 and 4.83 higher than $1.39.

- A Good Housekeeping approval yields a rank 1.5 better than no approval.

- A Guarantee yields a rank 4.5 higher than no Guarantee.

The Part-worth Approach

Which attributes have the most influence on the customer's likelihood of purchasing the product? Look at the attributes where there is the most spread from the best level of the attribute to the worst level of the attribute. This analysis is displayed in the following table.

Attribute	Spread	Ranking
Design	4.5 – (-3.5) = 8	1st
Brand	0 – (-2) = 2	4th
Price	7.67- 0 = 7.67	2nd
Approval	1.5- 0 = 1.5	5th
Guarantee	4.5 – 0 = 4.5	3rd

For example, we see the Package Design is the most important attribute and the Good Housekeeping approval the least important attribute. Most conjoint analysis programs display the "part-worth" for levels of each attribute graphically. To do this define

MAX SPREAD = Spread from worst to best for most important attribute.

In our example MAX SPREAD = 8.

The worst level of each attribute receives a rating of 0. Then the other levels for each attribute are graphed as

$$\frac{(\text{score for level of attribute}) - (\text{score for minimum level of attribute})}{\text{MAX SPREAD}}$$

For example

- Design B gets a part worth of 8/8 =1.
- Design C gets a score of 4.5/8 = .56.
- Design A gets a score of 0.

The part-worths for Design are graphed in Figure 57.5.

Figure 57.5 Part-worths for Package Design

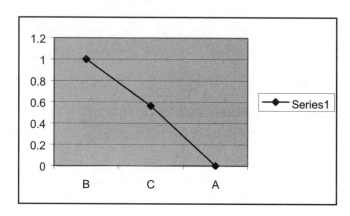

The graphs for the other part-worths follow:

Brand Scores

Figure 57.6 Part-worths for Brand

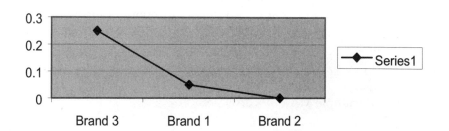

Figure 57.7
Part-worths
for Price

Price

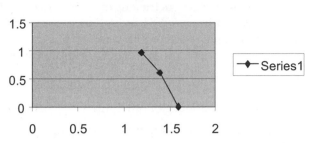

Figure 57.8
Parts-worth
for Approval

Approved?

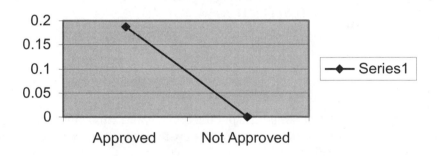

Figure 57.9
Parts-worth
for Guarantee

Guarantee?

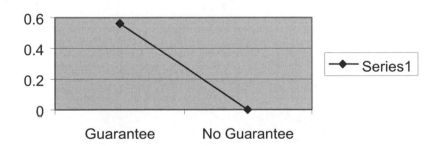

Expressing Attribute Importance in Terms of Price

A common way of expressing the importance of various levels of attributes is in terms of price. Note that the +4.83 coefficient of $1.39 price implies that a 20 cent increase in price to $1.59 results in a 4.83 reduction in ranking. Thus, each cent of price increase is roughly equivalent to .24 ranking points. Similarly, the +7.667 coefficient for $1.19 price implies that each cent we decrease price (between $1.39 and $1.19) improves our ranking by $\frac{7.67 - 4.83}{20} = .14$ ranking points. We can use these values to express the importance of other attribute changes:

- Changing Package Design from B to C is same as increasing Price from $1.39 to $1.54. (3.5/24 = 15 cents)

- Changing Package Design from B to A has same effect as increasing Price from $1.39 to $1.72. (8/24= 33 cents)

- A Good Housekeeping approval has same effect as cutting Price from $1.39 to $1.28(1.5/14 = 11 cents).

- A Guarantee has same effect as cutting Price from $1.39 to $1.07. (4.5/.14 = 32 cents)

- Brand 3's advantage over Brand 2 has the same effect as a Price cut from $1.39 to $1.25 (2/14 = 14 cents).

- If we obtained a Guarantee, we could raise our Price from $1.39 to $1.58 (4.5/24 = 19 cents) and the customer would view our product as favorably as before.

- If we obtained Good Housekeeping approval, then we could raise our Price from $1.39 to $1.45 (1.5/24 = 6 cents) and the customer would view our product as favorably as before.

Determination of Product Market Share

We now show how to use conjoint analysis to estimate a product's market share. We will also be able to determine how changes in the product's design will change its market share. We now assume that 14 market segments have been identified and the "average" regression equation for each segment is given in Figure 57.10 (see sheet **Segments** of file **conjoint.xls**).

Figure 57.10

	A	B	C	D	E	F	G	H	I	J	K
5	Segment	Size(000)	Intercept	A	B	Brand 1	Brand 2	1.19?	1.39?	Approved?	Guarantee?
6	1	10	4.83	-4.5	3.5	-1.5	-2	7.67	4.83	1.5	4.5
7	2	15	2	-6	5	1	2	9	6	2	3
8	3	20	5	-2	2	-4	-6	8	5	3	5
9	4	12	2	4	1	4	2	7	4	1	4
10	5	22	4.7	1	4	3	2	6	4	2	2
11	6	14	9	-6	-4	2	1	5	3	2	3
12	7	10	8	1	3	0	-2	4	3	1	2
13	8	15	2	4	-3	5	-3	9	7	2	1
14	9	8	2	-2	4	2	5	7	4	3	4
15	10	12	7	-4	-2	1	3	6	4	2	2
16	11	9	2	1	2	2	4	8	5	4	3
17	12	11	4.4	-6	5	-4	-2	6	4	5	2
18	13	8	7	-4	3	-1	3	4	3	2	3
19	14	14	2	2	2	2	-1	8	5	3	4

For example, Segment 14 consists of 14,000 people and from analyzing the rankings of representatives from that segment we found the average equation to be

Predicted Inverse Rank = 2 + 2*A + 2*B + 2*(Brand 1) - (Brand 2) +8*($1.19 Price) +5*($1.39 Price) + 3*(Goodhousekeeping) + 4*(Guarantee).

This segment prefers Package Designs A and B and Brand 1.

We now assume that there are 3 products in the market.

- Product 1 is Brand 1, uses package A, sells for $1.19 and has no Approval or Guarantee.

- Product 2 is Brand 2, uses Package B, sells for $1.39 and is Approved with no Guarantee.

- Product 3 is Brand 3, uses Package C, sells for $1.59 and is not Approved but has no Guarantee.

Currently Product 1 (our product) has a 30% market share, Product 2 has a 50% market share, and Product 3 has a 20% market share. Our goal is to come up with a model that accurately predicts current market share. Then the model can be used to determine how changes in product design will change market share. In the conjoint literature it is commonly assumed that a product's market share in a segment may be approximated by:

Market Share Prediction Formula

$$\frac{Product\ 1\ Predicted\ Inverse\ Rank^{\alpha}}{Product\ 1\ Predicted\ Inverse\ Rank^{\alpha} + Product\ 2\ Predicted\ Inverse\ Rank^{\alpha} + Product\ 3\ Predicted\ Inverse\ Rank^{\alpha}}$$

If $\alpha = 1$, this formula assigns the members of a segment to a product in proportion to the inverse rank the segment assigns to the product. For example, suppose Product 1 had an inverse rank of 12, Product 2 an inverse rank of 6, and Product 3 an inverse rank of 6. Then Product 1 would be assigned a 50% share of the segment and Products 2 and 3 would each be assigned a 25% share. If α is a large positive number, then the entire segment is assigned to the product with the highest inverse rank. To calibrate this model, we determine the value of α that yields predicted market shares for each product (given current attributes for each product) that most closely matches each firm's actual current share. We proceed as follows:

Step by Step

Step 1: Enter the coding and current market share for each product in rows 1-4.

Figure 57.11

	A	B	C	D	E	F	G	H	I	J	K
1	Current share			A	B	Brand 1	Brand 2	1.19?	1.39?	Approved?	Guarantee?
2	0.3	Our brand		1	0	1	0	1	0	0	0
3	0.5	Comp 1		0	1	0	1	0	1	1	0
4	0.2	Comp 2		0	0	0	0	0	0	0	1

Figure 57.12

	L	M	N	O	P	Q	R
1	Alpha	2.075613					SSE
2			Squared Error	0.001927	0.000352	0.000632	0.002911
3			Actual Share	0.3	0.5	0.2	
4			Predicted Share	0.3439	0.481241	0.174859	
5	Our Brand Score	Comp 1 score	Comp 2 Score	Our share	Comp 1 share	Comp 2 Share	
6	6.5	12.66	9.33	0.140706	0.561363	0.297932	
7	6	17	5	0.096428	0.837525	0.066047	
8	7	9	10	0.209145	0.352362	0.438494	
9	17	10	6	0.690824	0.229638	0.079538	
10	14.7	16.7	6.7	0.400179	0.521484	0.078337	
11	10	11	12	0.271832	0.331296	0.396872	
12	13	13	10	0.387583	0.387583	0.224834	
13	20	5	3	0.929564	0.052316	0.01812	
14	9	18	6	0.177108	0.746554	0.076338	
15	10	14	9	0.262187	0.527128	0.210686	
16	13	17	5	0.346895	0.605366	0.047739	
17	0.4	16.4	6.4	0.000393	0.875442	0.124165	
18	6	18	10	0.07317	0.715574	0.211255	
19	14	11	6	0.562282	0.340851	0.096867	

Step 2: Enter a trial value for Alpha in cell M1 (range name the cell alpha). In cells L6:N19 we compute the predicted inverse rank for each segment-product combination. For Product 1 and Segment 1 we compute the predicted inverse rank in cell L6 with the formula

=SUMPRODUCT($D$2:$K$2,$D6:$K6)+$C6.

Copying this formula to M6:N6 (and changing the 2 to a 3 in M6 and a 4 in N6) and then copying from L6:N6 to L7:M19 computes the predicted inverse rank for each Product-segment combination.

Step 3: In O6:Q19 we compute the predicted market share of each product in each segment. By using our Market Share Prediction Formula we obtain in cell O6 our prediction for Product 1 in Segment 1 with the formula

=L6^Alpha/($L6^Alpha+$M6^Alpha+$N6^Alpha).

Copying this formula to the range O6:Q19 computes the market share of each product for each segment.

Step 4: In O3:Q3 we enter the actual market share for each segment. Then in O4:Q4 we compute the predicted market share for each product. For Product 1 we compute in O4 the predicted market share for Product 1 with the formula

=SUMPRODUCT(O6:O19,$B$6:$B$19)/SUM($B$6:$B$19).

This simply divides the total number of customers predicted to buy Product 1 by the total number of customers. Copying this formula to P4:Q4 computes the predicted market share for each product.

Step 5: In O2:Q2 we compute the squared error of our prediction for each product's share. In O2 we compute the squared error of our prediction for Product 1's share with the formula

$=(O4-O3)^2.$

Copying this formula to P2:Q2 computes the squared error of our predictions for Product 2 and Product 3 market share.

Step 6: In cell R2 we compute the sum of the squared errors for our forecasts with the formula

$=SUM(O2:Q2).$

Step 7: We now use Solver to determine the value of α that minimizes the sum of the squared errors. Our Solver window follows:

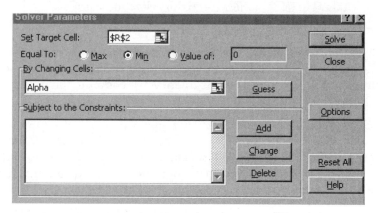

We checked the Assume Non-negative box because a negative value for α would imply a higher inverse rank leads to a lower market share. For Figure 57.12 we find $\alpha = 2.08$. The model predicts market shares of 34%, 48% and 17% respectively. Actual shares are 30%, 50%, and 20% respectively.

How Does a Product Change Modify Market Share?

Using our market share model we can determine how changes in our product will modify market share. More specifically, suppose Product 1 is our product. If we obtained Good Housekeeping approval and offered a Guarantee what would happen to our product share? To answer this question we copied the sheet Segments to a new sheet (**Guaranteeapp**) and changed the entries in J2 and K2 to 1 (see Figure 57.13).

Figure 57.13

	A	B	C	D	E	F	G	H	I	J	K
1	Current share			A	B	Brand 1	Brand 2	1.19?	1.39?	Approved?	Guarantee?
2	0.3	Our brand		1	0	1	0	1	0	1	1
3	0.5	Comp 1		0	1	0	1	0	1	1	0
4	0.2	Comp 2		0	0	0	0	0	0	0	1

From Figure 57.14 we find that our predicted market share is now 52%. We can now decide if it is worthwhile to offer a Guarantee and obtain Good Housekeeping approval. This type of what-if analysis can be used to determine the optimal product line configuration for a company. For example, should we sell a high price and low price product or just a low price product? How much is it worth to pay Michael Jordan to endorse a product? Questions like these can be attacked with conjoint analysis.

Figure 57.14

	L	M	N	O	P	Q
1	Alpha	2.075613				
2			Squared Error	0.047194	0.01949	0.006027
3			Actual Share	0.3	0.5	0.2
4			Predicted Share	0.517243	0.360392	0.122366

Remark

One drawback of our approach to conjoint analysis is that many consumers have difficulty ranking 18 products. An alternative approach (which uses Solver) requires consumers to make **pairwise comparisons**. For example, do you prefer Cheerios or Wheaties? Then Solver can be used to determine the weight a customer places on various attributes such as price, sweetness, nutritional value, etc.

References

1. Adleman, S., "Orthogonal Main Effect Plans for Asymmetrical Factorial Experiments," *Technometrics*, Vol. 4., 1962, pages 21-46.

2. Lehman, D., Gupta, S. and Steckel, J., *Marketing Research*, Addison-Wesley, 1998.

Chapter 58: Discrete Choice Analysis

Let's reconsider our carpet cleaning fluid conjoint example. We required the consumer to rank eighteen product profiles. In many cases this will be difficult. **Discrete choice analysis** simply requires the consumer to choose the **best product profile**. Here is an example (based on Kuhfeld, 1996).

Example 58.1

- Suppose a chocolate bar is specified by three attributes:
- Dark (defined by 1) or milk (defined by 0) chocolate.
- Soft (defined by 1) or chewy (defined by 0) chocolate.
- Nuts (defined by 1) or no nuts (defined by 0).

We want to determine the key factors that drive consumer chocolate preferences. For example, do people prefer nuts or no nuts? Does chewiness reduce the popularity of chocolate? To answer this question we asked 10 people to choose the best out of all eight possible combinations of chocolate. Three columns may specify the eight types of chocolate as follows: (see file **Chocolate.xls**.)

Figure 58.1

	B	C	D	E	F	G	H	I	J
1			Dark	Soft	Nuts				
2			1=dark 0 = milk	1=soft 0 =chewy	1=nuts 0=no nuts				
3									
4									
5		Weight	1.386293063	-2.1972262	0.84729703				
6		Choice	Dark?	Soft ?	Nuts?	Score	Exp(Score)	Prob of chosen	
7		1	0	0	0	0	1	0.0540001	
8		2	0	0	1	0.84729703	2.33333139	0.12600012	
9		3	0	1	0	-2.1972262	0.11111093	0.006	
10		4	0	1	1	-1.3499291	0.25925863	0.01399999	
11		5	1	0	0	1.38629306	3.99999481	0.2160001	
12		6	1	0	1	2.23359009	9.33331344	0.50399982	
13		7	1	1	0	-0.8109331	0.44444316	0.02399997	
14		8	1	1	1	0.03636392	1.03703317	0.05599989	
15									
16		Chosen	Frequency	Prob chosen					
17		2	2	0.01587603					
18		5	2	0.04665605					
19		6	5	0.0325201					
20		7	1	0.02399997					
21			Likelihood	5.7811E-07					
22			Ln(Likelihood)	-14.363497					

For example, Chocolate 1 is chewy milk chocolate with no nuts and Chocolate 4 is soft milk chocolate with nuts. Ten people were asked to choose their favorite chocolate. Two people chose Chocolate 2, two people chose Chocolate 5, five people chose Chocolate 6, and one person chose Chocolate 7.

Discrete choice analysis postulates a "weight" for dark, chewy and nuts (given in cells (D5:F5). Milk, soft and no nuts may be assumed (without loss of generality) to have a weight of 0. Each chocolate is then assigned a score equal to the sum of its weights. For example:

Chocolate 4 Score = Milk Weight + Soft Weight + Nuts Weight.

We hypothesize that the probability that a person will choose Chocolate I is given by $\dfrac{e^{Chocolate\ I\ score}}{\sum_{all\ j} e^{Chocolate\ j\ score}}$. This ensures that each Chocolate bar's chance of being chosen is non-negative and the sum of the probabilities that each chocolate bar is chosen add to 1. Also the higher the score for a chocolate bar, the higher the chance the chocolate bar will be chosen. We now choose the weights for dark, soft and nuts to **maximize the probability of the observed consumer preferences**. In our example the probability of observing the choices we have seen is given by

(Chocolate 2 Probability)^2(Chocolate 5 Probability)^2(Chocolate 6 Probability)^5(Chocolate 7 Probability)^1 (1).

Therefore we will choose our weights to maximize this probability. Actually, maximizing the **logarithm** of this probability will enable the ordinary Solver to easily solve the problem. Here is how we proceed:

Step by Step

Step 1: Enter trials weights in D5:F5.

Step 2: In G7:G14 compute the score for each Chocolate combination by copying from G7 to G8:G14 the formula

=SUMPRODUCT($D$5:$F$5,D7:F7).

Step 3: Compute e$^{Chocolate\ Score}$ in H7:H14 by copying from H7 to H8:H14 the formula

=EXP(G7).

Step 4: In I7:I14 compute the probability that each type of chocolate will be chosen by copying from I7 to I8:I14 the formula

=H7/SUM($H$7:$H$14).

Step 5: In E17:E20 compute each term in (1) by copying from E17 to E18:E20 the formula

=VLOOKUP(C17,Lookup,7)^D17.

The range lookup is C7:I14.

Step 6: In cell E21 we compute the likelihood of the observed choices with the formula

= *PRODUCT(E17:E20).*

Step 7: In cell E22 we compute the logarithm of the likelihood of the observed choices with the formula

=*LN(E21).*

Step 8: We now use Solver to choose weights that maximize the likelihood (more specifically Ln(Likelihood)) of our observed choices.

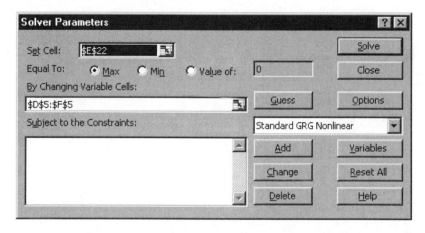

We find that dark chocolate is preferred to milk, chewy to soft, and nuts to no nuts. The biggest mover of consumer choice is chewy chocolate vs. soft chocolate. In column I we see the probability that each type of chocolate will be chosen. For Chocolates 5 and 6 our computed probability almost exactly matches the observed frequency with which these chocolates were chosen while for Chocolates 2 and 7 there is a fairly large difference between the computed and observed probabilities.

Reference

Kuhfeld, W., Multinomial Logit, Discrete Choice Modeling, SAS Institute, 1996.

Chapter 59: Discrete Choice II

Discrete choice analysis may also be used to determine price sensitivity and the power each brand has in a given market. The results of a discrete choice analysis can feed into an optimization model that yields a profit-maximizing price. Here is an example.

Example 59.1

100 people were shown 8 sets of products. Each set contained Brand 1, Brand 2, Brand 3, Brand 4, and the brand Other. The Other brand always sold for $4.99, but Brands 1-4 could sell for $3.99, or $5.99. For example, in Set 1 Brands 1 and 3 sold for $3.99, while Brands 2 and 4 sold for $5.99. Each person was asked to choose their **most preferred** product from each set. For example, for Set 1 we found that 4 people chose Brand 1, 29 chose Brand 2, 36 chose Brand 3, 21 chose Brand 4, and 10 chose the Other Brand. We want to use discrete choice analysis to understand how the brand and price determine the probability that a consumer will choose a given Brand, See file **Aggregratedata.xls.**

Figure 59.1 contains the Sets of products and consumer choices for each set.

Figure 59.1

	B	C	D	E	F	G	H	I	J	K	L	M	N	O	P	Q
1	pricewt	-0.16335														
2																
3	weight	-0.921468	-0.811721	-1.287514	-0.563605	-1.418506										
4	Set	Brand 1	Brand 2	Brand 3	Brand 4	Other	Br 1 like	Br 2 like	Br 3 like	Br 4 like	Other like					
5	1	3.99	5.99	3.99	5.99	4.99	0.207373	0.166929	0.143807	0.213937	0.1071	4	29	36	21	10
6	2	5.99	5.99	5.99	5.99	4.99	0.149578	0.166929	0.103728	0.213937	0.1071	12	19	22	33	14
7	3	5.99	5.99	3.99	3.99	4.99	0.149578	0.166929	0.143807	0.2966	0.1071	34	16	18	27	5
8	4	5.99	3.99	6.99	5.99	4.99	0.149578	0.231428	0.103728	0.213937	0.1071	13	37	15	27	8
9	5	5.99	3.99	3.99	5.99	4.99	0.149578	0.231428	0.143807	0.213937	0.1071	20	30	9	37	4
10	6	3.99	5.99	5.99	3.99	4.99	0.207373	0.166929	0.103728	0.2966	0.1071	31	12	6	18	33
11	7	3.99	3.99	5.99	5.99	4.99	0.207373	0.231428	0.103728	0.213937	0.1071	37	30	5	15	13
12	8	3.99	3.99	3.99	3.99	4.99	0.207373	0.231428	0.143807	0.2966	0.1071	16	14	5	51	14

Step 1: Enter trial weights for each brand (in cells C3:G3) and for price (in C1).

Figure 59.2

	H	I	J	K	L	M	N	O	P	Q
4	Br 1 like	Br 2 like	Br 3 like	Br 4 like	Other like					
5	0.20737318	0.166928746	0.143807229	0.213937362	0.10714	4	29	36	21	10
6	0.14957825	0.166928746	0.103728136	0.213937362	0.10714	12	19	22	33	14
7	0.14957825	0.166928746	0.143807229	0.29659975	0.10714	34	16	18	27	5
8	0.14957825	0.231427666	0.103728136	0.213937362	0.10714	13	37	15	27	8
9	0.14957825	0.231427666	0.143807229	0.213937362	0.10714	20	30	9	37	4
10	0.20737318	0.166928746	0.103728136	0.29659975	0.10714	31	12	6	18	33
11	0.20737318	0.231427666	0.103728136	0.213937362	0.10714	37	30	5	15	13
12	0.20737318	0.231427666	0.143807229	0.29659975	0.10714	16	14	5	51	14

	R	S	T	U	V	W	X
2					ln(prob)	-1246.020633	
3							
4	Prob 1	Prob 2	Prob 3	Prob 4	Prob other	Likelihood	ln(Like)
5	0.247112284	0.19891745	0.171365136	0.254934368	0.127670763	1.78E-72	-165.2099958
6	0.201775021	0.225180144	0.139925071	0.288592871	0.144526893	9.88E-70	-158.8901412
7	0.173112253	0.193192606	0.166433248	0.343265494	0.123996399	3.89E-69	-157.5189839
8	0.185624494	0.287198469	0.128725154	0.265493248	0.132958635	3.38E-66	-150.7522613
9	0.176829425	0.273590726	0.170007004	0.252913919	0.126658926	2.88E-65	-148.6114497
10	0.235178488	0.189311127	0.117636362	0.336368865	0.121505158	3.44E-73	-166.8522273
11	0.240124791	0.26797834	0.120110505	0.247725694	0.12406067	2.78E-66	-150.9485581
12	0.210243561	0.234631002	0.145797756	0.300705174	0.108622508	1.14E-64	-147.2370159

Step 2: The score for each item is Brand Weight + Price*Price weight. Then in cells H5:L12 we compute $e^{\text{Score for each item}}$ by copying the formula

=EXP(C$3+C5*$C$1)

from H5 to H5:L12.

Step 3: By copying from R5 to R5:V12 the formula

=H5/(SUM($H5:$L5))

we compute the estimated probability that each product in each set will be chosen.

Step 4: In W5:W12 we compute the likelihood of the observed preferences for each set by copying from W5 to W6:W12 the formula

=(R5^M5)(S5^N5)*(T5^O5)*(U5^P5)*(V5^Q5)*

Step 5: In X5:X12 we compute the logarithm of the likelihood for each set by copying from X5 to X6:X12 the formula

=LN(W5).

Step 6: In cell W2 compute the logarithm of the likelihood of the observed choices with the formula

=SUM(X5:X12).

Step 7: We now use Solver to determine the weights that maximize the log likelihood of the observed choices.

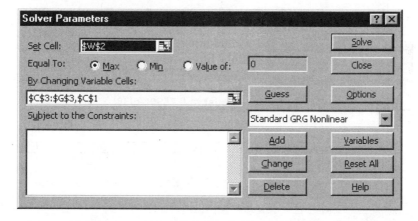

From Figure 59.1 we see that Brand 4 is most preferred and Other is least preferred. A price increase decreases the likelihood that a product will be purchased.

Optimizing Profitability

Suppose Brand 2 sells for $4, Brand 3 for $4.5, Brand 4 for $4.3 and Other for $5. Also assume that for Brand 1 it costs $2 to produce a unit of the product. What price for Brand 1 would maximize profit? Our work is in file **Optimizeprofit.xls**. See Figure 59.3.

Figure 59.3

	B	C	D	E	F	G
1	pricewt	-0.163351	cost	2		
2						
3	weight	-0.921468	-0.8117196	-1.287513	-0.563603	-1.418506
4	Set	Brand 1	Brand 2	Brand 3	Brand 4	Other
5	1	8.880863	4	4.5	4.3	5
6						
7			Brand 1 sales/cust	0.110315947		
8			Brand 1 profit/cust	0.759068938		

	H	I	J	K	L	M	N	O	P	Q
1										
2										
3										
4	Br 1 like	Br 2 like	Br 3 like	Br 4 like	Other like	Prob 1	Prob 2	Prob 3	Prob 4	Prob other
5	0.093278577	0.23105	0.132312	0.281954	0.106964	0.110315947	0.273251	0.156479	0.333453	0.126501322
6										

We entered the prices of each brand in cells D5:G5 and entered a trial Brand 1 price in cell C5. In cell E7 we recopy Brand 1's share (computed from discrete choice model in cell M5). Then in cell E8 we compute Brand 1's profit per potential customer with the formula

$= E7*(C5-E1).$

Now use Solver to find the profit-maximizing price.

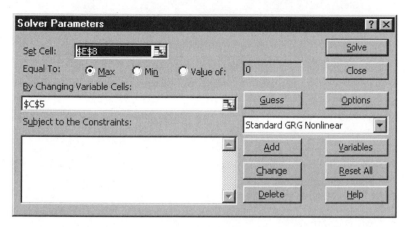

We find that a price of $8.90 with a resulting market share of 23.5% would result in a maximum profit of $0.76 per potential customer. Note that since our data only tested Brand 1 prices in the range $3.99-$5.99 we should probably constrain the Brand 1 price to be in this range. If we did the optimal price would come out to $5.99.

Chapter 60: Estimating Customer Preferences by Pair wise Comparisons

Another way to tease out customer preferences is to ask consumers to pair wise compare different products. As an example consider Cola sodas described by three attributes:

- Brand: Coke or Pepsi.

- Type of Soda: Diet or Regular

- Price of a Six Pack: $1.80, $2.20, $2.60, $3.00.

See file **Cokepepsi.xls**.

Here are the 16 products:

	F	G	H	I	J
1			0=Coke	0=Diet	
2			1=Pepsi	1= Reg	
3		Price	Brand	Diet	
4	1	1.8	0	0	
5	2	1.8	0	1	
6	3	1.8	1	0	
7	4	1.8	1	1	
8	5	2.2	0	0	
9	6	2.2	0	1	
10	7	2.2	1	0	
11	8	2.2	1	1	
12	9	2.6	0	0	
13	10	2.6	0	1	
14	11	2.6	1	0	
15	12	2.6	1	1	
16	13	3	0	0	
17	14	3	0	1	
18	15	3	1	0	
19	16	3	1	1	

We selected the following 8 products: 1, 4, 5, 8, 10, 11, 14, and 15. Then we asked ourselves to choose between each possible pair wise comparison of these products. There are 28 possible pair wise comparisons.

	L	M	N	O	P	Q	R	S	T	U	V	W	X	Y	Z
1			Price	Brand	Type										
2			-10	3	8	1									
3			2	3	4	2	3	4		2	3		2	3	
4	First	Second	P 1	B 1	Type 1	P2	B2	Type 2	P1	B1	T1	P2	B2	T2	Preferre
5	1	4	1.8	0	0	1.8	1	1	1.8	Coke	Diet	1.8	Pepsi	Regular	
6	1	5	1.8	0	0	2.2	0	0	1.8	Coke	Diet	2.2	Coke	Diet	
7	1	8	1.8	0	0	2.2	1	1	1.8	Coke	Diet	2.2	Pepsi	Regular	
8	1	10	1.8	0	0	2.6	0	1	1.8	Coke	Diet	2.6	Coke	Regular	
9	1	11	1.8	0	0	2.6	1	0	1.8	Coke	Diet	2.6	Pepsi	Diet	
10	1	14	1.8	0	0	3	0	1	1.8	Coke	Diet	3	Coke	Regular	
11	1	15	1.8	0	0	3	1	0	1.8	Coke	Diet	3	Pepsi	Diet	
12	4	5	1.8	1	1	2.2	0	0	1.8	Pepsi	Regular	2.2	Coke	Diet	
13	4	8	1.8	1	1	2.2	1	1	1.8	Pepsi	Regular	2.2	Pepsi	Regular	
14	4	10	1.8	1	1	2.6	0	1	1.8	Pepsi	Regular	2.6	Coke	Regular	
15	4	11	1.8	1	1	2.6	1	0	1.8	Pepsi	Regular	2.6	Pepsi	Diet	
16	4	14	1.8	1	1	3	0	1	1.8	Pepsi	Regular	3	Coke	Regular	
17	4	15	1.8	1	1	3	1	0	1.8	Pepsi	Regular	3	Pepsi	Diet	
18	5	8	2.2	0	0	2.2	1	1	2.2	Coke	Diet	2.2	Pepsi	Regular	
19	5	10	2.2	0	0	2.6	0	1	2.2	Coke	Diet	2.6	Coke	Regular	
20	5	11	2.2	0	0	2.6	1	0	2.2	Coke	Diet	2.6	Pepsi	Diet	
21	5	14	2.2	0	0	3	0	1	2.2	Coke	Diet	3	Coke	Regular	
22	5	15	2.2	0	0	3	1	0	2.2	Coke	Diet	3	Pepsi	Diet	
23	8	10	2.2	1	1	2.6	0	1	2.2	Pepsi	Regular	2.6	Coke	Regular	
24	8	11	2.2	1	1	2.6	1	0	2.2	Pepsi	Regular	2.6	Pepsi	Diet	
25	8	14	2.2	1	1	3	0	1	2.2	Pepsi	Regular	3	Coke	Regular	
26	8	15	2.2	1	1	3	1	0	2.2	Pepsi	Regular	3	Pepsi	Diet	
27	10	11	2.6	0	1	2.6	1	0	2.6	Coke	Regular	2.6	Pepsi	Diet	
28	10	14	2.6	0	1	3	0	1	2.6	Coke	Regular	3	Coke	Regular	
29	10	15	2.6	0	1	3	1	0	2.6	Coke	Regular	3	Pepsi	Diet	
30	11	14	2.6	1	0	3	0	1	2.6	Pepsi	Diet	3	Coke	Regular	
31	11	15	2.6	1	0	3	1	0	2.6	Pepsi	Diet	3	Pepsi	Diet	
32	14	15	3	0	1	3	1	0	3	Coke	Regular	3	Pepsi	Diet	

For example, first comparison is between Diet Coke priced at $1.80 and Regular Pepsi priced at $1.80. Then we indicate which product we prefer. For example, in the first comparison we preferred the second choice, which was Regular Pepsi priced at $1.80. See Column Z in which our preferences are entered.

	Z	AA	AB
1			
2			Sum
3			6E-08
4	Preferred	S1-S2	Reversal
5	2	-6.4535	0
6	1	2.18142	0
7	2	-4.2721	0
8	1	6E-08	0
9	1	2.27213	0
10	1	2.18142	0
11	1	4.45354	0
12	1	8.63496	0
13	1	2.18142	0
14	1	6.45354	0
15	1	8.72567	0
16	1	8.63496	0
17	1	10.9071	0
18	2	-6.4535	0
19	2	-2.1814	0
20	1	0.09071	0
21	2	6E-08	6E-08
22	1	2.27213	0
23	1	4.27213	0
24	1	6.54425	0
25	1	6.45354	0
26	1	8.72567	0
27	1	2.27213	0
28	1	2.18142	0
29	1	4.45354	0
30	2	-0.0907	0
31	1	2.18142	0
32	1	2.27213	0

In cells N2:P2 we enter trial weights for price, brand and type of soda. In cell Q2 we normalize these weights by ensuring that they add (in absolute value) to 1. Note that if weights add to +1 it probably means Brand with 1 and Type with 1 are preferred to Brand 0 and Type 0 while if weights add to −1 it probably means Brand 0 and Type 0 are preferred to Brand 1 and Type 1.

In cells AA5:AA32 we determine the "score" of Product 1 for each comparison less the score of Product 2 by copying from AA5 to AA6:AA32 the formula

$$=SUMPRODUCT(N5:P5,\$N\$2:\$P\$2)-SUMPRODUCT(Q5:S5,\$N\$2:\$P\$2).$$

The score of a product is (Price weight)*Price + (Brand weight)*Brand + (Type weight)*Type.

A preference reversal occurs when the product with the higher score in a comparison is not the most preferred product. In cells AB5:AB32 we compute the magnitude of all "preference reversals" by copying from AB5 to AB6:AB32 the formula

$$=IF(AND(Z5=1,AA5<0),-AA5,IF(AND(Z5=2,AA5>0),AA5,0)).$$

Then in cell AB3 we compute the sum of all preference reversals with the formula

$$= SUM(AA5:AA32).$$

We now use Evolver to determine a set of weights adding to one that minimizes the sum of preference reversals. We used Budget method and made sure that our initial changing cell values add to 1. Our Evolver window follows:

We find a price weight of –10, brand weight of 3, and type weight of 8 will result in **no preference reversals**. **These weights are not unique,** however. These weights imply that we prefer Pepsi to Coke and that preference is worth 3/10 = 30 cents. These weights also imply that we prefer Regular to Diet and the preference is worth 8/10 = 80 cents. Thus we see our preference for regular soda is more than twice as strong as our preference for Pepsi. By asking many people to do these pair wise comparisons we can determine market segments and use Evolver to determine a product line that will maximize profitability.

Chapter 61: Optimizing Channel Conflicts

An important problem in marketing is how to set prices in different channels in order to maximize a company's profitability. A company must realize that charging a low price in one channel will cannibalize sales in another channel. To optimize profitability we proceed as follows:

- Use Solver to determine a demand curve for each channel that gives the demand for the product in each channel as a function of the price in each channel.

- Use Solver to determine prices for each channel that maximize overall profitability.

Here is an example of this procedure. Our work is in file **Webretail.xls**.

Example 61.1

We are trying to sell a product on the Web and via retail. It costs us $12 to ready a unit for retail sale and $4 to ready a unit for Web sale. For various combinations of Web and retail prices the demand for the product in each channel (in thousands of units) are as follows:

	E	F	G	H	I	J	K	L
1								
2		Web cost	Retail cost					
3		$ 4.00	$ 12.00		b	f1	f2	
4					1173.1349	1.36287	-2.663275327	
5					a	e1	e2	
6					1000	-1.602234	0.319655116	
7	Web Price	Retail Price	Web Demand	Retail demand	Predicted Web	Predicted retail	SQ Err Web	Sq err retail
8	$ 20.00	$ 30.00	25	7	24.412621	8.100322	0.345013609	1.21070759
9	$ 30.00	$ 30.00	12	15	12.748966	14.07641	0.560949595	0.8530263
10	$ 40.00	$ 30.00	7	21	8.0406992	20.83373	1.083054866	0.02764543
11	$ 20.00	$ 40.00	28	3	26.764043	3.764922	1.527589177	0.58510597
12	$ 30.00	$ 40.00	16	7	13.976945	6.542527	4.092751245	0.20928156
13	$ 40.00	$ 40.00	7	8	8.8151787	9.683242	3.294873881	2.8333043
14	$ 20.00	$ 50.00	27	3	28.742829	2.078059	3.037451239	0.84997445
15	$ 30.00	$ 50.00	16	6	15.010323	3.611166	0.97946042	5.70652695
16	$ 40.00	$ 50.00	9	5	9.4669243	5.344693	0.218018301	0.11881313
17						SSE	15.13916233	12.3943857
18							27.53354801	

For example, if we charge $30 for the retail product and $20 for the Web product we expect to sell 25,000 units on the Web and 7,000 in retail.

We begin by estimating a demand function for each product. We will assume

Web Demand=a*(Web Price)^{e1}(Retail Price)^{e2}

Where a, e1, and e2 are unknown. It can be shown that a 1% increase in Web price will increase Web demand by e1% and a 1% increase in retail price will increase Web demand by e2%.

Similarly we estimate

Retail Demand=b*(Web Price)^{f1}(Retail Price)^{f2}

where b, f1, and f2 are unknown. It can be shown that a 1% increase in Web price will increase retail demand by f1% and a 1% increase in retail price will increase retail demand by e2%.

Step by Step

Step 1: We insert trial values of e1, e2, f1, f2, a, and b in I4:K4 and I6:K6.

Step 2: In I8:I16 we generate the predicted Web demand for each combination of prices by copying the formula

=a*E8^e1_*F8^e2_

from I8 to I9:I16.

Step 3: In J8:J16 we generate the predicted retail demand for each combination of prices by copying the formula

=b*E8^f1_*F8^f2_

from J8 to J9:J16 .

Step 4: In K8:L16 we generate the squared error for each forecasted demand by copying from K8 to K8:L16 the formula

=(G8-I8)^2.

Step 5: In K17:L17 we compute the sum of our squared errors for Web and retail demand by copying from K17 to K17:L17 the formula

=SUM(K8:K16).

Step 6: In cell K18 we compute the total squared error with the formula

=SUM(K17:L17).

Step 7: We now use Evolver to minimize the total SSE. Here is the Evolver window:

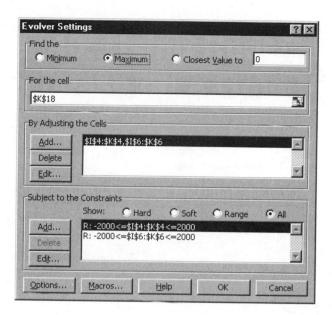

We minimize SSE (combining Web and retail SSE) by changing the parameters a, b, e1, e2, f1, and f2. We bound these parameters so we can use Evolver. We obtain the following demand curves (in thousands of units):

Web Demand = 1000(Web Price)$^{-1.6}$(Retail Price)$^{.32}$

Retail Demand = 1173.13(Web Price)$^{1.37}$ (Retail Price)$^{-2.66}$.

This indicates that for Web demand the price elasticity with regards to the Web price is -1.6 and the price elasticity with regards to retail price is .32. For retail demand the elasticity with regards to Web price is 1.37 and with regards to retail price is –2.66.

Now we use Solver to find the profit maximizing prices. We copied our work to a new sheet.

	E	F	G	H	I	J	K	L
1								
2		Web cost	Retail cost					
3		$ 4.00	$ 12.00		b	f1	f2	
4				Retail demand	1173.1349	1.36287	-2.663275327	
5					a	e1	e2	
6				web	1000	-1.602234	0.319655116	
7	Web Price	Retail Price	Web Demand	Retail demand	Predicted Web	Predicted retail	SQ Err Web	Sq err retail
8	$ 20.00	$ 30.00	20	7	24.412621	8.100322	19.4712277	1.21070759
9	$ 30.00	$ 30.00	7	15	12.748966	14.07641	33.05060643	0.8530263
10	$ 40.00	$ 30.00	1	21	8.0406992	20.83373	49.5714455	0.02764543
11	$ 20.00	$ 40.00	23	2	26.764043	3.764922	14.16802132	3.11495037
12	$ 30.00	$ 40.00	15	7	13.976945	6.542527	1.046641387	0.20928156
13	$ 40.00	$ 40.00	4	8	8.8151787	9.683242	23.18594636	2.8333043
14	$ 20.00	$ 50.00	24	3	28.742829	2.078059	22.49442234	0.84997445
15	$ 30.00	$ 50.00	16	6	15.010323	3.611166	0.97946042	5.70652695
16	$ 40.00	$ 50.00	7	5	9.4669243	5.344693	6.085715498	0.11881313
17						SSE	170.053487	14.9242301
18								
19		Web Price	Retail price					
20		50	19.71818308					
21		Web demand	Retail demand		-0.722214			
22		4.917707869	86.34483252					
23		Web profit	Retail profit					
24		226.214562	666.4252252					
25								
26		Total						
27		892.6397872						
28								

We entered trial prices in F20 and G20. Then in F22 we compute our Web demand

=a*F20^e1_*G20*e2_.

In cell G22 compute our retail demand with the formula

=b*F20^f1_*G20^f2_.

In F24 we compute our Web profit and retail profit by copying from F24 to G24 the formula

=(F20-F3)*F22.

In cell F27 we compute our total profit with the formula

=SUM(F24:G24).

We now use Solver to choose Web and retail prices that maximize profit. We do not allow prices too far out of line with the prices used to estimate the demand curves. Our Solver window is as follows:

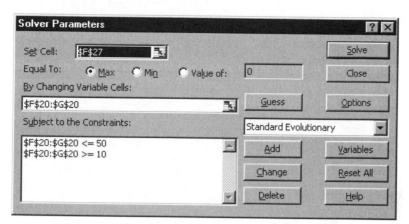

We assumed each price had to be between $10 and $50. We tried Solver and then Evolver. Evolver improved our answer slightly over the Solver answer. We found a $19.72 retail price and a $50.00 Web price. Basically, for our estimated demand curves Solver is telling us to close out the Web channel and just sell retail. This is probably because of the high negative elasticity of the Web price for retail demand. Of course, these numbers were made up and are not necessarily realistic.

Chapter 62: To Free PC or Not to Free PC?

Many companies have considered giving consumers a free PC in return for the consumer signing up for 3 years of Internet access. Whether or not the free PC is a good idea for a company like Microsoft depends on how likely it is for the customer to stay with MSN after the three years are up. We now use Monte Carlo simulation to analyze whether or not the free PC is a good idea. The key is to determine if our expected long-run profit from a current non-MSN (say AOL) customer is higher if we give them a free PC than if we do not give them a free PC. The major source of uncertainty is the probability that a consumer will "churn" or leave MSN during a year. We will run the numbers for an annual "retention rate" of 50%, 60%, 70%, 80%, and 90%. This corresponds to annual churn rates of 50%, 40%, 30%, 20%, and 10%. Our other assumptions follow:

- During a given year there is a 10% chance that an AOL customer will switch to MSN.

- Cost of PC is $1000.

- After three years price of Internet access will increase 3% a year.

- Current price of Internet access is $21.95 a month or $263.40 a year.

- Profits are discounted at 10% a year.

- All of Internet access fee is profit.

We begin (see Figure 62.1 and file **Freepc.xls**) by modeling the free PC situation. We use a RiskSimtable function to vary the retention rate from 50%-90%. An MSN customer switches to AOL during a year with a probability equal to 1 – retention rate. An AOL customer switches to MSN during a year with probability 0.1. We use the RiskBinomial random variable (with 1 trial) to model whether or not a customer switches providers during the year. A success indicates the customer does switch providers during the year.

Figure 62.1

	A	B	C	D	E	F
1						
2				Annual Internet price for 3 yrs	$ 263.40	
3				PC Cost	$ 1,000.00	
4				Retention Rate	0.5	
5				discount rate	0.1	
6				Price increase	0.03	
7				Switch back	0.1	NPV
8						442.0691
9	Time	With us?	Quit?	Comeback?	Revenue	Price
10	0	Yes	0	0	$ 263.40	
11	1	Yes	0	0	$ 263.40	
12	2	Yes	1	0	$ 263.40	$ 263.40
13	3	No	0	0	$ -	$ 271.30
14	4	No	0	0	$ -	$ 279.44
15	5	No	0	0	$ -	$ 287.82
16	6	No	0	0	$ -	$ 296.46
17	7	No	0	1	$ -	$ 305.35
18	8	Yes	1	0	$ 314.51	$ 314.51
19	9	No	0	1	$ -	$ 323.95
20	10	Yes	0	0	$ 333.67	$ 333.67
21	11	Yes	0	0	$ 343.68	$ 343.68
42	32	No	0	0	$ -	$ 639.34
43	33	No	0	1	$ -	$ 658.52
44	34	Yes	0	0	$ 678.28	$ 678.28
45	35	Yes	1	0	$ 698.63	$ 698.63
46	36	No	0	1	$ -	$ 719.58
47	37	Yes	1	0	$ 741.17	$ 741.17
48	38	No	0	0	$ -	$ 763.41
49	39	No	0	0	$ -	$ 786.31
50	40	No	0	0	$ -	$ 809.90
51						

Step by Step

Step 1: In B10:B12 we enter Yes to indicate that customer is locked into three years.

Step 2: In C10:D11 we enter 0 to indicate customer cannot quit or come back to MSN during years 0 and 1.

Step 3: In E10:E12 we enter the guaranteed revenue of $263.40 per year for Years 0-2.

Step 4: By copying from C12 to C13:C50 the formula

$$=IF(B12="Yes",RiskBinomial(1,1-\$E\$4),0)$$

we determine each year whether or not the customer left MSN.

Step 4: By copying from D12 to D13:D50 the formula

$$=IF(B12="No",RiskBinomial(1,\$E\$7),0)$$

we determine whether or not the customer left AOL and "saw the light" at MSN.

Step 5: By copying from B13 to B14:B50 the formula

$$=IF(C12=1,"No",IF(D12=1,"Yes",B12))$$

we determine the status of the consumer at the beginning of each year. If she left MSN they are not with us. If she left AOL they are with us. Otherwise the customer is where she was last year.

Step 6: By copying from F13 to F14:F50 the formula

$$=E12*(1+\$E\$6)$$

we generate the annual price of Internet access for all later years.

Step 7: By copying from E13 to E14:E50 the formula

$$= IF(B13="Yes",F13,0)$$

we compute our revenue for Years 3-40. These formulae only credit us with revenue if the customer is with MSN at the beginning of the year.

Step 7: Our total NPV is computed in cell F8 with the formula

$$=-E3+(1.1)^0.5*NPV(E5,E10:E50).$$

Note that we are assuming that all revenues are concentrated entirely at the midpoint of the year.

Step 8: After selecting cell F8 as an output cell and running 400 iterations and 5 simulations we obtain the output in Figure 62.2.

Figure 62.2 Free PC

	I	J	K	L	M	N
11		0.5	0.6	0.7	0.8	0.9
12	Name	NPV	NPV	NPV	NPV	NPV
13	Description	Output (Sim#1)	Output (Sim#2)	Output (Sim#3)	Output (Sim#4)	Output (Sim#5)
14	Cell	F8	F8	F0	F8	F8
15	Minimum =	-312.9916	-312.9916	-312.9916	-312.9916	-312.9916
16	Maximum =	1371.322	1766.705	2061.116	2219.835	2489.985
17	Mean =	262.6483	391.318	584.2987	871.8735	1375.437

For example, our mean NPV per customer is $262.65 with a 50% retention rate and $1375.44 with a 90% retention rate.

Per Customer NPV with No Free PC

We now determine the mean NPV per customer when no PC is given out. See file **Nopc.xls** and Figure 62.3. We essentially begin with the customer **being an AOL customer** and have them cycle back and forth between AOL and MSN. The price of Internet access increases at 3% a year beginning with Year 1.

Figure 62.3

	A	B	C	D	E	F
1						
2				Annual Internet price for 3 yrs	263.4	
3				PC Cost	0	
4				Retention Rate	0.5	
5				discount rate	0.1	
6				Price increase	0.03	
7				Switch back	0.1	NPV
8						420.6533
9	Time	With us?	Quit?	Comeback?	Revenue	Price
10	0	No	0	0	0	263.4
11	1	No	0	0	0	271.302
12	2	No	0	0	0	279.4411
13	3	No	0	1	0	287.8243
14	4	Yes	1	0	296.459	296.459
15	5	No	0	0	0	305.3528
16	6	No	0	0	0	314.5134
17	7	No	0	0	0	323.9488
18	8	No	0	0	0	333.6672
19	9	No	0	0	0	343.6773
20	10	No	0	0	0	353.9876
21	11	No	0	0	0	364.6072
22	12	No	0	0	0	375.5454
23	13	No	0	0	0	386.8118
24	14	No	0	0	0	398.4161
25	15	No	0	0	0	410.3686
26	16	No	0	0	0	422.6797
27	17	No	0	1	0	435.3601
44	34	Yes	1	0	719.5839	719.5839
45	35	No	0	0	0	741.1714
46	36	No	0	0	0	763.4065
47	37	No	0	0	0	786.3087
48	38	No	0	0	0	809.898
49	39	No	0	0	0	834.1949
50	40	No	0	0	0	859.2208

Figure 62.4 gives the mean NPV for each retention rate

**Figure 62.4
No Free PC**

	H	I	J	K	L	M
10		0.5	0.6	0.7	0.8	0.9
11	Name	NPV	NPV	NPV	NPV	NPV
12	Description	Output (Sir	Output (Sir	Output (Sir	Output (Sir	Output (Sir
13	Cell	F8	F8	F8	F8	F8
14	Minimum =	0	0	0	0	0
15	Maximum =	1978.099	2292.075	2705.659	2826.379	3251.432
16	Mean =	545.9941	647.8163	775.262	975.1291	1301.218
17	Std Deviati	362.435	435.6406	518.7365	617.9836	766.7444

Note that when the retention rate is less than 80%, the No PC strategy is better. Somewhere in the 80%-90% retention rate range the Free PC strategy becomes superior!

Chapter 63: Working With Text Functions

Often we receive a file where the text is not in the form we want. It is therefore important to learn how to manipulate text in spreadsheets. Here is an example:

Example 63.1

In the file **Lenora.xls** we are given the Product ID, Product Description, and Price of several computer units. To analyze this data, we need to have a single column containing just the Product ID, a single column just containing the Product Description, and a single column just containing the price. We know that the Product ID takes up 12 characters.

Figure 63.1

	A
1	Product ID Description Price
2	
3	
4	32592100AFES CONTROLLERPENTIUM/100,(2)1GB H 304.00
5	32592100JCP9 DESKTOP UNIT 225.00
6	325927008990 DESKTOP WINDOWS NT 4.0 SERVER 232.00
7	325926008990 DESKTOP WINDOWS NT 4.0 WKST 232.00
8	325921008990 DESKTOP, DOS OS 232.00
9	325922008990 DESKTOP, WINDOWS DESKTOP OS 232.00
10	325925008990 DESKTOP, WINDOWS NT OS 232.00
11	325930008990 MINITOWER, NO OS 232.00
12	
13	32593000KEYY MINI TOWER 232.00

Solution

The key to this problem is a knowledge of several neat Excel text functions: the LEFT, RIGHT, MID, and LEN functions. Here's how things go.

Step by Step

Step 1: To extract the product ID we need to extract the 12 leftmost characters from Column A. To do this copy from B4 to B5:B13 the formula

   =LEFT(A4,12).

This formula simply extracts the 12 leftmost characters from the text in cell A4. This, of course, yields our product ID.

	B
3	Product ID
4	32592100AFES
5	32592100JCP9
6	325927008990
7	325926008990
8	325921008990
9	325922008990
10	325925008990
11	325930008990
12	
13	32593000KEYY

Step 2: To extract the product price we note that the price takes the last 8 digits of each cell. This is because two blank spaces were inserted after each price. This means we need to extract the rightmost 8 characters in each cell. To do this copy from cell C4 to C5:C13 the formula

=RIGHT(A4,8).

This formula extracts the rightmost 8 characters in cell A4.

	C
3	Price
4	304.00
5	225.00
6	232.00
7	232.00
8	232.00
9	232.00
10	232.00
11	232.00
12	
13	232.00

Step 3: Extracting the product description is much trickier. Note that if start extracting with the 13th character and continue until we are 8 characters from end of cell we will have what we want. Copying the following formula from D4 to D5:D13 does the job:

   =MID(A4,13,LEN(A4)-8-12).

Note LEN(A4) returns total number of characters in cell A4. This formula (MID for Middle) begins with the 13th character and goes on to extract a number of characters equal to the total number less the twelve at the beginning (Product ID) and the eight on the end (Product Price). This simply leaves the product description!

	D
3	Product Description
4	CONTROLLERPENTIUM/100,(2)1GB H
5	DESKTOP UNIT
6	DESKTOP WINDOWS NT 4.0 SERVER
7	DESKTOP WINDOWS NT 4.0 WKST
8	DESKTOP, DOS OS
9	DESKTOP, WINDOWS DESKTOP OS
10	DESKTOP, WINDOWS NT OS
11	MINITOWER, NO OS
12	
13	MINI TOWER

Concatenation

Suppose we have the Product ID in Column B, the Price in Column C, and the Product Description in Column D. Can we somehow put them together to recover our original text? Text can easily be combined using the CONCATENATE function. Copying from E4 to E5:E13 the following formula recovers our original text.

=CONCATENATE(B4," ",D4," ",C4)

	E
3	Concatenation
4	32592100AFES CONTROLLERPENTIUM/100,(2)1GB H 304.00
5	32592100JCP9 DESKTOP UNIT 225.00
6	325927008990 DESKTOP WINDOWS NT 4.0 SERVER 232.00
7	325926008990 DESKTOP WINDOWS NT 4.0 WKST 232.00
8	325921008990 DESKTOP, DOS OS 232.00
9	325922008990 DESKTOP, WINDOWS DESKTOP OS 232.00
10	325925008990 DESKTOP, WINDOWS NT OS 232.00
11	325930008990 MINITOWER, NO OS 232.00
12	
13	32593000KEYY MINI TOWER 232.00

This formula starts with the Product ID in cell B4. Then the "" inserts a space. Then we add the Product Description from cell D4. Then we add another space. Finally, we add the price from cell C4. We have now recovered the entire text for each computer!

Chapter 64: More on Text Functions

Continuing with our product ID, description, and price example how would we extract the price if each price could use a different number of digits? This is a much harder problem. We proceed as follows:

- Use the TRIM function to delete excess spaces between words and at end of each cell.

- Determine that the maximum number of digits used is 8 in a price and the minimum used is 4. Then we extract rightmost 8, 7, 6, and 5 digits from each cell.

- Then use the VALUE function to convert these cells to numbers. If extracted text is not a number, the #VALUE error will appear.

- Convert any #VALUE error to a price of 0.

- Now extract maximum price in each row and you have the answer.

See Figure 64.1 and file **Rightprice.xls**, sheet **Price**.

Figure 64.1

	B	C	D	E	F	G
2						
3	Product ID Description Price		Extract			
4			rightmost 8 digits			
5		Need last 8 digits maybeonly last 4	8	7	6	5
6		Trim it	Right 8	Right 7	Right 6	Right 5
7	32592100AFES CONTROLLERPENTIUM/100,(2)1GB H 3304.00	32592100AFES CONTROLLERPENTIUM/100,(2)1GB H 3304.00	3304.00	3304.00	304.00	04.00
8	32592100JCP9 DESKTOP UNIT 25.00	32592100JCP9 DESKTOP UNIT 25.00	IT 25.00	T 25.00	25.00	25.00
9	325927008990 DESKTOP WINDOWS NT 4.0 SERVER 232.00	325927008990 DESKTOP WINDOWS NT 4.0 SERVER 232.00	R 232.00	232.00	232.00	32.00
10	325926008990 DESKTOP WINDOWS NT 4.0 WKST 232.00	325926008990 DESKTOP WINDOWS NT 4.0 WKST 232.00	T 232.00	232.00	232.00	32.00
11	325921008990 DESKTOP, DOS OS 2.00	325921008990 DESKTOP, DOS OS 2.00	OS 2.00	OS 2.00	S 2.00	2.00
12	325922008990 DESKTOP, WINDOWS DESKTOP OS 232.00	325922008990 DESKTOP, WINDOWS DESKTOP OS 232.00	S 232.00	232.00	232.00	32.00
13	325925008990 DESKTOP, WINDOWS NT OS 23200.00	325925008990 DESKTOP, WINDOWS NT OS 23200.00	23200.00	3200.00	200.00	00.00
14	325930008990 MINITOWER, NO OS 232.00	325930008990 MINITOWER, NO OS 232.00	S 232.00	232.00	232.00	32.00

	H	I	J	K	L	M	N	O	P	Q	R
3											
4		Convert them to values							Real price		
5					If not a number set price to 0				is biggest number you got		
6	Value 8	Va;ue 7	Value 6	Value 5	New Value 8	New Value 7	New Value 6	New Value 5	Actual price		
7	3304	3304	304	4	3304	3304	304	4	3304		
8	#VALUE!	#VALUE!	25	25	0	0	25	25	25		
9	#VALUE!	232	232	32	0	232	232	32	232		
10	#VALUE!	232	232	32	0	232	232	32	232		
11	#VALUE!	#VALUE!	#VALUE!	2	0	0	0	2	2		
12	#VALUE!	232	232	32	0	232	232	32	232		
13	23200	3200	200	0	23200	3200	200	0	23200		
14	#VALUE!	232	232	32	0	232	232	32	232		

Step 1: Copy from C7 to C8:C14 the formula

> =*TRIM(B7).*

This will trim excess spaces between words and to right of last price digit.

Step 2: We see the largest price (23200.00) requires 8 digits and the smallest price (2.00) requires 4 digits. We now find last 8, 7, 6, and 5 digits in each cell. To do this copy the formula

> =*RIGHT($C7,D$5)*

from D7 to D7:G14.

Step 3: By copying from H7 to H7:K14 the formula

> =*VALUE(D7)*

we convert each text to value. Note that if any letters are included we receive a #VALUE message.

Step 4: By copying from L7 to L7:O14 the formula

> =*IF(COUNT(J7)=1,J7,0)*

we keep the price if it exists and replace all #VALUE cells by 0 (COUNT() will return a 1 if a number is in a cell and 0 otherwise).

Step 5: Now we find the actual price as the largest of the 4 numbers in columns L:O by copying from P7 to P8:P14 the formula

> = *MAX(L7:O7).*

This seems like a lot of work but if you have 50,000 rows consider the alternative!

Here is another example. A Microsoft finance employee regularly (this is a real situation!) receives a 5000-row spreadsheet in which each row adds up sales from three regions. Her job is to extract the sales for each region. An easy way to do this is to first use Edit>Replace to delete the = sign from each sum and leave text. Then we find all + signs and first determine all text to the left of first + sign (this is sales in first region). Next determine all text between the first and second + sign (this is sales in second region). Finally determine all sales in the third region as all text to the right of the second + sign. See file **Rightprice.xls** sheet **Sales Stripping** and Figure 64.2.

Figure 64.2

	B	C	D	E	F	G	H
1							
2	Total	First +	Second +	First Sale	Second Sale	Total Length	Third Sale
3	10+300+400	3	7	10	300	10	400
4	4+36.2+800	2	7	4	36.2	10	800
5	3+23+4005	2	5	3	23	9	4005
6	18+1+57.31	3	5	18	1	10	57.31

Step by Step

Step 1: Use Edit>Replace to replace each = by a space. This yields the text in Figure 64.2.

Step 2: Find the first + in each row by copying from C3 to C4:C6 the formula

$= FIND("+",B3,1).$

This finds first + in B3 beginning first character. Note + must be enclosed in ""

Step 3: To find 2nd + in each row use =FIND function beginning right after first +. Just copy from D3 to D4:D6 the formula

$= FIND("+",B3,C3+1).$

Step 4: In E3:E6 we compute sales in first region by extracting all text to left of first + sign by copying from E3 to E4:E6 the formula

$= LEFT(B3,C3-1).$

Step 5: In F3:F6 we compute sales in second region by extracting all text to right of first + sign and left of 2nd + sign. This requires we use the MID function. Copy from F3 to F4:F6 the formula

$= MID(B3,C3+1,D3-C3-1)$.

This formula begins 1 character after first + and takes all characters between 1st and 2nd +. This yields, of course, the sales in the 2nd region.

Step 6: Before obtaining the sales in the third region, we need to determine total number of characters in each row. Then we can use the MID function beginning one character to right of 2nd + and continuing (Length of cell) −(Placement of 2nd +) characters to obtain the last sales. Copying from G3 to G4:G6 yields the number of characters in each row

$= LEN(B3)$.

Step 7: Copying from H3 to H4:H6 the formula

$= MID(B3,D3+1,G3-D3)$

yields the sales in the final region!!

An Easier Approach: Just try the Text to Columns option in the Data menu, and make the Delimeter a + sign.

Chapter 65: Playing Craps with @RISK

Craps is a very complex game. With @RISK it is easy to estimate the probability of winning at craps. Here is a description of craps.

Example 65.1

In the game of craps a player tosses two dice. If on the first toss a 2, 3, or 12 results the player loses. If on the first toss the player rolls a 7 or 11 the player wins. Otherwise the player continues tossing the die until she either matches the number thrown on the first roll (called the point) or tosses a 7. If you roll your point before rolling a 7 you win. If you roll a 7 before you roll your point you lose. By complex calculations it can be shown that the player wins at craps 49.3% of the time. Use @RISK to verify this.

Solution

The key observation is to note that we do not know how many rolls the game will take. It can easily be shown that the game is very unlikely to require more than 30 dice rolls so we will "play out" 30 dice rolls. After each dice roll we keep track of the game status

- 0 = Game lost.
- 1 = Game won.
- 2= Game still going.

Our output cell will keep track of the status of the game after the 30th toss. A "1" will indicate a win and a "0" will indicate a loss. Our work is in the file **Craps.xls**.

Figure 65.1

	A	B	C	D	E	F	G	H	AD	AE	AF	AG
1	TOSS#		1	2	3	4	5	6	7	29	30	
2	Die Toss 1		4	3	3	6	1	4	1	4	4	
3	Die Toss 2		3	5	5	2	6	5	6	5	4	
4	Total		7	8	8	8	7	9	7	9	8	
5	GAME STATUS		1	1	1	1	1	1	1	1	1	
6	0=LOSS	WIN??		1								
7	1=WIN											
8	2=STILL GOING	95% CI							Result			
9	LOWER									1		
10	UPPER									2		
11										3		
12										4		
13										5		
14										6		
15												
16									Simulation Results for craps.XLS			
17												
18									Iterations= 4000			
19									Simulations= 1			
20									# Input Variables= 60			
21									# Output Variables= 1			
22	95% CI for WInning at Craps								Sampling Type= Latin Hypercube			
23	Standard Deviation		0.499711						Runtime= 00:00:26			
24	Lower Limit		0.467493						Run on 6/26/00, 2:05:33 PM			
25	Upper Limit		0.498507									
26	Sample Size		4000						Summary Statistics			
27												
28									Cell	Name	Minimum	Mean
29									C6	WIN??	0	0.483
30												

Step 1: In B2 we use the "discrete uniform random variable" to generate the roll of the first dice on the first toss with the formula

  =RiskDuniform($AD$9:$AD$14).

The RiskDuniform function ensures that each of its arguments is equally likely. Therefore each die has an equal (1/6) chance of yielding a 1, 2, 3, 4, 5, or 6.

Copying this formula from the range B2:AE3 generates both dice rolls for 30 tosses. Note that we have hidden roles 8-28.

Step 2: In B4:AE4 we compute the total dice roll on all 30 rolls by copying from B4 to C4:AE4 the formula

  =RiskDuniform($AD$9:$AD$14).

Step 3: In cell B5 we determine the Game Status after the first roll with the formula

  =IF(OR(B4=2,B4=3,B4=12),0,IF(OR(B4=7,B4=11),1,2)).

Note that a 2, 3, or 12 will result in a loss, a 7 or 11 will result in a win, and any other roll will result in the game continuing.

Step 4: In cell C5 we compute the status of the game after the second roll with the formula

  =IF(OR(B5=0,B5=1),B5,IF(C4=$B4,1,IF(C4=7,0,2))).

Note that if the game ended on the first roll, we maintain the status of the game. If we make our point we record a win with a "1". If we roll a 7 we record a loss. Otherwise the game is still going.

Copying this formula from C5 to D5:AE5 records the game status after rolls 2-30.

The game result is in AE5, which we copy to C6 so we can easily see it. After running 4,000 iterations with output cell C6 we obtain a 48.3% chance of winning. With 10,000 iterations we usually obtain a probability very close to 49.3%.

Chapter 66: Simulating the NBA Finals

Our Indiana Pacers came within two plays (one horrible foul call on Dale Davis in Game 6 and Travis Best missing a shot in Game 4) of winning the 2000 NBA championship. Before the series, what was the probability that the Lakers would win the series?

From the Sagarin ratings (found at http://www.kiva.net/~jsagarin/), we found that the Lakers are around 4 points better than the Pacers. The home team has a 3-point edge and games play out according to a normal distribution with the mean equal to our prediction and a standard deviation of 12 points. In file **Finals.xls** and Figure 66.1 we simulate the NBA 2000 Finals. Recall the Lakers are home during Games 1, 2, 6, and 7 while the Pacers were home during Games 3-5. I went to the awesome Game 5! Note we make the series always go 7 games because we do not know when it will actually end. If the Lakers win at least 4 of the 7 games they win the series, which is indicated by a "1" in cell I14. We have named the cells in D2:D5 with the range names given in C2:C5.

Figure 66.1

	B	C	D	E	F	G	H	I
1	NBA Finals 2000							
2		IND	5					
3		LA	9					
4		HE	3	Game	Home	LA Forecast	LA Margin	LA Win
5		STDEV	12	1	LA	7	1.312640391	1
6				2	LA	7	0.911581437	1
7				3	IND	1	-0.423239113	0
8				4	IND	1	22.02026177	1
9				5	IND	1	-13.825966	0
10				6	LA	7	-5.963644407	0
11				7	LA	7	-2.505744158	0
12							LA total wins	3
13								
14							LA Wins series?	0
15								
16								
17								
18		Name	NPV	LA Wins series? / LA Win				
19		Description	Output	Output				
20		Cell	[]Sheet1!F{	[finals.xls]Sheet1!I14				
21		Minimum =	0	0				
22		Maximum −	0	1				
23		Mean =	0	0.796875				

We proceed as follows:

Step 1: In G5:G11 we generate our forecast for each game by copying the formula

$$=IF(F5="LA",HE+LA-IND,-HE+LA-IND)$$

from G5 to G6:G11.

**Step 2: In H5:H11 we generate the Lakers margin of victory in each game as
normally distributed with a standard deviation of 12 and mean given in column
G.** Just copy from H5 to H6:H11 the formula

$$=RiskNormal(G5,STDEV).$$

**Step 3: In I5:I11 we determine if the Lakers won the game by copying from I5 to
I6:I11 the formula**

$$=IF(H6>0,1,0).$$

**Step 4: In cell I12 we compute the total number of Lakers wins in the series with
the formula**

$$=SUM(I5:I11).$$

Step 5: Note that if the Lakers win at least 4 games they win the series. In cell I14
we determine if the Lakers win the series with the formula

$$=IF(I12>=4,1,0).$$

From the @RISK output we find the Lakers had an 80% chance to win the series.
The bookmakers had LA as a 7-1 favorite which means (after taking out a 10%
profit) they believed the Lakers had around a 90% chance to win.

Chapter 67: Database Statistical Functions

Suppose you have a sales database that records each sale made by a company and records the size of the sale, the salesperson and location of the sale. There are many questions that come to mind that we would like to answer.

- How much did we sell in each region?

- How much was sold by each salesperson?

- How much did each salesperson sell in each region?

These questions can easily be answered with pivot tables but sometimes it is easier to use Excel's database statistical functions to answer these questions. Essentially with a database statistical function we can add (with DSUM), average (with DAVERAGE) or count (with DCOUNT) all items in a column that are in a row which satisfies fairly complex criteria. The syntax, for example, of the DSUM function is as follows:

=DSUM(Database, Name of Column to Sum, Criteria).

The use of database statistical functions is best explained by example.

Example 67.1

The file **Databasefunctions.xls** contains a sales database. Each row of the file contains the following information describing a sales transaction:

	D	E	F
9			
10	Region	Salesperson	Units Sold
11	Midwest	Heather	204
12	East	John	337
13	Midwest	John	297
14	South	Heather	474
15	West	Calista	372
16	West	Calista	465
17	West	Jill	424
18	West	Calista	254
19	South	Calista	44
20	East	Jill	108
21	South	Jill	96

- Region of country

- Salesperson

- Number of Units Sold.

We would like to answer the following questions:

- Total units sold in the Midwest.

- Units sold by Heather in the East.

- Units sold by Heather or sold in East.

- Units sold by Heather or John in the East.

- Number of transactions in East region.

- Number of transactions with greater than average sales.

Solution

The key to using the database functions is understanding a criteria range. The first row of any criteria range contains the names of columns from the database. The rows below the first row of the criteria range describe criteria that must be met for the function to add or count entries in the "column to sum" or "column to count." The key is to remember that multiple criteria in the same row are treated as "AND" and multiple criteria in different rows are treated as "OR".

	H	I	J	K	L
9					
10	Part a	Sold in Midwest	236164		
11	Part b	Sold by Heather in East	55558		
12	Part c	Sold by Heather or in East	413966		
13	Part d	Sold by Heather or John in East	118339		
14	Part e	Number of East transactions	970	970	
15	Part f	Number of > Average transactions	1916		
16	Part a	Region			
17		Midwest			
18					
19	Part b	Salesperson	Region		
20		Heather	East		
21					
22	Part c	Salesperson	Region		
23		Heather			
24			East		
25					
26	Part d	Salesperson	Region		
27		Heather	East		
28		John	East		
29					
30	Part e	Region			
31		East			
32					
33	Part f	Big			
34		FALSE			

| **Part a** | Enter in cell J10 the formula |
| **Solution** | |

$$= DSUM(Sales, "Units\ Sold", I16:I17).$$

This adds up in Sales database (cells D10:F3861) all entries in Units Sold column That match Midwest in the region column.

| **Part b** | Enter in cell J11 the formula |
| **Solution** | |

$$=DSUM(Sales, "Units\ Sold", I19:J20).$$

This formula adds up all entries in Units Sold column of Sales range that have salesperson Heather and Region East.

| **Part c** | Enter in cell J12 the formula |
| **Solution** | |

$$=DSUM(Sales, "Units\ Sold", I22:J24).$$

This formula adds up all entries in Units Sold column of Sales range that were sold by Heather **or** were sold in the East.

| **Part d** | Enter in cell J13 the formula |
| **Solution** | |

$$=DSUM(Sales, "Units\ Sold", I26:J28).$$

This formula adds up all entries in unit sold column that were sold by Heather in East (row 27) or by John in the East (row 28).

| **Part e** | Enter in cell J14 the formula |
| **Solution** | |

$$=DCOUNT(Sales, "Units\ Sold", I30:I31).$$

This formula counts the number of rows in Sales range for which the region is East.

| **Part f** | Enter in cell J15 the formula |
| **Solution** | |

$$=DCOUNT(Sales, "Units\ Sold", I33:I34).$$

Here we are using a **computed criteria**. The statement in I34

$$=F11>AVERAGE(F:F)$$

causes our function to count any row in database where Units sales exceeds average of Unit Sales column. Note for a computed criteria the first row of criteria must be **not be a heading in the database**.

Chapter 68: Analyzing Data by Resampling

In a well-known study (see Efron (1993)) whose purpose was to determine whether or not taking aspirin prevents heart attacks, 11,141 men took one aspirin every other day for 20 years. 104 had heart attacks and 11,037 did not have heart attacks. 11,223 men participated for 20 years and did not take aspirin. 189 of these men had heart attacks and 11,034 did not have heart attacks. The question is whether or not taking an aspirin every other day reduces a man's risk of heart attack. From Figure 68.1 we find that .93% of all men taking aspirin had a heart attack while 1.69% of all men not taking aspirin had a heart attack. This appears to be strong evidence in favor of the hypothesis that taking an aspirin every other day reduces a man's risk of heart attack. In fact, it appears that men taking aspirin every other day are .93/1.69 = 56% as likely to have a heart attack as men who do not take any aspirin. What we really want, however, is a confidence interval (say 95%) on the following

ratio: $R = \dfrac{probability\ of\ heart\ attack\ with\ aspirin}{probability\ of\ heart\ attack\ without\ aspirin}$. If a 95% confidence interval

for our estimate of this parameter does not include one, then we can be quite sure that taking aspirin does significantly reduce the risk of a heart attack.

Figure 68.1

	A	B	C	D	E	F
2		Aspirin and Heart Attacks				
3			HA	NHA	Prob HA	Prob NHA
4	11141	Asp	104	11037	0.009335	0.9906651
5	11223	No Asp	189	11034	0.016964	0.9903958

To construct a 95% confidence interval for R we use the Resampling technique. **We simply regenerate our data** (11,141 results for people taking aspirin and 11,223 results for people not taking aspirin) by **sampling with replacement** from our data. In other words, we generate 11,141 people each having a .0093 chance of heart attack and 11,223 people each having a .0169 chance of a heart attack. When the dust clears, we look at the ratio of the fraction of people in the first sample that had heart attacks to the fraction of people in the second sample that had heart attacks. We perform this procedure many (say 1000) times and use Targets(2.5%) and Targets(97.5%) to obtain a 95% confidence interval for the ratio R. Here is an outline of the procedure. See file **Aspirin.xls** and Figure 68.2.

Figure 68.2

	E	F	G	H	I	J
7					Asp/Nasp	
8		0.0103222	0.017019		0.606526	
9		Asp	Nasp			
10	1	0	0			
11	2	0	0			
12	3	0	0			
13	4	0	0		Name	Asp/Nasp
14	5	0	0		Description	Output
15	6	0	0		Cell	I8
16	7	0	0		Minimum	0.416376
17	8	0	0		Maximum	0.764204
18	9	0	0		Mean	0.555647
19	10	0	0		Std Deviati	7.01E-02
20	11	0	0		Variance	4.92E-03
21	12	0	0		Skewness	0.439414
22	13	0	0		Kurtosis	2.835917
23	14	0	0		Errors Calc	0
24	15	0	0		Mode	0.50368
25	16	0	0		5% Perc	0.446613
26	17	0	0		10% Perc	0.467332

Step 1: Copy from F10 to F11:F11150 the formula

=RiskDiscrete($G$4:G$5,E$4:F$4).

This generates 11,141 possible heart attack results (1 = heart attack, 0 = no heart attack) with a .0093 chance of heart attack. In short, we are replaying out our sample data from the group of men who took aspirin.

Step 2: In a similar fashion by copying from G10 to G11232 the formula

=RiskDiscrete($G$4:G$5,E$5:F$5)

we generate 11,223 possible heart attack results (1 = heart attack, 0 = no heart attack) with a .0169 chance of heart attack. In short, we are replaying out our sample data from the group of men who did not take aspirin.

Step 3: In F8 we compute the fraction of men in our sample of aspirin takers who had heart attacks with the formula

= SUM(F10:F11150)/11141.

Step 4: In G8 we compute the fraction of men in our sample of non-aspirin takers who had heart attacks with the formula

= SUM(G10:G11232)/11223.

Step 5: In cell I8 we compute the estimate of our ratio R with the formula

=*F8/G8.*

Step 6: After running 1000 iterations and obtaining the 2.5 percentile and 97.5 percentile with Targets option we find we are 95% sure that R is between .44 and .70. In short, we are 95% sure that men who take an aspirin every other day are between 44% and 70% as likely to have heart attacks as men who do not take an aspirin.

Reference

Efron, B., and Tibshirani, R., *An Introduction to the Bootstrap*, Chapman and Hall, 1993.

Index